Reader's Digest Paperbacks

Informative.....Entertaining.....Essential.....

Berkley, one of America's leading paperback publishers, is proud to present this special series of the best-loved articles, stories and features from America's most trusted magazine. Each is a one-volume library on a popular and important subject. And each is selected, edited and endorsed by the Editors of Reader's Digest themselves!

Berkley/Reader's Digest books

THE AMERICAN SPIRIT
THE ART OF LIVING
DRAMA IN REAL LIFE®
"I AM JOE'S BODY"
KEEPING FIT
THE LIVING WORLD OF NATURE
LOVE AND MARRIAGE
RAISING KIDS
SECRETS OF THE PAST
TESTS AND TEASERS
UNFORGETTABLE CHARACTERS
WORD POWER

KEEPING FIT

FIT

THE EDITORS OF

Reader's Digest®

A BERKLEY/READER'S DIGEST BOOK
published by
BERKLEY BOOKS, NEW YORK

KEEPING FIT
A Berkley/Reader's Digest Book/published by arrangement with
Reader's Digest Press
Printing No. 8
PRINTING HISTORY
Berkley/Reader's Digest edition/May 1981

ISBN: 0-425-05017-3

Grateful acknowledgment is made to the following organizations and individuals for permission to reprint material from the indicated sources:

Macmillan & Company Pub., for "The Wisdom of the Body" from the book THE ART OF MINISTERING TO THE SICK by Dr. Richard C. Cabot and Rev. Russell L. Dicks, copyright © 1936 by Macmillan & Co.; renewed 1964 by Russell Dicks. *The New York Times* for the following: "Your Aching Back" by Gilbert Cant, copyright © 1974 by New York Times Co., "What Happens When You Sleep?" by Gay G. Luce and Julius Segal, copyright © 1966 by New York Times Co. and "The Fastest Diet— Is It For You?" by Michael Goodwin, copyright © 1976 by New York Times Co.; "Ladies and Gentlemen—Be Seated Properly" by Janet Travell, M.D. reprinted from *House Beautiful*, copyright © 1955 by the Hearst Corporation, all rights reserved; New York Magazine Corp. for "Do Body Rhythms Really Make You Tick?" by Vicki Goldberg, copyright © 1977 by New York Magazine Corp.; South Illinois Press for "Exercise in the Office" by Robert R. Spackman Jr., copyright © 1968 by South Illinois Press; *Today's Health* for "Do We Eat Too Much Meat?" by Daniel Grotta-Kursha, copyright © 1974 by the American Medical Assn.; *Glamour* and Elizabeth Whelan for "What's Your Food I.Q.?" by Elizabeth Whelan, copyright © 1974 by the Conde Nast Publications Inc.; *American Home* for "A Way to Reduce Your Chances of Getting Cancer" by Jane Brody, copyright © 1977 by American Home Pub. Co.; Ms. Carol Schindler Brand for "Your Mind Can Keep You Well" by John Schindler, M.D. condensed from a talk over the University of Wisconsin Radio Station, WHA; *U.S. News and World Report* for "The Secret of Coping with Stress" by Dr. Hans Selye, copyright © 1977 by U.S. News and World Report; *Executive Health* for "But Hard Work Isn't Bad for You" condensed from ON STRESS AND THE EXECUTIVE by Hans Selye, copyright © 1973 by Executive Publications; William Morrow & Co. Inc. for "THE RE-LAXATION RESPONSE" by Herbert Benson, M.D. condensed from THE RELAXATION RESPONSE, copyright © 1975 by William Morrow & Co.; *National Observer* for "Your Personality May Be Killing You" condensed from STAY CALM–STAY ALIVE by Patrick Young, copyright © 1974 by Dow Jones & Co., Inc.; *Parade* for "The Heart Test That Could Save Your Life" by Arlene and Howard Eisenberg, copyright © 1974 by Parade Publications; Walker & Co. for "Stay Slim for Good" excerpted from STAY SLIM FOR GOOD by E. Ann Sutherland and Kalman Amit, copyright © 1976 by Amfern Psychological Consultants Ltd., by permission of the publisher, Walker & Co.; New York Sunday News for "The Prime Time of Life" by Jill Newman, copyright © 1976 by New York News Inc.; *Woman's Day* for "Clues to Live Longer; Staying Younger" condensed from A LIFE STYLE TO AVOID AGING by Patrick McGrady Jr., copyright © 1977 by Fawcett Publications; "How to Feel Fit at Any Age" from AEROBICS by Kenneth H. Cooper, M.D., M.P.H. copyright © 1968 by Kenneth Cooper and Kevin Brown, reprinted by permission of the publisher, M. Evans & Company Inc. New York; "Run Your Way to Happiness" condensed from THE COMPLETE BOOK OF RUNNING, copyright © 1977 by James Fixx, published by Random House; *New England Journal of Medicine* for "Anatomy of an Illness" by Norman Cousins, copyright © 1976 by Mass. Medical Society, this material also appears in *Saturday Review* May 28, 1977; *New York Magazine* for "How Much Stress Can You Take?" by Dr. Thomas Holmes.

Contents

The Wisdom of the Body **1**

WALK TALL
The Magic of Good Posture **7**
Step Lively! **11**
Your Aching Back **14**
Be Seated—Properly **19**

TIDES OF LIFE
What Happens When You Sleep **25**
Biorhythms: A Key to Your Ups and Downs **30**
Five Rules for Waking Up Alert **37**
Do Body Rhythms Make You Tick? **42**

SHAPE-UPS
Six Seconds for Exercise **49**
Everybody's Belly-Dancing **54**
Pumping Iron **58**
Exercise in the Office **62**

YOU ARE WHAT YOU EAT

Do We Eat Too Much Meat? **69**
What's Your Food I.Q.? **73**
A Vital Ingredient May Be Missing in Your Diet **78**
To Reduce Your Chances of Cancer **83**

THE BREATH OF LIFE

Take a Deep Breath **89**
Your Lungs **93**
Do You Really Know How to Breathe? **98**

EMOTIONS COUNT

Your Mind Can Keep You Well **103**
How Much Change Can You Take? **109**
To Beat Stress: Do Your Own Thing **110**
But Hard Work Isn't Bad for You **114**
The Relaxation Response **117**
Your Personality May Be Killing You **121**

CHECK IT OUT

What ECG Tells the Doctor About Your Heart **129**
...And the "Stress Test" ECG **133**
New Light on a Hidden Killer **136**

THE RIGHT DIET FOR YOU

Think Before You Diet **143**
Nibble That Fat Away **147**
Your Best Weapon Against Overweight **154**
Stay Slim—For Good **157**
The Fastest Diet—Is It for You? **162**

LIVING LONGER
When Do You Hit Your Prime? **169**
Add Years to Your Life **172**
Clues to Living Longer, Staying Younger **176**

MUSCLES IN MOTION
Get Fit and Stay Fit, With Aerobics **183**
Run Your Way to Happiness **197**
Tennis, Everyone? **201**
Hop, Skip and Jump **205**
The Pulse Test **209**
Striding—The Most Natural Exercise **213**

INSULTS TO THE BODY
What Happens When You Smoke **219**
Poisoning Ourselves With Noise **224**
Alcohol and Your Brain **231**
Super Athletes—or Monsters? **236**
Marijuana: More Dangerous Than You Know **241**

PERSONAL EXPERIENCES
Return From Despair **247**
How I Solve My Energy Crisis **253**
Anatomy of an Illness **257**

The Wisdom of the Body

by Richard C. Cabot, M.D., and Russell L. Dicks

IN BOSTON an elderly man with a ruddy, fresh complexion stepped off the curb without looking and was struck by an automobile. Taken to the Massachusetts General Hospital, he died within an hour. When his wife was asked about her husband, she declared that he had never been sick in his life. He was a most active person both in mind and body.

Yet this is what was found upon examination: (1) healed tuberculosis of both lungs; (2) cirrhosis of the liver, with all the blood going around his liver by a new set of roads; (3) chronic kidney trouble, but with enough reserve kidney tissue to function despite the destruction of portions of both kidneys; (4) hardening of the arteries and compensatory enlargement of his heart. No doubt he had had high blood pressure for a long time. All this he never knew. He was a well man despite four potentially fatal diseases inside of him.

When a vessel's rudder is damaged in a storm a "jury rudder" is often rigged. This man's body was full of "jury" arrangements. Four vital organs had these compensatory defenses, *but he was a going concern.*

"When you understand a great deal about the human body and its resources for health, you wonder why anyone is ever sick," the late Dr. Walter Cannon once said. Any physician knows that if given rest, proper food and ease of mind 90 percent or more of his patients get well. As a ship rights herself after a squall has keeled her over, so the body rights itself after the minor squalls that strike it daily in health and after the tempests of disease.

The organs of the body have a reserve that can be called upon in need. When a man suffers from tuberculosis of the lungs, part of the lung is destroyed, but he has a great deal more lung tissue than he needs. He can call upon his reserve and get along, as the great Doctor Trudeau did at Saranac for nearly 40 years of hard work, though he had only a part of one lung still healthy.

Experiments have shown that one can remove more than two fifths of the liver, and the remaining part will still carry on. When we see a surgeon cut and tie 30 or 40 blood vessels in the course of an operation, we may wonder what is to become of the blood that should circulate through them. The answer is that we have many more than we need. Each of us has about 22 feet of intestine. Three or four feet can be removed and hardly be missed.

When heart disease takes the form of valvular inflammation and deforms the valve, the situation is as if one of the doors of a room were stuck halfway open. A person could not live if it were not that, as the deformity gradually occurs in the valve, the heart gradually thickens and so strengthens its own muscle. A heart that is ordinarily the size of a fist will become as big as two or even four fists, because it must.

How does a surgeon dare to remove a diseased kidney? Because, as one kidney is removed, the other begins to grow, double its size, and does the work of two. All the details are rebuilt—and the architecture of a kidney is far more complicated and differentiated than the architecture of any ordinary building. This ingenious ability has been called "the wisdom of the body."

Another natural defense of the body is rest. If you sprain your wrist, even before the doctor comes nature splints it by making it so sore and stiff that you hesitate to move it. If a person is strained emotionally or physically beyond a certain point of exertion or terror, nature says, "Take a rest," and he faints.

If you wound your finger with a dirty splinter, festering occurs. This is one of the most dramatic and wonderful things that happen in the human body. What is this stuff called "pus"? It is the dead bodies of the white corpuscles which have come to fight the bacteria and have died in the attack. They make a wall of defense between the attacking bacteria on one side and the free circulation on the other. Almost every case of appendicitis would be fatal if this wall were not built by nature around the diseased appendix. It shuts in the inflammation until the surgeon operates.

God's plan provides a great healing power in ourselves that makes for health, a never-slumbering intelligence which doctors try to imitate and supplement with medical and surgical work. In our fight against disease we always have this prodigiously ingenious and powerful force at work on our side.

WALK TALL

The Magic of Good Posture

by Warren R. Young

How much would you give for a formula guaranteed to make you look younger, brighter, more attractive—and *feel* that way, too? Probably a lot. Yet the secret is built right into the human body, *your* body. All you have to do is take a few moments every now and then to check up on your *posture*.

The formula sounds so simple it's scarcely to be believed. After all, who doesn't know by natural instinct how to sit on a chair, lie on a bed, walk down the street or just stand up? Well, chances are you may not. The mechanics of balancing our bodies against the ever-tugging pull of gravity—which is what posture is all about—are more complicated than you may imagine.

Good posture has never been more vital, both psychologically and physically, than in today's tense, push-button, sit-down world. Posture is so basic to the human condition that we all rely upon it to make instant judgments of others. A slumping figure betrays advancing age, and nothing signals to us that someone is a "loser" more surely than a defeated slouch. By the same token, nothing more effectively rolls back the years or creates an aura that a person is one of life's "winners" than a well-poised body, a head held high.

Besides affecting your appearance and mental state, posture habits can also influence your kidneys, stomach, reproductive organs, heart, lungs and brain. Eliminating round shoulders, a hunched back and muscular tenseness can help you breathe more deeply, prevent the cramping of your heart and send more oxygen to your brain cells. Digestion and metabolism may also improve with posture improvement. Says Dr. Allen S. Russek, formerly a rehabilitation specialist at New York's Rusk Institute. "By the way a person walks into my office, I can often recognize some chronic problem he may have."

The impact of posture on social image, personal morale and general health can, in fact, change a person's life. One career woman in her late 30's came to Dr. Russek seeking relief from incessant back pains and chronic fatigue. "Professionally, she was successful—a personnel interviewer with a responsible job." he recalls, "although because of her back problems she had to wear a massive corset to work. But she had atrocious posture and a walk that was almost comic.

"After posture retraining and specific muscle-strengthening exercises, she learned to walk, stand and sit properly. The pain subsided, and she discarded the corset. Gradually her entire personality changed. She began smiling more often, and discovered that she was attractive to men. Before long she was going out dancing."

Good posture is the proper relationship of the segments of the body to each other, whether you are standing, walking, sitting or lying down. This involves the orchestration of 639 muscles, 206 bones, dozens of organs, hundreds of sensing structures, thousands of communication circuits and gallons of body fluids.

But four main sections of the body are the keys: the feet and legs; the pelvis; the spine; and the shoulders and head. When all is well with our posture, in the side view a vertical line will run from your earlobe through your shoulder, your hipbone and your anklebone. If it does not, you have fallen into one or more posture errors. These are the three most common:

1. Swayback. Many people harmfully exaggerate the spine's natural curves when they try hardest to "stand straight." Mistakenly attempting to snap to stiff attention, they raise their buttocks high. This tilts the front of the pelvis down, makes the belly sag outward and increases the arch in the small of the back. Some people make the same mistake when walking or sitting, especially in overly soft chairs, sofas or auto seats. Other contributing causes of swayback are sleeping on the stomach or flat on the back; pregnancy; and potbelly. Swayback can generate agonizing lower-back pain.

2. *Splayfeet*. Some people stand and walk with their feet angling outward rather than properly parallel. Kneecaps should turn out slightly, and feet should point straight ahead, a combination which automatically lifts the arches, stretches the toes, places calves and thighs in position to give powerful support, and helps to tighten buttocks. The results of splayfeet are a tendency to flattened feet, less efficient walking, off-balance standing, and lower-extremity fatigue.

3. *Shoulder-head slump*. Round shoulders and a heavy-hanging head are among the worst penalties we pay for our sedentary habits. Bending long hours over a desk, hunching toward a car's steering wheel, watching TV from a typical soft or "easy" chair—these all encourage you to curve your shoulders ahead and jut your head forward, imposing intolerable strains on your upper back and neck. The problem is merely intensified if you try to compensate for the lowered head by raising the chin, instead of pulling the head back above the spine with the chin kept down. Shoulder-head slump causes the muscles to become tight in the chest and front of the neck, weak at the back of the neck and between the shoulder blades; breathing is hindered.

To avoid these errors and improve your posture, here are some basic suggestions.

• **Learn the right "body feel."** Since good posture is something you achieve with your body, you must *learn* it in your body and not just in your mind. First, you must imitate the correct "form" and then practice it until it becomes habit. Use a full-length mirror to check if your earlobe, shoulder, hipbone and anklebone are in line. An excellent way to get the feel of the way your back should be is to stand 12 inches away from an unobstructed flat wall, with back to the wall. Then, bending your knees, "sit" on an imaginary support with your back and head against the wall. Next, tighten abdominal and buttock muscles in order to tilt the pelvis up in front and down in back. Try to eliminate the arch of the "small of the back" as completely as you comfortably can. Keep chin down. Now, keeping your back and head flat against the wall, slowly inch your feet back to the wall and straighten your legs until you are in a standing position. This is correct standing posture. Finally, walk around the room, maintaining the same posture; then place your back against the wall again to see if you have held the good form.

• **Get fit.** To keep good posture after you have found it, you need to get fit and stay fit with sensible exercise. The best exercises for preventing or overcoming swayback are those that will strengthen the abdominal muscles. Just try sucking in your gut and feel the strain disappear from the small of your back. If you do sit-ups—probably the best gut-strengthening exercise—have another person hold your ankles down, or brace your feet under a heavy chair, to avoid undue strain; then curl your back upward to a sitting position.

A second valuable exercise is the pelvic tilt. Lie on your back (in bed or on the floor) with legs bent, knees high and feet on the surface you are lying on. Then, press the small of your back hard against floor or bed. At the same time, tighten your buttocks and abdominal muscles. Tuck your chin in, and without holding your breath, press your neck and back flat with as much strength as you can muster, for a slow count of five. Then relax.

A third exercise is leg raising. While lying with back and neck flat, raise each leg several times, first with the knee bending as far as possible toward the head, then with the knee straight. Beyond these three exercises, jogging and isometric exercises can work wonders for your posture.

• **Be hard-nosed about soft seats.** Choose firm, level chairs or sofas to sit on. Adjust your automobile seat closer to the steering wheel, and tilt it as nearly upright as you can. Seat belts can ease some of the strain on your back, too, especially if you place a hard pillow under your shoulder blades.

• **Practice, practice.** At any pause in your daily routine, check to make sure that your feet are parallel; tighten your abdominal muscles and tuck your tail under; pull your head and shoulders back without raising your chin; and breathe deeply.

A few weeks of observing these principles of good posture will assure you of a quadruple reward:

Other people will subconsciously regard you as a more successful and more attractive person.

Your improved bearing will automatically make you feel more confident and more in command of your daily life.

You will feel toned-up and healthier.

And as these three benefits begin to become evident, each will subtly reinforce the others—all of which can add a great deal to the pleasure and success of your life's journey.

Step Lively!

by Myron Stearns

WITHOUT being aware of it, you walk at least two or three miles, possibly six or eight, every day—stepping from room to room, about an office, to the car and back, shopping. Hours of it. But *how* you walk rarely occurs to you. Why should it? You developed your own particular walk so long ago it has become a part of you.

But the way you walk is also a part of your posture—so much so that it helps determine how you feel at the end of the day. Consequently, you can improve your sense of well-being by learning to walk better.

Just what is a good walk? Lulu E. Sweigard, a long-time teacher of posture at New York University and a leading authority, said: "An ideal walk is easy, graceful and rhythmical, with no waste motion. You step straight ahead, using the whole length of the foot. Try to avoid twisting or swaying your hips. Breathe deeply, as though you were breathing up and down through a well in the center of your body, clear down to your diaphragm. Your three big weight-masses—hips, chest and head—should be in an erect straight line.

"We develop our walk pattern as children," Dr. Sweigard continued. "Later, all sorts of things—sickness, badly fitting shoes, the habits of people about us—change this pattern."

Take the matter of toeing in or out. Our American Indians toed straight ahead; they were natural walkers and covered great distances tirelessly. But from childhood most of us have been taught to "toe out." It's supposed to look better. Yet it means loss of efficiency, rolling forward off the side of the foot, increasing the danger of an inturned instead of a straight ankle.

Notice the way others walk. Mabel Elsworth Todd, a young semi-invalid in a Massachusetts town, began watching from her bedroom window the walks of passers-by. Many of them, instead of carrying themselves blithely erect, walked in sort of toppled S pattern: forward to the hips, slanting backward from hips to shoulders, and then the head thrust forward again. You can observe the same thing in the walk of many acquaintances. How much unnecessary work, Mabel Todd wondered, did muscles have to do when a person walked that way, instead of with the big weights (hips, chest and head) balanced one directly above the other? She started thinking about the degree of muscle-strain that might be saved. Eventually she regained her health and became one of the country's most distinguished teachers of posture.

As you watch others walk, you will become increasingly aware of your own walking habits. And if they are wrong habits, you will see how they may be corrected.

"Many people," Dr. Sweigard said, "take steps that are too short or too long. Each person has to find his own right step, of course. If the other things are right—toes straight ahead, legs swinging straight ahead with a minimum of wiggling or swaying of the hips, shoulders relaxed, letting the arms swing naturally, good breathing and rhythm—the length of your step will regulate itself without exaggerated effort on your part."

Listening to the way individuals walk—perhaps in a corridor outside an office, in the hallway of an apartment building, coming up the steps to your home—will explain better than words the matter of rhythm. You will note that few people walk with any bounce or lilt. One foot usually comes down harder than the other—a step that is anything but rhythmical. Or you may hear the uncertain, foot-dragging shamble of a tired or listless person. Presently you will find yourself listening to your own walk and trying to make it more rhythmical, more alive and enthusiastic.

New walking habits can be formed only through constant, concentrated practice. But the rewards are well worth looking for. Anything that you can learn to do with greater ease and less effort, hour after hour and day after day, will increase your chance for better health. Consider how the blood, after being pumped from the heart through the arteries far out to the extremities, manages to get back to the heart again, largely against the pull of gravity. Among other things it's helped along by innumerable tiny muscle tissues within the veins. Like all our muscles these tend to take their tone and vigor from the condition of the greatest in each group; improve your big walking muscles, among the strongest in your whole body, and your entire circulatory system, prime key to health, is bettered.

The greatest reward of all, however, is the sheer joy of walking. When I was an undergraduate in California I left a camping party one moonlight night and walked 15 miles back to the college campus. I did it in just under three hours, carried along by a tremendous elation that I still remember. I became more and more aware of that miraculous thing, the human body: my body, functioning in what seemed perfection. I have never forgotten the thrill of it. And I have recaptured it, in part, over and over again, in the course of less ambitious walks.

Blind men tell me that one of the most important things in their training is to learn to step out boldly and confidently; once they learn that, other things come easier. To improve your walk does not require the courage needed by a blind man to step off into blackness; but it does require confidence, self-discipline and the conviction that you are improving yourself.

Remember that both your mind and your emotions are inextricably related to your muscles and your muscle tone. By improving your walk—and by *walking*—you will improve your posture, benefit your general health and add to your sense of fitness and well-being.

Your Aching Back

by Gilbert Cant

IT IS AT least as common as the common cold, and far more disabling. It causes the nation, by conservative estimate, a loss of 200 million man-days of work a year. And the misery it spreads is immense: no fewer than eight million Americans are reported to be under treatment of some kind for it every day of the year.

"It" is low-back pain. And for Western, civilized man it is the epidemic plague of the 20th century's second half.

Millions of casualties inevitably ask, "Why *me?* What's the cause of my pain?" They get a bewildering variety of answers. One textbook lists no fewer than 103 causes. Clearcut cases—the two Kennedy brothers, John and Ted for example, whose back pains were caused by direct physical injury—are the exception. In other cases the triggering event is only superficially clear. Doctors know that a hard sneeze or cough puts great strain on the lower back and may throw it "out of whack." But this does not explain why *one* particular sneeze should do so. In fact, doctors don't know why.

There are many more, equally painful, cases in which nothing is "out of joint," but where muscles and ligaments are protesting some maltreatment. Working for years at a desk, under the stress and strain of a competitive office situation, causes many persons to tense up. They contract their muscles until these finally remain contracted for long periods, causing discomfort. Another backache-producing factor is the automobile. Not only does it keep people from walking moderate distances—a valuable preventive exercise—but it condemns them to the worst possible sitting posture, slumped in an over-stuffed seat which has no support for the small of the back.

You can get low-back pain from being overweight. Tumors, both benign and malignant, may be responsible for backaches, and the various forms of arthritis and rheumatism are frequent causes. And Dr. John Sarno, of the Institute of Rehabilitation Medicine in New York City believes that emotions—tensions, anxiety, depression—are a significant factor in at least 80 per-cent of back troubles.

With so many causes of low-back pain, what's the cure? Exercise. For the back that aches simply because it has not been given enough activity, and has therefore lost muscle tone, appropriate exercise may be an essentially complete cure. In the more severe cases, including many resulting from acute injury and even the relatively few that require surgery, muscle-building exercises can so restore the back that it will not give pain again. But these exercises must be repeated, day in and day out, year after year.

A little lesson in anatomy helps understand back pain. Na-ture gives the human body 33 separate vertebrae, extending from the base of the skull to where other animals have a tail. An X ray of the normal spine viewed from the side shows a gentle, double-S, reverse curve, a configuration essential to proper balance and weight bearing. If the vertebrae were piled vertically on top of one another like bricks, the spine would have only 1/16th as much strength as it has with its curves.

When you bend forward, backward and sideward, each ver-tebra moves in relation to those above and below it. To ensure smooth interplay, the spine has shock absorbers between the vertebrae: the discs that have acquired such notoriety in talk about "slipped discs." In fact, as Dr. Lawrence W. Friedmann of the Nassau County Medical Center in New York, points out, "slipped disc" is only a slip in terminology. A disc, as such, can't slip.

Looking like a Life-Saver without a hole, the disc has an outer ring of tough material, anchored to the vertebrae above and below it by thin sheets of cartilage. The precious core of the disc, the part that does the shock absorbing, is a capsule of gelatinous matter. In the young, this highly compressible capsule is about 88-percent water. As you get older, water content of the gel gradually falls to about 70 percent, and the capsule loses much of its compressibility. This sets the scene for the possibly catastrophic development known as the slipped, alias "ruptured," alias "herniated," disc. Such ruptured-disc material may bulge, for example, through the rear part of the outer ring and exert pressure on the nerves, triggering severe pains in the lower back, and on down to the toes.

It is because of their severity and the possibility they may require surgery, rather than their frequency, that the ruptured-disc cases attract so much attention. A study by Columbia University and New York University showed that of 5000 patients with low-back complaints, 81 percent had no skeletal disorder—nothing wrong with either bones or discs. Their troubles came from muscles, ligaments or tendons, due to strain, sprains, poor posture or lack of exercise. And, in this regard, doctors agree on three main points:

• If a backache victim has no skeletal disorder, he does not need surgery. No ifs, ands or buts.

• Even among those who have skeletal disorders, the vast majority—up to 90 percent, say some authorities—still do not need surgery. Their cases can best be treated by "conservative management"—that is, through rest and a regimen of exercise supervised by a professional.

• In the 10 percent of skeletal disorder cases that would seem to require an operation, the decision should be made only after consultation with both a neurosurgeon and an orthopedist, and only after a battery of searching tests has pinpointed the location and severity of the disorder. (Recently, doctors at Massachusetts General Hospital began using an enzyme injection to shrink slipped discs without surgery.)

But what is the prognosis for the great mass of low-back patients with milder, nonskeletal disorders? The first thing that nature does when you strain or sprain your back is to "splint it"—*i.e.*, provide it with a rigid support—by throwing the nearby muscles into spasm. Though painful, this reaction can help effect a cure. If, for instance, you were a Neanderthal man and had just thrown your back out killing a bear, you would first lie down, groaning, and probably keep your back to the fire. After about three days of limited activity your muscles would relax enough to let you hobble about. Increasing exercise would soon repair your muscles so that these would continue to support your back.

The caveman's regimen is just about what most doctors will

prescribe for you today. First, bed rest. (Use a firm mattress, preferably with a plywood board underneath.) But not too much of it—the caveman's three days will be right for most uncomplicated cases. If you stay in bed for weeks you will get up worse, not better, because of further deterioration in muscles that were probably too weak to begin with. (Painkillers such as aspirin and liniments give no more than symptomatic relief.)

Most doctors think warmth—from a heating pad, say, or a soothing hot tub—can be helpful. Moderate heat will help you relax, and thus ease some of the pain. Surprisingly, cold may also be recommended. As a home remedy, this means an ice pack. (Doctors use the far more potent spray can of ethyl chloride, a muscle-relaxant often given athletes.) When chilled, the spasm-racked muscles sometimes go comfortably numb and relax. Gentle massage by a fond spouse can also be soothing for both muscles and mind.

Because low-back pain is so often inexplicable and intractable, most physicians derive little satisfaction from treating it, and so have neglected it. This has left the field open for osteopaths and chiropractors and their controversial manipulative treatments. Now, no less eminent a medical authority than Dr. Howard A. Rusk, head of the Institute of Rehabilitation Medicine, is interested in researching the possible uses of acupuncture. And Dr. Friedmann reports occasionally striking results for it in pain relief.

But, after doctors and therapists have done all they can for your aching back, it remains true that only *you* can cure your back trouble and prevent future attacks. The almost universally approved prescription is at least a half-hour of exercise daily, or two 15-minute periods if that fits your schedule better, as prescribed by your doctor (preferably a specialist in physical medicine or an orthopedist).

Exercises, yes—but for what muscles? No fewer than 140 muscles are involved in the support of the back and control of its movements, and laymen expect these to be located in the back itself. Not so. Of the four most important groups sustaining the back, one set is out in front—the abdominal muscles, too often miscalled "stomach muscles." When these are flabby, the weight of the abdominal contents is thrown forward, tending to pull the spine with it. The old parade-ground command "Suck in that gut!" is a sound injunction for everyday life. The simple act of frequently tightening the belly muscles will eventually strengthen them, and take strain off the spine.

Dr. Rusk points out that many exercises to strengthen the back can be carried out inconspicuously, while seated in a conference or waiting in a queue. The pelvic tilt, or "tucking your tail under" by squeezing the buttocks together, is one of these. Another is tightening those abdominal muscles. Such simple maneuvers, combined with a daily half-hour of exercise, should do the trick of keeping your back in business. But it takes what no doctor can prescribe—willpower.

Be Seated—Properly

by Janet Travell, M.D.

YOU WOULDN'T dream of buying shoes that don't fit. You wouldn't sleep in a bed that's too short. But have you considered the chairs you sit in? One can go into most homes and not find a single chair that's properly designed to support the person sitting in it. And this poor design, which violates the principles of human physiology, is one of the major reasons for the muscular pain which afflicts vast numbers of people.

Most people think that comfort in a chair implies something soft and yielding. The truth is that the more a chair is used for relaxing, the more important it is to have the bony framework of your body held up by that chair. Many now realize that sleeping on too-soft beds (which let the body sag, gradually straining joints, ligaments and muscles) gives them backache. But few are aware of the ill effects of too-soft chairs.

When you sit in a chair that is not right for you, your muscles are compelled to do the work the chair should do. If the natural body weight that keeps muscles stretched to a comfortable tension is modified by an unnatural position, as when the arm is pushed up by an arm rest, then the muscles take up the slack and shorten; when the shortening is prolonged, they cramp and become painful. If the muscles are *overstretched* from sitting improperly, they fail to keep the ligaments and joints in line, and the sagging of the body results not only in muscle injury but in joint strain, too.

Most chairs have at least one of nine major faults:

No support for the lower back. This is probably the commonest fault in furniture, and it leads to acute physical discomfort. Hours of "relaxing" in a chair that fails to support the lumbar region may cause so much muscle fatigue that you become tense, nervous and worn out. A chair back should have some extra padding to fit your lower back. If it hasn't, you can achieve this effect by propping a small cushion against the small of your back. Also, an occasional chair is more likely to be comfortable if it has an opening between the backrest and seat, allowing clearance for body spread.

Back too scooped. To support your back properly, a chair should allow your shoulder blades to drop back slightly behind the center of your spine. But a high-back scooped chair like the barrel or Windsor chair rounds your back, rolls your shoulders forward and may cause severe muscle strain. Libraries, conference rooms and restaurants commonly have the scoop-backed chair. What a pity, for these are just the places where one should be able to lean back and relax in comfort!

Too-high arm rests. These push your shoulders upward and forward. As a result, after any length of time, cramped muscles may cause stiffness and pain across the shoulders and in the back of the neck.

The big upholstered armchairs that look so comfortable are often bad offenders because, when you sink down, the arm rests become too high. A desk or work table that's too high in relation to your chair has the same effect.

Insufficient slope to the back. Any chair with a nearly vertical back forces you to droop forward in a round-shouldered position. The familiar straight dining-room chair, the erect ballroom chair, and the gilt French parlor chair so charming to the eye may be menaces to the human frame if sat in for any length of time.

I recall attending a medical convention where an audience of 500 doctors sat in beautiful little straight ballroom chairs. After half an hour I never saw so much squirming and turning. Every one of those restless people was trying to find a position that would allow him to relax and lean back. If the backs of these chairs had been tilted 15 to 20 degrees behind the vertical, they would have been more comfortable.

On easy chairs and sofas, loose back cushions are useful to provide an adjustable incline.

Back too short. Have you ever come out of the movies with a stiff and aching neck? If the back of the movie seat were high enough to support your upper back and neck, you'd be more comfortable. Try the back row some evening and lean your head against the wall. If practical neck rests could be devised for movie and theater seats, they would add immeasurably to one's enjoyment. Usually, I advise patients with shoulder and neck pains not to go to the theater or movies until they are 90 percent recovered.

Jackknifing at hips or knees. The ideal sitting position requires at least a 90-degree angle at the waist and also at the knees. If your hips and knees are jackknifed into an angle sharper than that, overstretching of the back muscles follows, together with shortening and cramping of the muscles behind the bent knees, including the calf muscles.

Jackknifing at the hips occurs in any chair which has a seat that sinks way down but a relatively firm front edge—as, for example, an automobile driver's seat when the springs are old and saggy. If you keep driving for very long, your back muscles protest. One solution is a wedge-shaped cushion that raises the seat at the back and makes it horizontal.

Chairs that give you "shelter legs." During World War II, physicians in London noted an astonishing number of cases of swollen feet. It was found that these people had been sleeping at night in air-raid shelters, in folding deck chairs. Circulation of the blood to and from the lower legs was partially cut off by pressure which the edge of the chair exerted underneath the thigh, just above the knees, where the main artery and veins cross the bone. The result was pain and swelling. Any chair or sofa with a high, hard front edge may produce this condition.

Chairs with bucket seats. The bucket chair now in vogue has a definite fault. Nature supplies you with bony structures in the middle of each buttock to support the weight of the body when you are sitting. The bucket seat undoes this work of nature. It puts the weight on the *sides* of the buttocks, so that the center sags, rolling the thighs inward. This distortion, if it lasts, causes discomfort.

The wrong size for you. Women with short legs should be especially mindful of the chairs they sit in. When feet dangle without touching the floor, the weight of the legs compresses the blood vessels under the thighs and shuts off circulation. The average straight chair measures 17 inches from the front of the seat down to the floor. But some women have legs that measure only 15 or even 14 inches from underneath the knee to the heel. A small footstool can often solve this problem.

In selecting chairs, you should know your measurements and those of other members of the family—the length of legs from knee to floor, and from hip to knee. Thus you can tell right away whether a chair is the right height from the floor and whether its seat is the right depth.

Actually, our ancestors in this country had some chairs more comfortable than most of ours. Long ago they discovered that one of the best chairs in the world is the now old-fashioned cane-seated porch rocker with high back. This rocker has low enough arm rests. It gives support to the upper shoulders and neck. It has a firm flat back that can be padded to fit the lumbar region by adding a small cushion. It can be tilted back to ensure sufficient "slope." And the motion of rocking favors circulation by alternately relaxing and contracting the muscles and so keeps them from getting stiff.

There's no such thing as one chair to fit every person, nor is there one chair to suit every purpose. But, with awareness of the general principles involved, you may find it easier to select chairs that will make sitting more comfortable and restful.

TIDES OF LIFE

What Happens When You Sleep

by Gay Gaer Luce and Julius Segal

EACH NIGHT, as most of us begin the small rituals that set the stage for bed, sleep laboratories are being geared for action in a number of major hospitals and universities throughout the country. The preparations center around a brain-wave amplifying and recording device: the electroencephalograph, or EEG machine.

The pace of discovery by the sleep scientists in the last couple of decades has been startling. A vast new library of information, based on studies of laboratory animals and human volunteers, has been compiled in the U.S.A., Europe, U.S.S.R., Mexico, Japan and elsewhere.

Sleep may feel like a blanket of darkness, punctuated by dreams; a time when the mind stops functioning. Nothing could be less true. All night a person drifts down and up through different levels of consciousness, as on waves. With the EEG machines and other sensors that record body temperature, pulse, respiration and the like, researchers have charted the stages of the long night's journey.

It begins while the subject is still awake, but his brain waves, which have been low, rapid and irregular, show a new pattern: the alpha rhythm, an even rhythm of about 9 to 12 cycles per second. This is a state of serene relaxation, devoid of concentrated thought.

Now the alpha waves grow smaller, as the subject passes through the gates of the unconscious. He may be wakened for a moment by a sudden spasm that causes his body to jerk. This is the "myoclonic jerk," resulting from a tiny burst of activity in the brain. It is related to the epileptic seizure, yet is normal in all human sleep. It is gone in a fraction of a second. Descent continues and soon the subject is truly asleep.

Here in Stage I, the pattern of the sleeper's brain waves is small and pinched, irregular and rapidly changing. The sleeper may be enjoying a floating sensation or drifting with idle thoughts and dreams. His muscles are relaxing, his heart rate is slowing down. He awakens easily, and might insist he had not been asleep.

After a few minutes the sleeper descends to another level, Stage II. Now his brain waves trace out quick bursts—a rapid crescendo and decrescendo, resembling a wire spindle and unmistakable on the EEG chart; the eyes roll slowly from side to side, but if the experimenter gently opens a lid the sleeper will not see. Still, the sleeper descends—to Stage III. It is characterized by large slow waves that occur about once a second. The sleeper's muscles are very relaxed and he breathes evenly. His heart rate slows. His temperature is declining. His blood pressure drops.

Some 20 or 30 minutes after he first falls asleep, the sleeper reaches Stage IV, the deepest level. It is marked by large, slow brain waves, called delta waves, that trace a pattern resembling jagged buttes. Stage IV is a relatively dreamless oblivion. The breathing is even, heart rate, blood pressure and body temperature slowly falling.

But after 20 minutes or so in the depths, the sleeper begins to drift back up from Stage IV through lighter levels. By the time he has been asleep for about 90 minutes, he will show brain waves of the lightest sleep, even resembling those of waking. Still the sleeper is not easy to awaken, lying limply, his eyes moving jerkily under closed lids as if watching something. He is in a special variety of Stage I, known as REM (for "rapid eye movement") sleep. If awakened now he could almost certainly remember dreaming, probably in vivid detail.

After perhaps ten minutes in the REM state, the sleeper will probably turn over in bed and begin shifting down the levels of sleep again to the depths, to return in another hour or so for a longer REM dream. Each night the entire cycle is repeated about four or five times.

For present sleep researchers, two stages are of particular interest: REM sleep, the most spectacular; and delta sleep, which comes the closest to what most of us think of as deep, restorative slumber.

The profound unconsciousness of the delta sleep predominates in the first part of the night but lessens its hold on us toward morning. In the early 1960s, Dr. Wilse B. Webb and his associates at the University of Florida deprived volunteers of their delta sleep for two nights—not awakening them, but nudging them back toward lighter sleep whenever they approached this deepest stage. On the next night they indulged in more delta sleep than usual, as if making up the loss. This is the first phase to be made up when one has been totally without sleep.

Delta sleep is a curious phase of seeming unconsciousness. Certain brain cells appear to fire less frequently—yet the brain is not inactive. Evidence suggests that activity is altered in central regions of the brain where sensory impulses are converted into what we know as perception or sensation. This strange brain function may be related to certain peculiar disorders. Delta sleep, for example, is a time of bedwetting. It is then that night terrors may cause a child to shriek—and to continue screaming for his mother even when seated on her lap or clasped in her arms, and on awakening to remember only fright, no dream details. And, strangely enough, it is in the delta period of slow-wave oblivion that somnambulists begin their sleepwalking.

Somnambulism has often been associated with dreaming. Sleepwalkers have been known to drive cars, climb trees, even commit murder—giving dream explanations later. On occasion, laboratory volunteers when awakened from delta slumber have recalled some vague but thoughtlike fragment. It may be that many more dreams than we know lie buried in this deep slumber.

Those dreams we do remember are probably from the final REM period out of which we may awaken in the morning. When a person enters a REM period after quiet sleep, his already relaxed musculature becomes flaccid. His closed eyes dart—sometimes furiously—and his face twitches. His breathing and pulse become irregular. Blood pressure fluctuates. Oxygen consumption rises, as does brain circulation and brain temperature. Adrenal hormones in the blood increase.

It is like a physiological storm, comparable to a state of fright or excitement—yet no one has established any clear connection between this body intensity and the intensity of the dream. People have reported most innocuous dreams after their records showed remarkable physiological changes.

Experiments have revealed that our dreams take place in real time, although a few may occur in split seconds. Anyone who has watched the half-open, darting eyes of a dreaming pet, or the movements of a child's eyes under closed lids, would swear that they were following the events and action of an internal movie. But this may not be so. Rapid eye movements also occur in the congenitally blind, who do not dream in visual images but in terms of touch and sound. In sleep, they happen when bursts of bioelectric activity invade the visual region of the brain, stimulated perhaps by rhythmic activity deep below in the brain stem.

Doctors have long conjectured that violent or disturbing dreams might be the cause of nighttime heart attacks. Nocturnal angina attacks have correlated with the REM intervals, and these are the times when ulcer patients have shown peaks in their abnormal gastric secretion.

As a person is awakened from REM periods in the course of a night, his dreams often progress from vague and almost thoughtlike incidents, revolving about his everyday realities— job or studies, home and friends—to dreams growing more vivid, detached from reality and bizarre as the night wears on. This trend may offer a clue to the nature of dreaming. It may be a time in which a person assimilates his present life into the whole of his past.

Neurophysiologists, studying cats, have found unusual activity during REM sleep in the brain centers associated with memory and emotion. Perhaps new memories are being filed with the old, in a hierarchy of association—in the process unloosing a horde of details from the files of past memory.

Both delta sleep and REM sleep seem to be essential. Dr. William C. Dement of Stanford University observed that when he deprived subjects of REM sleep (permitting them all other phases), both people and animals invariably gave signs of mounting change in the brain, even when their behavior seemed unaffected. On each successive night of deprivation, a person would try more and more often to "dream." When finally left to sleep uninterrupted, he would go into an orgy of REM sleep, as if making up the loss.

Abnormally little REM sleep has been noted in the records

of some mentally ill and senile patients, among restless sleepers who are also psychologically disturbed, and among people who have taken heavy doses of alcohol, barbiturates, amphetamines or other drugs. The biochemistry of dreaming is now the focus of much research. Some scientists foresee the possibility that some mental illness may be ameliorated by a kind of dream therapy—a drug to enhance REM sleep. It may be triggered by neurochemicals produced and used in the body and brain— several substances, among them microscopic doses of LSD, have increased this kind of sleep in man.

We know now that sleeping pills, alcohol, barbiturates and tranquilizers do not induce normal sleep. They alter the usual pattern, generally reducing the REM phase. Stimulants such as amphetamines also have this effect.

Even more important is the gradual revelation that poor sleep and insomnia arise from a multitude of causes. When a person persistently fails to sleep, we have to look for the *specific* cause, and only a doctor can determine what drug will give him rest. The sedative that soothes one patient may keep another awake, or drive a depressive into deeper despair.

What does sleep do for us? What are its mysterious restorative functions? Such questions remain unanswered.

We can demonstrate that it is essential by taking it away for just a few days. As the days go by, the people taking part in such experiments become irritable, lapse into infinitesimal blackouts called microsleeps. Memory falters. They are beset by visual illusions, sensations, nonsensical thoughts, a sense of disorientation. Finally they begin to act like psychotics. The turning point into delirium comes for many at about 100 hours.

Chronic sleep loss, far more common and less dramatic, has been studied in several laboratories. A person who abbreviates his sleep to four hours or less will change his sleep pattern. He will maximize some stages at the expense of others—often showing more delta and REM sleep, and less of the transitional light levels. There are people who seem to manage on a couple of two-hour naps instead of a night's sleep.

Some scientists conjecture that we may shrink our sleep time down to the essential stages, eliminating hours of transitional light stages. Some say that we will do away altogether with sleep, adding 20 useful years to the normal lifetime. At this point in our knowledge, however, we can invent no substitute.

Biorhythms: A Key to Your Ups and Downs

by Jennifer Bolch

WE'VE ALL HAD DAYS when we can't seem to do anything right—days when we feel irritable, depressed, unable to concentrate, inexplicably tired or vaguely ill. On the other hand, we've all experienced golden days when everything goes right—when we feel energetic, strong, happy and bright.

What's the difference between our "good" and "bad" days? There are, of course, many factors that influence how we feel. One theory that has gained prominence involves the fascinating—and controversial—study of biorhythms.

Derived from the Greek words *bios*, life, and *rhythmos*, a regular or measured motion, biorhythms (according to some researchers) reflect the apparent ebb and flow of life energy. There are many kinds of body rhythms; the three discussed here are a physical cycle 23 days long, an emotional cycle of 28 days, and a 33-day-long intellectual cycle. Drawn on a graph, they appear as three graceful curves. Each cycle begins the day a person is born and begins again every 23, 28 and 33 days thereafter for the rest of his life, as in this sample graph of the first month of a person born on October 1:

When the curve is above the center line, the biorhythm is said to be "high," with energy to spare. For example, on a physical high we tend to be energetic, strong, full of vitality. On an emotional high, we're apt to be most creative, artistic, aware and cheerful. On an intellectual high, we're able to think quickly and logically, and to solve complex problems.

When the curve is below the center line, the biorhythm is

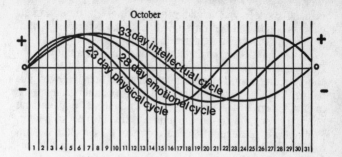

"low," in a recharge period. Physically, we tend to tire more quickly, feel dragged out and succumb to colds or other ailments. Emotionally, we're apt to feel moody, irritable or depressed. And intellectually, we may find concentrating or remembering difficult, and we may get distracted easily and be more likely to use poor judgment.

The day any of the curves crosses the center or zero line is called a "critical" day, when our system seems to be in flux or transition and hence is unstable. Critical days are days when things are most likely to go wrong. People are more likely to get sick, or seem to lack coördination and are therefore accident-prone on such days. But remember: biorhythms don't predict what will happen. All they do is tell us our tendency to behave in certain ways at certain times. If we are informed about the tendency, we can usually overcome it by awareness and willpower.

The theory of biorhythms is not accepted by everyone. To Andrew Ahlgren of the University of Minnesota's Chronobiology Lab, the 23-, 28-, and 33-day cycles are "basically a put-on, with no scientific basis whatsoever." Prof. Michael Persinger of the Environmental Psychophysiology Laboratory at Laurentian University in Ontario agrees, calling the three cycles "highly unlikely."

But other respected authorities, including Dr. Philip A. Costin, a director with a national research agency in Canada, and Prof. Douglas Neil, a researcher at the Naval Postgraduate School in Monterey, Calif., believe that biorhythms are a definite factor in our lives. Indeed, scientists and students of human behavior have long been amassing evidence of their existence. As far back as Hippocrates' time, that venerable medical pioneer was advising his followers to observe their patients' good and bad days and to take those regular fluctuations into account in their treatment.

In the first decade of the 20th century, a German physician, Dr. Wilhelm Fliess, and Hermann Swoboda, an Austrian psychologist, after studying the fluctuations of their patients' ailments, feelings and behavior, and then examining thousands of case histories, discovered independently the 23-day physical biorhythm and the 28-day emotional cycle. Two decades later, Prof. Alfred Teltscher of the University of Innsbruck in Austria discovered the 33-day intellectual cycle by studying the performance records on exams of hundreds of high-school and college students.

It was George Thommen, a Swiss-born businessman, who brought the European science of biorhythms to the attention of the American public. He first heard of biorhythms while visiting his native Switzerland in 1946. After a catastrophic head-on train wreck, a friend of his, Hans Frueh, did biorhythm graphs for the engineers and firemen on both trains, discovering that three were on critical days and one on a triple low. Thommen paid little attention to Frueh's work until an almost identical head-on train collision the following year in Gallitzin, Pa., started him wondering. He drew up biorhythm charts for the engineers and firemen and found one engineer on a double critical day, the other engineer and one fireman on critical days, and the second fireman on a triple low. Thommen plunged into the study of biorhythms, and went on to write *Is This Your Day?*, the first and one of the largest-selling books in English on the subject.

Today, thanks in great part to calculators, computers and books of code numbers that have simplified the mathematics of biorhythms, a growing body of evidence is being collected and analyzed by researchers at more than a dozen U.S. and Canadian universities. Much of it indicates that there probably is something to the biorhythm theory, and suggests potential application.

For example, biorhythms' apparent correlation with plane accidents is chilling. According to Bernard Gittelson, author of *Biorhythms: A Personal Science*, in 10 of 13 recent major commercial- and private-plane crashes attributed to pilot error, the pilot or co-pilot was on a critical day. Most airlines deny their involvement with biorhythms, but Gittelson, who serves as biorhythms consultant to dozens of firms, counts several airlines among his clients.

Industry is also paying special attention to biorhythms, for they promise a new way to cut accident rates and save money. Wycoff Co. Inc., a small package express firm, provides biorhythm charts to the 60 drivers in its Pocatello/Idaho Falls, Idaho, terminal; forewarned to be extra careful on critical days, these drivers cut their accident rate by two thirds. AT&T in New York programmed its computer to produce biorhythm charts.

Biorhythms have potential applications in many human endeavors, including medicine. At the late Dr. Franz Wehrli's clinic in Locarno, Switzerland, operations were scheduled according to patients' and doctors' biorhythms. Only emergency surgery was performed on a patient's critical days, and no surgeon operated on his own critical days. The clinic reduced its postoperative-complications rate by 30 percent.

Some marriage counselors are using biorhythm charts to help couples see why they get on each other's nerves and fight on certain days. Couples learn when to make an extra effort to compensate for their mate's low or critical days. Even the oddsmakers are in the act: Professional handicapper Ken Cammisa says he increased his win factor from 64 percent to 87 percent by taking into account the charted biorhythms of the athletes he handicaps.

To be sure, the evidence on biorhythms is not all in. Clearly they are *not* fate, fortune-telling or predestination, being at most only one of many factors which determine how we act. But they are also fascinating and more than a little persuasive. Perhaps psychologist Douglas Neil puts it best when he says, "Biorhythms are a small but significant piece of the complex puzzle of human behavior."

How to Chart Your Own Biorhythms

1. Multiply your present age by 365.
2. Divide your present age by four. Add the whole number you get to the answer of Step 1. Disregard any remainder.
3. Count the number of days from your last birthday to the first day of the chart (the first day of the month you want to study), including your birthday and the first day of the

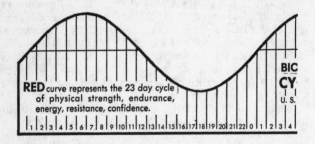

RED curve represents the 23 day cycle of physical strength, endurance, energy, resistance, confidence.

1 2 3 4 5 6 7 8 9 10 11 12 13 14 15 16 17 18 19 20 21 22 0 1 2 3 4

BIC CY U. S.

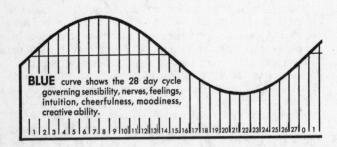

BLUE curve shows the 28 day cycle governing sensibility, nerves, feelings, intuition, cheerfulness, moodiness, creative ability.

1 2 3 4 5 6 7 8 9 10 11 12 13 14 15 16 17 18 19 20 21 22 23 24 25 26 27 0 1

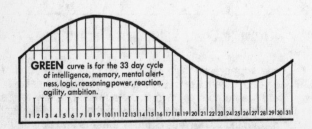

GREEN curve is for the 33 day cycle of intelligence, memory, mental alertness, logic, reasoning power, reaction, agility, ambition.

1 2 3 4 5 6 7 8 9 10 11 12 13 14 15 16 17 18 19 20 21 22 23 24 25 26 27 28 29 30 31

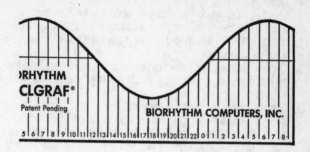

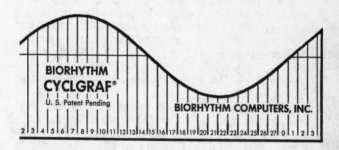

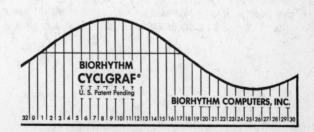

chart. Add that answer to your total from Steps 1 and 2. Now you have the number of days you have lived, from the day you were born to the first day of the chart.

4. Divide (by long division, not a calculator) that total number of days by 23, 28, and 33. Keep track of your remainders; they're important.

5. Cut out the curved rulers on pages   , and paste them on cardboard, cutting the cardboard to the shape of the rulers.

6. On the physical-cycle ruler, find the number representing the remainder you got when you divided the number of days yhou have lived by 23 and place that number over Day 1 on the chart, lining up all lines on the ruler with the lines on the chart. Be sure the ruler's zero line—the line that goes horizontally across the center of the ruler—is on the zero line of the chart. Trace the curve on the chart in red. That is your physical biorhythm for the month.

7. Follow the same procedure with the numbers representing remainders you got when you divided 28 and 33 into the number of days you have lived, lining up the remainders on the emotional- and intellectual-cycle rulers with Day 1 on the chart. Draw those curves in blue and in green. They will be your emotional and intellectual cycles for the month.

8. To check your biorhythms for any day during the month you have charted, look for the date along the bottom of the chart. Note where the curves cross that date's lines. If they cross above the center or zero line, you're high in that cycle that day. If they cross below the zero line, you're low. If a curve crosses a date directly on the zero line, that's a critical day. If two curves cross each other above or below the line, that may be a critical day as well. The day before and day after a critical day are called semi-critical days and also deserve extra caution and awareness.

Five Rules for Waking Up Alert

by Warren R. Young

ALL MY LIFE I have considered myself a true-born member of a vaguely romantic, slightly daring fraternity: the Night People. Late of evenings, when Day People are ready to slide into bed, a Night Person may be enjoying a peak of energy. We are the ones who can outlast others at working (or playing) into the wee hours—and frequently find reasons to do so.

Yet, for many of us, there is a sad side to being a Night Person. Waking up early is a joyless ordeal. Like a cranky car on a cold winter's morning, we have to fight our way through layers of lethargy. Also, the world—bosses, for example—instinctively prefers the early starter. In the marriage nest, too, a difference in waking-up styles can introduce thorns of contention. In fact, it is a rare drowsy owl who does not *himself* harbor a grudging suspicion that the early bird is a fellow of superior feather.

Like millions of other Night People, I had assumed that I was locked into a lifelong sequence of morning "wearies" by my individual body chemistry. Day People are apt to regard the Night Person as a slugabed, who could get going if he would just put his mind to it. Who is right? I finally decided to ask the experts, and here is what I learned.

Night People are partly right: the agonizing slowness with which we become alert and energetic in the morning is not imaginary but a physical reality. The medical term is *dysania*. However, a Night Person doesn't necessarily have to *stay* one. "The waking process is complex," says Milton DeLucchi, a

Houston neurophysiologist who has conducted studies on the sleeping patterns of astronauts and aquanauts. "But many people can retrain themselves to go through it more efficiently." What is required is a simple, planned program to synchronize certain living habits and certain subconscious mechanisms more closely with nature's harmony. I found that this can be accomplished by following five basic rules:

1. Just enough sleep. Everyone knows that sleep is essential to survival. Although individual sleep needs vary, each person has one best length of sleeping time, and this changes little throughout his adulthood. Tests conducted by psychologist Wilse B. Webb, at the University of Florida Sleep Laboratory, show that for nine out of ten people, normal sleeping time lies somewhere between 5 and 9 hours; for the vast majority, it is between 7½ and 8 hours.

Interestingly, getting too *much* sleep, compared with your need, can be just as disruptive as too little. Sleeping more than ten hours (except when catching up after a genuine sleep shortage) makes a person feel listless, irritable and fuzzy-minded.

The ideal amount of sleep for you is that which, got most nights (and assuming you follow the other four rules below), enables you to wake up spontaneously, feeling reasonably cheerful, refreshed and eager to meet the morning.

2. Respect your rhythms. Even though you routinely log the proper amount of sleep, it may not be totally fulfilling if you get it on erratic schedules. The body is, after all, a wondrously complex affair, thrumming and humming with electrical and mechanical activities of which we are seldom aware, filled with chemical seas of hormones and other body fluids. Normally these interrelated currents ebb and flow like tides, and they follow remarkably persistent patterns—different when you are asleep and when you are awake.

When you suddenly alter your sleeping-waking habits, some of your bodily "tides" may be upset. After a week or two of living on a new schedule, as night-shift workers and jet-age travelers know, *some* of your body's internal cycles adapt fully to the new timing; some may persist weeks longer—at cross-purposes with the others. The altered balance of vital body chemicals, in turn, can disrupt the quality of your sleep and have you waking up feeling "out of joint."

The way to put Rules 1 and 2 into practice is to adopt a *fixed* bedtime, starting about eight hours before the time you regularly need to get up. In two weeks you should have a clear idea of your normal sleeping time, and be well on the way to regularizing your internal cycles. After that, you may break routine once in a while. But most nights, get just enough sleep and respect your rhythms.

3. Wiggle yourself awake. In the moments after consciousness softly begins to make its morning reappearance, you can help it shine through the cobwebs with a series of simple stratagems. Contrary to common belief, your brain is not switched off by sleep; it stays active, like a car engine running but with the clutch disengaged. The trick is to smoothly reconnect your mind to the waiting machinery of your body—which is rested and ready to go—and set it in motion.

As you lie there, halfway between oblivion and wakefulness, bend one little finger. Once. Twice. Believe it or not, that tiny action may help nudge you toward waking up. Now, another finger—and then all ten. Now your toes: wiggle them three times, alternating with the fingers of each hand. Be very careful to count each wiggle.

The secret of all this is not physical exercise but attracting your mind's attention with a little series of external sensations and rudimentary cerebral action. After five seconds of it, you may not yet feel very lively, but chances are that you are more awake than asleep—a major turning point.

Now take one deep breath, and hold it while you count to seven. Next, try to involve each area of your body in movement. Swing one arm across your chest, then the other. Bend each leg. Gently, twist your neck back and forth. Try stretching. As soon as possible, sit up, put your feet on the floor and limber your shoulders by hunching them high, then letting them sag. Count to five in each position. Repeat four times. Stand up, and stretch your arms high for a count of ten. Then lower head, arms and trunk until fingers are close to the floor, letting the knees bend as you relax into this position and holding the pose for a count of 15. Repeat this stretch-and-sag sequence four times.

"Performing easy flexibility drills starts one off with less actual strain than merely getting dressed in a sort of semi-stupor," says Dr. Warren R. Guild, Harvard Medical School cardiologist. They can get your bloodstream flowing, your lungs pumping, and your brain synapses snapping with a vitality and vigor you otherwise might not enjoy until noon.

4. Keep the familiar fresh. You are now awake, but not yet safely into high gear. The secret is to start off with activities simple enough for you to perform successfully, with no great physical exertion. But humdrum habits alone can bore you into a return to drowsiness. To prevent monotony—to keep the familiar fresh—change your regimen and routine from day to day. Confront yourself with small, non-critical choices such as deciding what to have for breakfast rather than eating exactly the same thing. Indulge in some unharried small-talk with family or neighbors. Spend a few minutes organizing your day's schedule. Take a different route to work and look for a glimpse of something new. None of this is frivolity; it is a practical method to heighten your alertness throughout the day.

5. Expect to like it. Every sleep researcher I spoke to emphasized that one of the most important influences on the way you wake up is your psychological "set" toward waking itself—the attitude built up by your memories of previous mornings. Anything you can add to make your mornings serene but interesting and cheerful will help you wake up better. In fact, the best morning exercise of all can be the careful flexing of the lower facial muscles—commonly called a smile.

If you have been waking poorly, try to pinpoint what lies in store for you during the coming day that you may subconsciously be wishing to avoid. Then, see if you can predict something enjoyable or exciting that may also be expected.

One businessman who felt grouchy every morning decided the reason lay in his unhappiness with his job. He couldn't afford to quit. So he at least eased his mood problem by setting his alarm for a half-hour earlier, and spending the extra time each morning working on an elaborate birdhouse for his backyard. Just before going to sleep he would concentrate on this project, planning the small but satisfying progress he would accomplish on it the next morning. When he awoke, he usually felt rested and relaxed. I have other friends who look forward to waking up, eager to study the sports pages of the morning paper, or to work the crossword puzzle.

In my own case, the five rules have helped me learn why the morning world is considered by many to be the sweetest part of day. One's sharpened senses quickly learn to bask in the fresher smell of morning breezes, to notice the subtle pinks and blues painted on the early sky.

Even if you never become a full-fledged Day Person, the

shedding of at least some of the morning pains and pessimisms brought on by *dysania* can end that dismal old feeling that the sun comes up too early. Once you learn how to partake in the poetry of the dawn, you can move zestfully into each morning, enjoying the quickened pace of your personal high gear.

Do Body Rhythms Make You Tick?

by Vicki Goldberg

THE LABORATORY of Human Chronophysiology, Montefiore Hospital, the Bronx, 3 p.m. A tube through which blood can be drawn is attached to the arm of Barry Perlmutter, asleep on the bed. A machine records information from electrodes on Perlmutter's head: rapid-eye-movement sleep, jerky squiggles as he grinds his teeth. An automated thermometer flashes his temperature every minute. Perlmutter has been isolated from all time cues for 15 days. He thinks it's been 13, since he's only slept 13 times, once for 16 hours straight. (Afterward, he said, "The best dreams I ever had." He then stayed awake for 33 hours. "Seemed a short day," he said.)

Perlmutter is being paid to participate for 3½ weeks in a study of biological rhythms. These rhythms determine hormone production, heartbeat, mental agility, powers of concentration, nighttime dreams or daytime fantasies; each dances to a specific beat. In time-free experiments like this one, most people forget the 24-hour day and adopt a schedule slightly different. Some experimental subjects "free-run" wildly, stretching time like an elastic band. Perlmutter lunches at what he takes for midday, which may actually be 4 a.m., when his hormones have practically fallen asleep. Several of his rhythms have drifted out of phase, so he doesn't eat with gusto. His body is internally desynchronized. Various interior clocks are obviously ticking, but they refuse to match the environment's schedule unless nudged by external signs, like dawn or the alarm clock.

The Montefiore laboratory is investigating the difference

between "larks"—people who rise in the morning wide-awake and singing—and "owls"—nighttime people who get the early-morning drears. The owl's temperature rises more slowly in the morning and peaks later in the afternoon. Dr. Elliot D. Weitzman, chairman of the department, speculates, "There may be real personality differences between larks and owls." Researchers in Britain agree: larks, with their speedy start-of-the-day temperature rise, are apparently more introverted than owls. Could introversion be tied more to inborn body rhythms than to upbringing?

Our rhythms do influence our moods. University of California researchers studied 36 healthy male college students and found they were most depressed and inefficient in early morning, least depressed and most efficient in late afternoon. Mood level tended to rise with the daily temperature curve. Every 90 minutes or so, moreover, there seems to be a fluctuation in intensity of daydreaming, and some researchers speculate that the brain shifts back and forth all day between right- and left-hemisphere dominance. Two psychologists have warned that personality tests might show different results at different times of day. Your response to a Rorschach test (a personality test based on ink-blot recognition) could seem outrageous at high points in your fantasy cycle, or dull at a quiet period.

Women's mood-swings, of course, can be traced over monthly cycles with changing hormone levels. It's possible that men's hormone levels shift in a monthly cycle as well. Beard growth, which is regulated by hormones, appears to follow biological rhythms measured in weeks.

Each of us has an interior drummer that continually coördinates the rhythmic fluctuations of hormones, moods, sleep and waking; neither our well-being nor our sanity can easily march to a different beat. More and more, mental illness is being measured in terms of wobbling rhythms. Thus, severe depression pushes time largely out of joint, sleep rhythms disintegrate, and cortisol, an adrenal hormone involved in stress reactions, is secreted at higher than normal levels. (After treatment and clinical improvement, these rhythms approach normalcy.) It's also thought manic depressives may suffer from desynchronization of several hormone rhythms. Some say man's triumphs over nature—especially artificial light and heat—have deprived our lives of a natural cadence and contributed to increased mental disorder.

When we eat can also affect the coördination of our rhythms. When volunteers at the University of Minnesota ate only one meal a day, and that in the morning, the pancreatic hormones insulin and glucagon in their bloodstreams peaked within a few hours of each other. Perfectly normal: insulin lowers and glucagon raises blood-sugar levels, keeping them under control. But when the subjects ate their only meal at night, insulin and glucagon peaked further apart, and their carbohydrate-control systems were altered.

The future medical implications of being able to separate rhythms by mealtimes are enormous. In a world food shortage, it would help to know which calories, taken when, could keep a hungry man alive. We know that mice die if they eat at the wrong time of day. At the University of Minnesota, mice housed individually in cool cages were allowed to eat only during the first four hours of light, when they would normally be resting. Most died. When fed only during the first four hours of darkness, most survived. Understanding our own vital mealtimes could possibly spell life or death for the undernourished or very ill.

Knowledge of biological rhythms could help explain how a body adjusts to its environment. In an experiment at Harvard Medical School in Boston, a squirrel monkey lives in a whiteporcelain box that feels like the tropics inside. This monkey is in trouble: since he lives in constant light, without sunrise and sundown to set his interior clock, his rhythms have desynchronized, and he can no longer adapt to temperature change. Normally, if air temperature drops, an animal's system revs up to keep him warm. Not this monkey's. When the outside temperature falls, his body temperature falls with it, as much as four degrees. This is added evidence that desynchronization of rhythms can disrupt the body's capacity to keep its internal state constant no matter how the environment varies. Without such a capacity, the body can't deal with external challenges anymore.

The 24-hour day has both traps and enchanted moments. Births and deaths occur most frequently in the small hours of the morning, and all creatures, including man, are more vulnerable at certain times. A sudden loud noise will kill genetically susceptible mice at certain hours of the day, but not at others. Far less pentobarbital is needed to sedate mice during their resting hours than during their active period.

Clearly you cannot fly in the face of time. All these facts about muted or enhanced sensitivity are important elements in chronotherapy, a new branch of medicine that takes account of body rhythms. Sometime in the future, it may change the treatment of cancer; it has already been effective in animal experiments. For example, at the Universities of Arkansas and Minnesota, leukemic mice treated chronotherapeutically had double the survival rate of mice on equal doses of drugs every three hours, even though both groups of mice received the same total amount in any 24-hour period.

The trick is to find the right rhythms. Certain cancerous tumors have rhythms different from the body's; they have lost contact with the drummer. Someday we may be able to chart fluctuations in DNA synthesis or tumor-cell divisions and attack at the right time to cause maximum damage to the cancer. The best time to apply drugs or radiation might be when DNA synthesis is at a low point, to inflict minimum damage on surrounding healthy tissue.

When we finally learn to tell biological time, even operating-room schedules will change. At the Chronobiology Laboratories in Minnesota, skin grafts were most successful on mice if done at certain times of day. Studies have not yet been made on optimal times to do human transplants.

We have time in our hearts, in our hands, and in our every cell. Scientists are searching for these tiny clocks and for the master clocks which keep the whole system coördinated. If they find them, maybe we can learn how to keep them *wound*.

SHAPE-UPS

Six Seconds for Exercise

by Keith Monroe

To MANY of us, exercise is a bore or chore. Yet it needn't be. Without workouts at a gym or a "daily dozen" every morning, we can still get needed exercise and keep ourselves in trim by using odd moments during the day—those few seconds spent waiting for a traffic light, telephoning, standing in line.

The peppy Charles F. Kettering of General Motors, who worked at full speed until his death at 82, never took any formal exercise; instead, he just didn't wait for elevators. Whenever he had to visit upper-story offices or laboratories he walked up at least two floors and down three. Theodore Roosevelt built his scrawny neck to a solid muscular one by kneading it in spare moments. For years Darryl F. Zanuck, the movie mogul, swung a polo mallet in his office while dictating or phoning. This was not Hollywood eccentricity, but a method of strengthening the wrist and forearm. More and more doctors and trainers are advocating these simple practices.

"What *kind* of exercise is more important than *how much*," said the late Dr. Arthur H. Steinhaus, dean and professor of physiology at George Williams College. "In a German laboratory where I worked, it was discovered that a muscle can grow at only a certain rate—and a very small amount of the right exercise will start it growing at that rate. If you contract any one of your muscles to about two thirds of its maximum power and hold that for six seconds once a day, the muscle will grow just as fast as it can grow.

"Every day there are bound to be intervals when you have

six seconds to relax. They can make a tremendous difference. Pull in your stomach. Pull up your chin. Wriggle. Yawn. Stretch. Do these exercises on company time. Do them while going from one place to another. Weave them into the day's routine."

Gene Tunney advised: "Take *regular* exercise—not violent weekends of golf, or sporadic bursts of squash, but a daily drill that becomes as much a part of your life as brushing your teeth."

Many show-business stars make idle seconds count to help their health and appearance. Hugh O'Brian, the actor, has an unobtrusive habit of pressing the clenched fist of one hand forcibly into the open palm of the other, at waist level, whenever he stands talking with someone. It keeps his forearms and biceps powerful. Singers have an exercise for the moments when, sitting in their cars, they wait for traffic lights to change. Borrowing an idea from Indian yoga, they slowly pull in the stomach, sucking the diaphragm up and up until the whole abdomen is flat from groin to chest—then little by little release it. When you first try this, it can make you lightheaded if you tighten too hard. Jane Powell warns: "Begin gently. But keep at it. It's the simplest trick I know for building good posture and a flat tummy."

For muscle tone, Dr. Steinhaus advocated a few seconds of planned exercise while toweling yourself after a bath. "Loop the towel behind your neck," he suggested. "Then pull your chin in, pull forward on both ends of the towel and resist the towel with your neck as hard as you can, for just six seconds. Do it only once. Now slide the towel down to the small of your back. While pulling forward on the towel, resist by contracting the muscles in your buttocks and your belly. Push back hard against the towel and count six. Now that's done. Loop the towel under your toes and pull up with both hands while your toes push down. Hold it for six seconds, then let go. Once on each foot and you're done for the day."

U.S. Navy submariners, cramped into small space, have learned to keep fit without moving more than a few inches. Lying flat on their bunks, they put hands under head, lift the head while resisting with the neck, and keep lifting until chin touches chest. Then they let the head down slowly. Or, in rising to a sitting position, they arrest the motion part-way up, hold it a few seconds and sink back again. These brief drills are good for anyone.

You may want to try a few moments of similar exercise yourself. At night in bed, stretch all over slowly and luxuriously, like a cat. Then start at your toes and work up to eyelids and scalp, tensing each muscle for a moment, then relaxing it. You'll probably be almost asleep when you finish.

In the morning, a simple breathing exercise can help rouse you and clear out cobwebs. As you lie half-awake take the deepest breath you can; fill your lungs with air. Then close your mouth, pinch your nose and lie still. Time it, and you'll be amazed to find that you can hold your breath without discomfort for twice as long as usual. And when you finally let your breath out you'll be wide-awake.

Now you can limber up before getting out of bed. Lie on your back, stretch your arms overhead till you feel the pull all the way down to your waist. Hold them there a moment; then drop them limply. Next kick the covers off and raise your legs. Then lower them—but don't let your heels quite touch the bed. Repeat this several times. At first you'll feel a strain on your stomach muscles, but after a few days your midsection will begin to firm up.

While dressing, stand on one foot as you put on your shoe and tie the shoelaces. You may have to start by putting your foot in the shoe on the floor and leaning against a wall while tying the laces. However you do it, daily repetitions will tighten your stomach and give you stronger, suppler legs and feet.

When you think about it, you'll be surprised to notice how many brief periods of idleness there are in your day: riding to work, waiting at a counter for a clerk's attention, sitting at your desk or standing by your workbench between chores. Put some life into those intervals! Use them for a "seventh-inning stretch."

If you want to firm a flabby chin, you can. Push your chin out, pull it back, drop it, lift it. Then give yourself a five-second massage under the jaw. To tone the muscles around your midriff, draw your abdomen up and in whenever you think of it, whether sitting or standing. At the phone, instead of doodling, use your free hand to knead your belly or give it a gentle pummeling. Dave Garroway would hold an umbrella or golf club out in front of him with the heavy end away, flipping it up and down. You'd be surprised how this tightens the torso muscles.

Perhaps you bulge and wobble at the seat. Ever notice that truck drivers nearly always have firm hindquarters? So do cow-boys. That's because they constantly bounce up and down. Try it yourself. Pick out a hard chair in home or office. Bounce on it a few times whenever you're alone. Vary the routine by extending your legs and shifting your weight from side to side.

For spine-straightening, stand with your back to a wall and try to push firmly up against it so you're touching from head to heels—buttocks, shoulder blades, if possible every vertebra. You'll feel a strong pull along your backbone and neck. This stretching is recommended by physical culturists to improve posture, get rid of aches in back or neck and make you feel alive all over.

The "heel stretch" is a favorite of health experts for use while sitting at a desk or table. You needn't get out of your chair to do it. Just lift your feet and push the heels forward as if trying to push a wall away. Bring your toes up—so you feel the muscles in back of your knee pulling like a rope—count six, and slowly relax.

Dr. Jay A. Bender, as director of the physical-fitness program of Peoria, Ill., said, "All you need do is *use your muscles correctly* as you go through a routine day at home or office." If you pick up something from the floor, for example, don't spraddle your legs and bend. Put one foot forward and kneel erectly. Or, when it's a light object, keep your knees stiff and reach straight down. For variety, squat and rise like a jack-in-the-box; it tightens flabby legs.

When you must wait in line, teeter on your toes a few times to uncramp foot and leg muscles. Put your hands in your pockets and clench and unclench the fingers to get the blood speeded up. Take a whopper of a breath and see how far you can expand your belt. Deep-breathing exercises should be employed every day. When you go up stairs, climb slowly with head and chest high and stomach muscles tight. If you can, walk up two steps at a time, or even three.

Basically, there are nine essential exercises which authorities advise you to take every day, in doses of a few seconds at a time:

1. *Stretch*—while sitting, lying or standing.
2. *Straighten your spine*—while standing with your back against something straight.
3. *Roll your neck*—up, down and around.
4. *Suck in your stomach*—while sitting or bending over.

5. *Expand your chest.*
6. *Flex your arms*—by pushing, pulling and reaching.
7. *Bend your legs*—by squatting, climbing and walking.
8. *Limber your toes and feet.*
9. *Firm your muscles*—by bouncing, pinching, kneading, pummeling.

A little of each of these every day, and you'll be slimmer, stronger and peppier. Try them and see!

Everybody's Belly-Dancing

by James Stewart-Gordon

FLASHING-EYED CIA CIREL stepped before an enthusiastic audience of students and housewives at New York University's Loeb Student Center. The slender, exotically costumed teacher of Middle Eastern dancing at N.Y.U. demonstrated the bouncy movements of the *khaslimar*, the classic dance of welcome that for generations made sheiks and sultans hurry home. As Cia's heavenly hips, cascading black hair and twitching tummy wove an Arabian Nights spell, onlookers spontaneously began moving their shoulders, arms and hips in time to the music.

After the performance, a young student turned to his neighbor, a sturdy matron, and asked, "What interested you in belly-dancing?" The woman, who moments before had been swaying like Scheherazade, replied, "Anything that can combine weight reduction with sex has got to be a gift from heaven."

According to its teachers and devotees, belly-dancing consumes 350 calories an hour, develops a slender waist, teaches graceful movements, and presents sex with a smile instead of a leer. With such potential it seems no great wonder that so many women today want to learn how to do it. From Anchorage, Alaska, to Palm Springs, Fla., more than 5000 professionals are offering Oriental-dance instruction. Belly-dancing is now being taught on college campuses, at YWCAs, in department stores, shopping malls, homes and studios. Suburban housewives are forsaking the bridge table in squadrons for instructions in hip twisting, veil movement and shoulder isolation.

Whatever their reasons for seeking the secrets of the seductive shimmy, most student belly-dancers agree that it makes them feel joyous and alive. A New York schoolteacher boosts its exercise potential: "It is more suitable to a woman than calisthenics—but boy does it leave you stiff afterward!" A young woman in Los Angeles left the ballet to devote herself to belly-dancing, "because it offered a wider means of self-expression." A 32-year-old Washington, D.C., nurse, who goes to class three times a week, says simply, "Belly-dancing makes me feel like a temptress."

The origins of this dance are said to lie in fertility rites practiced in Egypt long before the time of the pharaohs. From Egypt, versions of the dance spread throughout the Mediterranean—most notably among the harems of Turkish sultans and their nobles. Since a sultan's harem might house 500 wives and concubines, only the best dancers could hope to attract his attention. Competition in the art became extremely keen. At the same time, punishment for any outsider caught gazing was instant death, so little descriptive material has survived.

After the fall of the sultans in 1921, the center of interest in belly-dancing shifted to Cairo, where a nightclub called the Casino Opera opened in 1925. Dancers from all over the Middle East worked their magic there, earning dowries and admirers.

But in 1953, with the accession of Gamal Abdel Nasser to power, belly-dancers were discouraged from performing in Cairo on the ground that their art was not dignified. Cairo's loss proved to be our gain. Star dancers traveled to the United States, where genuine interest in Oriental dancing was soon aroused. American girls began to be recruited into the dancers' ranks. Physical-education teachers discovered that belly-dancing involved movements which play one muscle against the other, strengthen the back, make the spine more supple, improve breathing and are fun to do. Changing its name to Mideastern folk dancing, they put it on their curriculums.

According to Serena, a leading teacher, performer and author of *The Serena Technique of Belly-Dancing*—and, in private life, Mrs. Alan Wilson—there are nine basic body positions Oriental dancers can learn, offering an almost limitless number of movements and variations. Concentrating on her form rather than locomotion, a highly trained belly-dancer can get volumes of subtle meaning in the twitch of a hip or the ripple of a tummy. Her muscle control is incredible. Many experts are able to slide to their knees, lean backward, touch the floor with their heads, drop a coin on their stomachs and flip it in the air.

Traditional instruments play a special role in all Oriental dancing. The whine of the flute inspires arm undulations reminiscent of a serpent. The twanging of the oud, an 11-stringed ancestor of the lute, helps shoulders rotate. The zing of the zither-like kanoun provokes a more lightsome touch.

As belly-dancers swirl through their routines, they snap their zills—small brass finger cymbals tuned to various pitches. A good player uses her zills to talk to the audience, signal other dancers or issue a bristling challenge to her musicians to match her movements. For each thrust of the dancer's hips, ripple of her belly or shake of her shoulders, the challenged musician will have a different answer. At the finale, his flying fingers will rip out the music in machine-gun-like bursts, while her replying hips swing in answer with the force of an atomic-powered pendulum.

Side by side with the growth of belly-dancing's popularity is a movement to have it taken seriously as an art form. New York City teacher-dancer Ibrahim "Bobby" Farrah and his troupe, considered by many experts to be the foremost Middle Eastern dancers in the world, want to preserve the original forms of belly-dancing, which Farrah has researched in travels through the East. By contrast, Serena wants to develop them along American lines, away from old rules. Her model is the American-born Ruth St. Denis, who, along with her partner, Ted Shawn, pioneered Oriental dancing in this country more than 60 years ago.

Most teachers seem to stress the joy in the dancing. Scheherazade, of Hartsdale, N.Y., tells her beginners to "feel their feet are nailed to the floor and to write their names with their hips." "In the beginning," Cia Cirel says, talking about her own teaching methods, "student belly-dancers are caught up in the glamour and fantasy of the veils, music and movement. Then, once their bodies have reacted to the discipline, they realize how much fun they are having."

One step beyond the obvious pleasure is the mystery which, for thousands of years, has kept belly-dancing alive as something more than pure entertainment. The expert dancer can induce a form of self-hypnosis called trance dancing. She feels as though she has left her body and is floating in air. She becomes euphoric and finds powers of creating and invention beyond her normal capability.

On a recent evening, I visited a small theater on New York's West Side to see Serena and her troupe perform. The house-lights lowered, the orchestra of oud, guitar and two drums began its beat, and the stage came alive with slender women in bangles and beads. Serena appeared, dominating the stage. She danced slowly at first, then with her zills challenged the musicians. They answered, and the dancing became faster. Every portion of Serena's body seemed to move independently. Her stomach flickered in and out like a tongue of flame.

When I left the theater I was still under Serena's spell. I felt an open-sesame to the harem's haunting mysteries. "Where to?" the taxi driver asked. I gave him my address, but at every corner we passed, I looked—in vain—for a veiled figure who might beckon me through the streets of old Baghdad back into the magical world of the Arabian Nights.

Pumping Iron

by Alfred Steinberg

WHEN MY SON dragged a barbell set through the cellar door, I wasn't at all pleased. Arne was a slim 14-year-old, and his main interest was the piano, on which he practiced long hours. My wife and I were certain that weight lifting would strain his abdominal muscles or damage his heart.

Nothing of the sort happened. After a month of fearful listening to clanging iron in the basement, we were happy to note Arne's improved posture and the spring in his walk. His ability in other sports showed visible gains. He became an excellent wrestler, could run half a mile without breathing hard, and could throw a ball much farther than any of his friends.

Nevertheless, my skepticism about weight lifting remained until four years later, when I visited him at Baltimore's Peabody College Conservatory, which he was then attending. By this time his shoulders were thick and hard, his arm muscles bulged and his stomach felt like a piece of wood. He was continuing his barbell work at the local Y.M.C.A.

Arne's interest in weight lifting started when he attended a lecture-demonstration by Robert Hoffman, who in 1964 was coach of the U.S. Olympic weight-lifting team for the fifth time. Hoffman, then 65, was six feet three inches tall, with a ramrod stance, a 53-inch chest and 250 pounds of hard weight. A successful businessman, he is still an enthusiastic muscle man. "You are your own sculptor," he insists, "You can mold and shape your body, and weight lifting can help you do it."

During his many decades of promoting weight lifting, Hoffman coached and built up many athletes. Yet his main interest has lain in making non-athletes—both men and women—aware of their bodies' welfare. He believes that everyone can and should be in good trim, as resoundingly healthy as he has always been. He has tirelessly promoted this cause through books, magazines, lectures and pamphlets. My family and I, and 15 million others around the world, can testify that his methods work.

Hoffman defines weight lifting as the simple raising and lowering of a barbell—or small dumbbells—to exercise different combinations of the 720 muscles in your body. A barbell is a five-foot-long metal bar, on the ends of which you can lock discs weighing from 1¼ pounds up. Using the smaller discs, even a frail man—or a woman—can perform the identical exercises that champions do. As strength grows, the weights can be increased little by little.

After observing my son's success, I could no longer excuse the roll around my middle, my flabby arms and disappearing chin. Arne's original barbell set was still in the basement with the instruction book listing different exercises. One day when no one was looking, I embarked on my first tentative adventure in weight lifting.

I carefully followed the detailed instructions to avoid strain. For one exercise I lay on my back, gripping the ends of a five-pound dumbbell and raising it from my thighs to over my head. By inhaling deeply as I raised it, exhaling as I lowered it, I could *feel* my chest expanding. The suggested routine required only about ten minutes every other day, doing ten repetitions of each exercise with light weights.

Surprisingly, there was no tiredness after each session, but a new, alert physical self-awareness. There was the constant incentive of graduating to heavier weights—an incentive that simple calisthenics lack. After a few months, suit jackets were growing snug across the shoulders, two inches had disappeared from my waist, the double chin had begun firming up.

Noting these clear improvements, my wife and 16-year-old daughter began to show a lively interest. They had always assumed that weight lifting was not for women and were surprised to learn that a number of women do exercise in this way. One pretty mother of five was told by her doctor that weight lifting had made the birth of her children easier because it had so notably improved her muscle tone. Women often exercise with no weights at all on the bar. (The bar alone with its end collars weighs 15 pounds.)

My wife and daughter were also concerned lest it develop bulging muscles. They discovered that women who do weight-lifting exercises—especially those devised for particular parts of the body—simply develop firmer flesh and trimmer lines. My wife did sit-ups and leg raises, and was pleased to find her hips and legs getting slimmer, while her posture improved.

The result I noticed most was that weight lifting gave me a sense of physical well-being I had not known since youth. I walked with a spring in my step, could clear a snow-filled walk without any sense of exertion. I came to realize that the body I had always taken for granted is a gift that deserves thoughtful care.

In the mid-1960s I visited Hoffman at York, Pa., where, in addition to his manufacturing operations, there are offices for his publications and other business activities, plus an excellent gym. He was in his 20s, manufacturing and selling oil burners, when he bought his first barbell set. While traveling on business he took along a small barbell set and exercised in the evening. In time his strength so increased that he could put 325 pounds overhead. In 1924, he organized the first national weight-lifting tournament in the United States—and won it.

Continued lifting brought improvement in other sports as well. In 1926, he was a member of Philadelphia's national champion Vesper Boat Club crew, international hexathlon champion, heavyweight weight-lifting champion again, national champion in the quarter-mile canoe race and at canoe tilting.

As a sideline, he started manufacturing barbells in one of his plants during the '30s. Then in the late '40s, says Hoffman, "I took stock of myself. I had all the money I needed—my health was excellent, and I decided to spend as much time as possible helping others improve theirs."

At that time the medical profession tended to look down its nose at weight lifting as a health aid. There were objections that it would make the exerciser muscle-bound and slow him down in sports requiring speed, coördination and agility. Dr. Peter Karpovich, professor of physiology at Springfield College, Mass., with Dr. W. S. Zorbas, tested 600 young people. The 300 who were weight lifters, with well-developed muscles, proved far speedier than those who were not. The results, said Karpovich, "were surprising to the investigators, too." Dr. Karpovich also examined the common belief that weight lifting produces ruptures. In his survey of 31,702 weight lifters, only five had hernias.

As for the belief that weight training can strain the heart, a physical-fitness specialist reports in *Strength and Health*, "The heart is a muscle and responds to exercise by getting stronger. By the time you have a muscular body your heart is prepared to keep it nourished. Progressive weight training will not injure a 'normal' heart."

Today many doctors weight-lift. At Moss Rehabilitation Center in Philadelphia—as at a number of other rehabilitation centers—graded weight lifting is the basis for most of the muscle-strengthening exercises. And weight-trained athletes include some of the best-known men in the sports world—including pole vaulters, golfers, runners, high jumpers, base-ball and tennis players.

Hoffman, still active at age 81, advises beginners with bar-bells to start slowly. "Train, don't strain," he says. "It took you years to get into your present condition, and you will need some time to work out of it. As your outer muscles strengthen, the internal muscles that hold your organs in place and keep them operating efficiently will also improve. At most, three months of training should begin to reward you with improved health and a prouder body." He emphasizes, too, that weight lifting alone cannot ensure good health. The observance of sane rules for diet, sleep, and the like are at least as important.

For workouts, Hoffman suggests a time before dinner or during the evening. "Odd as it may sound," he says, "if you come home from work tired or with a headache, exercise will often be the best antidote. It not only speeds the circulation and aids respiration—it sweeps the cobwebs from your brain."

Exercise in the Office

by Robert R. Spackman, Jr.

ARE YOU getting an hourglass figure with all the sand in the bottom? Is the floor getting farther away when you bend over to touch your toes? Can you look down and see your feet when you're standing up straight—or is there a Milwaukee tumor (beer belly) out in front? Do your legs shake like jelly when you walk? Have you noticed that you avoid stairs, or pull yourself up them by the handrail?

We are mechanized in almost everything we do. Know-how has taken the physical labor out of manufacturing jobs. We ride power mowers instead of pushing the hand mower. Typewriters, computers and business machines work with the lightest touch. Our homes are electric; the housewife must beware lest she get calloused fingers from pushing buttons.

Even in sports we have taken exercise away. We have golf carts to eliminate walking and ski lifts to take us to the top of the slope. Instead of rowing, we use motorboats. We are weekend athletes, or maybe only TV sports watchers.

Yet we all *need* daily exercise. The body remains strong only if it is used. Those parts involved in our usual daily regimen remain in reasonably good tone; those parts we don't use get weaker. More than 60 percent of the people in physicians' offices are underexercised. The only time many people step up their heart rates (the heart is a muscle and needs daily exercise) is when they get excited, smoke cigarettes or run across the street to avoid being hit by a car.

The only answer seems to be to make exercise part of your

daily activities, like brushing your teeth and combing your hair every morning. And while any exercise program should have a certain amount of vigorous activity, such as running or jogging, there are other calmer yet beneficial exercises that can be done almost anywhere.

For example, as you brush your teeth, pull your stomach muscles in tight and pinch your buttocks together. Stand on one leg when you put on your underwear and stockings instead of sitting down. If you walk to a commuter train, take big steps, breathe deeply and walk on your heels to stretch your heel cords. If you're driving (or riding in) a car, pull in your stomach muscles every time you stop for a street light. Hold them tight until you start the car again. Don't ride elevators—walk up at least a floor or two.

If you are a housewife, do stretching exercises while making the beds. Every so often stop whatever you're doing for a moment, rise on your toes on one leg and hold for six seconds. When you take the baby out of the crib, slowly lift him overhead four or five times. As you do the dishes, do deep knee bends slowly.

Many other exercises you can do while working at home or in your office. Don't answer the first ring of a phone; sit there, pull your stomach muscles in tightly and hold until the second ring. After the call, attempt to pull the phone apart, holding this position for six seconds before you hang up (next time, try pushing it together). After a client leaves your office or after coffee with a neighbor, push yourself up from your chair with your arms, keeping your legs extended. There are exercises you can do to improve your body—as part of your daily activities—from the time you get up in the morning until you go to bed at night.

Take a look in your mirror. The average American is ten or more pounds overweight. Many people can't understand why they are tired most of the time and fatigue so quickly with a little activity. But when you carry extra weight, your body has to work harder than normal. Working harder, the muscles fatigue. When fatigue sets in, muscles get tight, and the blood supply cannot circulate. With impaired circulation, the muscles ache and you have pain.

With daily on-the-job exercise, you can gain strength, and with more strength you will not have the fatigue and pain. (You might also cut out some of your snacks and lose the extra weight.) Before you begin an exercise program, have a physical examination. In most cases your physician will tell you that such a program is the best idea you ever had. He will also indicate what exercises would be best for you.

Do exercises slowly for the first week. Feel your way along so as not to hurt yourself with too vigorous contractions of the muscles. Always exercise short of the point of pain. Remember that at first you will have a little muscle soreness. Keep exercising—after a few days the muscle soreness will leave you.

Here are a few exercises almost anyone can fit into his schedule, using any time available and repeating at least three times during the day.

• *Neck extension*. Place hands behind your head with the fingers laced together. Attempt to push your head backward for six seconds (counting one-thousand-one, one-thousand-two, etc.) as you resist with your hands. Resist with head forward, then straight, and all the way back. Stretch your neck as far as you can in all directions.

• *Squeeze the desk together*. Sit at your desk; attempt to compress it by pulling your arms together, resisting for six seconds. This exercise helps to keep the chest muscles strong and the bust firm. Use stove, refrigerator, wardrobe or any other convenient item of furniture.

• *Shoulder flexion*. Sit at your desk (or table) and raise your arms forward until the backs of your hands are touching the underside of the desk in front of you. Keep your stomach muscles tight and your back straight. Attempt to lift the desk, pushing for six seconds; then relax. Vary this exercise by standing in a doorway and trying to push its two sides apart with the backs of your hands.

• *Back exercise*. Bend over at the waist, holding your legs with your hands behind the knees. Pull your stomach muscles in and attempt to straighten your back. Resist back extension with your hands and hold for six seconds. Try this exercise anytime your back feels tired, but remember to stretch and loosen up the back before and after.

• *Straight leg raising backward*. Lean over a table. Slowly raise one leg as high as possible (for six seconds). Slowly return to the starting position. Alternate legs. Vary by raising leg with knee bent.

• *V sit-ups*. You can do this one in bed. Raise both legs and your upper body simultaneously—keeping your legs straight, with arms out straight for balance. Hold this V position for six seconds, slowly returning to the starting position. Three repetitions of this exercise will help you to relax so you can get a good night's sleep.

• *Hip flexion.* Sit on a sofa with your feet under the coffee table. Hold the top of the table for stabilization. Raise one leg—keeping the knee straight—until the toes touch the table. Try to lift the table with the straight leg for six seconds; relax. Alternate legs.

• *Stretching on the stairs.* Stop as you go up the stairs, hold onto the rail and place the balls of your feet on the edge of a stair. Slowly rise on the toes as high as possible; stretch. Slowly lower down beyond the edge of the stair, stretching the heel cords.

In choosing specific exercises, think about your job. Do you work in an office? Are you a schoolteacher? Do you work on an assembly line? Do you drive a truck? How can you exercise on your job? Make a list of exercises you can do daily as you go about your tasks.

Many people wonder how to *remember* to exercise. They start off exercising regularly for a few days or a week, and then they get busy and forget all about it. Here are a few helpful hints. Try sticking pieces of adhesive tape around to jog your memory; for example, a small piece of adhesive tape on the corner of your mirror will remind you to pull in the abdominal muscles as you shave or comb your hair. Or choose exercises that you can do whenever you hear a bell or the phone.

Remember, if you can move a muscle you can strengthen it. It doesn't matter how old you are—if you start slowly and add resistance slowly, your strength and range of motion will increase. So begin today. Tomorrow you'll be a day older.

I have never seen anyone who could move a muscle and was willing to work who couldn't gain strength and have a more active life. You've reached middle age when your weight lifting consists of standing up.

YOU ARE WHAT YOU EAT

Do We Eat Too Much Meat?

by Daniel Grotta-Kurska

THE average American has been conditioned to believe that only a meat-based diet can provide the nutrition necessary for good health. Traditionally, we are a nation of carnivores, consuming some 15 pounds of meat per person, per month. (The Japanese, by contrast, eat only about a half pound of meat per person, per month.)

Does this great U.S. "meat gorge" make nutritional sense? *Is* meat necessary to our health?

Scientists have long classified meat as "first-class" protein and vegetables as "second-class" protein, thereby implying that non-animal protein is somehow inferior. Current evidence, however, points to other conclusions. For example:

• Statistically, vegetarians in the United States are thinner, healthier and may live longer than meat eaters.

• Meat, especially in the large quantities Americans are accustomed to eating, may be harmful to the body.

• Protein from non-flesh foods can be an adequate nutritional substitute for meat protein, particularly when supplemented with modest amounts of protein from milk and eggs.

Protein is essential to life. It is the substance that the body uses to build and replenish organs, skin, cartilage, nails, hair, muscle, and the organic framework of bones. The proteins our bodies use are composed of 22 amino acids. The human metabolic system can produce 14 of these on its own, but the remaining eight must be obtained from food. Hence their name—the "essential" amino acids. To be useful to a person, the totality of food proteins must be "complete"—all eight essential amino acids must be ingested more or less simultaneously, and in the right proportion. Incomplete proteins cannot be used to build muscle and tissue; they often end up as stored fat or are utilized for energy.

Meat is a complete protein because all eight essential amino acids are present in the proper proportion. Vegetable foods are incomplete proteins, in that they lack one or more of these acids.

But it is possible to satisfy your protein needs by a proper intermixing of plant proteins. You just have to make sure that you use the right combination. Wheat, for example, which has a deficiency in the amino acid *lysine* but an abundance of sulfur-containing amino acids, can be combined with beans, which have the opposite enrichment combination. Taken together, they complement each other to form a nearly complete protein.

Nutritionists use two basic criteria in evaluating protein sources: quality and quantity. Quality refers to the usability of protein by the body. This factor is expressed on a scale of 0 to 100. The Food and Agricultural Organization of the United Nations gives meat a protein quality rating of 67—higher than that of most plant proteins, with the exception of whole rice (70), and below that of cheese (70), fish (80), milk (82) and eggs (95).

In terms of quantity, 15 to 30 percent of the total weight of flesh food is usable protein—lamb rates the lower figure and turkey the higher one; the rest is water, fat and trace minerals. On the other hand, soybean flour is 40 percent protein; Parmesan cheese, 36 percent; and peas, lentils, and dried beans between 20 and 25 percent. Grains are fairly low in quantity (8 to 15 percent) but, surprisingly, so are milk (4 percent) and eggs (13 percent).

All this means that, in general, one has to eat proportionately less meat than vegetable protein sources to obtain the same amount of usable protein. But non-flesh alternatives are perfectly adequate.

Balanced against this, however, are the *disadvantages* of a diet heavy in meat. For one thing, the primary problem most American meat eaters face is not a deficiency of protein (most of us get all we need, and then some), but an excess of calories—because the meat we eat so much of is so larded with saturated fat. A number of nutritional studies have concluded that vegetarians who eat a proper diet easily meet their protein and caloric needs. Most meat eaters, however, consistently exceed their limits in calories and, as a consequence, tend to weigh more.

"Forty percent of the fat in our diets comes from meat," says Dr. Fredrick Stare, founder of the department of nutrition at the Harvard School of Public Health. "This fat is heavily—about 40 percent—of the saturated, cholesterol-producing variety. With the exception of eggs and dairy products, non-animal foods have *no* cholesterol." A study conducted by Dr. Stare and Dr. Mervyn Hardinge showed that vegetarians have consistently lower levels of serum cholesterol than do meat eaters.

Meat eaters also may be bothered by poor elimination. Food with a low fiber content, such as meat, moves sluggishly through the digestive tract, making stools dry and hard to pass. Vegetables, by contrast, retain moisture and bind waste bulk for easy passage.

But still the question remains: *Is* a vegetarian diet more healthful than a meat diet? Nutritionists have yet to agree on an answer. But evidence suggesting this conclusion is offered by anthropologists. Field investigations of certain non-meat cultures have documented the excellent health and longevity enjoyed by people such as the Hunzas of Pakistan and the Otomi Indians of Mexico. During World War I, Denmark consumed far less meat than usual because of the British naval blockade. Nutritionists who studied the people during the war concluded that general health had improved. Similarly, Norway adopted a vegetarian diet during World War II, and there was a significant drop in heart disease. Both nations, however, reverted to meat diets as soon as the crises passed, and subsequent studies showed that the temporary health advantages apparently subsided.

Such evidence, of course, is inconclusive, and many nutritionists remain unconvinced of the superiority of vegetarianism. They point out that certain vegetarian diets can lead to serious nutritional problems. For example, a strict macrobiotic diet (based largely on brown rice) can induce scurvy, anemia, hypocalcemia, emaciation and loss of kidney function. Other equally ill-advised vegetarian diets have resulted in beriberi, rickets, pellagra and severe vitamin deficiencies.

For people who are following, or plan to adopt, a vegetarian diet, here are a few basic guidelines:

• Cut sugar, fat and oil calories in half. Replace meat with increased intake of legumes, nuts, or textured vegetable protein such as soyburgers.

• Eat more grains and cereals, plus such things as raw carrots, beet roots, dried fruits and salads.

• Include cottage cheese, low-fat milk and eggs in your diet. To retain vitamins and minerals, cook vegetables for the shortest time and in as little water as possible. Eat fruit.

For pure vegetarians—who do not use dairy products or eggs—the following points are also important:

• Increase intake of leafy green vegetables.

• Consume a variety of plant foods—grains, fruits, vegetables, nuts—sufficient to meet caloric needs.

• Use fortified soy-milk preparations and textured vegetable proteins. Take vitamin B-12.

It may be helpful to remember that the word "vegetarian" is derived from the Latin word *vegetus,* which means "whole, sound, fresh, lively." "Vegetarianism is a humanitarian crusade," sums up Jay Dinshah, founder of the North American Vegetarian Society. Perhaps it is. From a nutritional standpoint, it may not be a bad idea, either.

What's Your Food I.Q.?

by Elizabeth M. Whelan

TODAY we need all the help we can get in sifting food facts from fads. Health foods, organically grown foods, massive doses of vitamins—all have reputable backers as well as cranks and faddists on their side. Fortunately, much has now been learned about these controversial food areas. To see if you are up to date on the constantly emerging facts, take this test. The answers, or facts, appear below each statement.

Organically grown foods are more nutritious than "chemically fertilized" foods: *Yes or No*.

Repeated scientific studies have concluded that organic foods—those naturally fertilized—are nutritionally indistinguishable from those fertilized by chemicals. *All* fertilizers, whether commercially processed or derived from living organisms, must be broken down to their inorganic components, such as nitrogen, postassium and phosphorus, before the plants can use them. When the fertilizer is transformed into nutrients, the plant cannot identify its origin. So you can't increase the vitamin content of an apple by altering the way it is grown. Its nutritional quality is largely genetically determined.

The non-use of pesticides by organic farmers produces a different problem: a significantly higher probability of crop failure. Contrary to popular belief, organic foods have no special immunity to insects. According to Norman E. Borlaug, a Nobel Prize-winner for his work in developing new strains of wheat, "If the use of pesticides in the United States were to be completely banned, crop losses would probably soar to 50 percent, and food prices would increase four- to five-fold." Given the recent direction of food prices, this is no small consideration.

Natural foods are safer than "artificial" foods: *Yes or No*.

"Natural" means free of additives—an unadulterated product of Mother Nature. But, under some circumstances, "natural" can also mean harmful—even life-threatening. Natural foods can deteriorate faster than those protected by additives. Sometimes the changes they undergo result in molds and other types of growths which have been linked with cancer and other diseases. It has been shown, for instance, that peanut meal can become contaminated with potent cancer-causing molds (aflatoxins). Mold growths on rye, wheat and sweet potatoes can pose equally serious problems. Even when fresh, some natural foods, such as bracken and sassafras roots, can wreak havoc with health.

There are some highly relevant statistics for those who fear links between food additives and cancer. These statistics clearly indicate that the rise in cancer deaths in the United States in the last 45 years can be attributed to an increase in lung cancer and the associated increase in cigarette consumption since the early 1940s. There is no such linkage of food additives with cancer. The frequency of cancer in nearly all other bodily sites—for instance, the stomach, which one might suspect could be affected by additives—has declined or stabilized.

Those who are alarmed about additives might look at some of the ways that additives have made our food healthier and safer. If nitrates and nitrites are omitted from processed and smoked meats, protection against botulism must be found. The fortification of foods with vitamins C and D and iodide has all but eliminated scurvy, rickets and goiter. New scientific findings strongly suggest that certain preservatives (BHT and BHA in particular) may decrease the incidence of stomach cancer. This protective action has been demonstrated in laboratory animals, and is suggested by the statistics on human disease. After BHT and BHA became widely used as antioxidants in the late 1940s the rate of stomach cancer began to fall; in countries such as Hungary, West Germany and Poland, where these preservatives were not used, the rates of this form of cancer remained relatively high.

Vitamin E has special preventive and curative powers: *Yes or No*.

Vitamin E has been touted to promote physical endurance and sexual potency, improve sperm quality, prevent miscarriage, protect against air pollution, and both prevent and cure heart attacks, muscular dystrophy, ulcers, cirrhosis of the liver and cancer. These claims are all scientifically undocumented. The claims of vitamin E's wonders are derived from laboratory-animal experiments where vitamin-E deficiencies were induced. Diseases did develop in these animals. Health enthusiasts drew analogies to humans. Their arguments, however, were faulty. Scientists have established that vitamin E is so widely distributed in the foods we eat (vegetable oils, whole grains, soybeans, leafy green vegetables) that it is almost impossible to develop a deficiency.

Extra doses of vitamin A contribute to strength and vitality: *Yes or No*.

Vitamin A plays a vital part in vision, children's growth and bone development, the health of the skin and mucous membranes. It is found in eggs, butter, fortified milk, meats and liver; deep-yellow and dark-green vegetables contain carotenes, substances which the body can convert to vitamin A. A well-balanced diet supplies adequate vitamin A; extra doses can be dangerous.

In 1856, an arctic explorer and his companion feasted one night on polar-bear liver, and shortly thereafter recorded symptoms of vertigo, violent headache and nausea. A century later, diners enjoying shark liver reported the same effects. Both groups had eaten food which contained an extraordinary amount of vitamin A, and they were experiencing its toxic effects.

In the early 1970s, while few people included polar-bear or shark livers in their diet, many were taking high supplementary doses of vitamin A and suffering from intracranial pressure and violent headaches. In addition, there were deaths from cirrhosis of the liver among food faddists who used inordinate amounts of carrot juice each day to wash down their vitamin-A capsules. Concerned about this massive self-medication, the Food and Drug Administration a few years ago restricted over-the-counter vitamin sale. It is no longer possible to purchase high doses of vitamin A without a prescription.

Large amounts of vitamin C may be dangerous: *Yes or No*.

The controversy about vitamin C began when Nobel-Prize-winner Linus Pauling presented his theory that massive doses of vitamin C (up to 20 times the recommended daily allowance) would prevent colds, and even larger doses would cure them. Dozens of attempts have since been made either to confirm or to deny this theory. The results are at this point inconclusive. Some studies show a slight decrease in the incidence of colds with vitamin-C therapy; other studies show no effect at all.

Meanwhile, doctors are concerned about the possible side effects of massive self-administration of this vitamin. (The recommended daily requirement is provided by a glass of orange juice or a serving of tomatoes.) Some people taking heavy doses develop diarrhea. Studies suggest that massive doses may also increase the chance of developing kidney stones. And some scientists have advanced the hypothesis that large amounts of vitamin C may reduce female fertility by changing the nature of the secretions around the cervix. Attention is also being given to the notion that high doses of vitamin C can lead to a dependency.

Lecithin is nature's protection against heart attacks: *Yes or No*.

Lecithin is a natural emulsifying agent. It has been used for many years in mayonnaise, salad dressings and chocolate to maintain the stability of the oil ingredients. Recently lecithin has been glorified as the key to preventing heart attacks. Some food faddists contend that it can also cure arthritis, high blood pressure and gall-bladder problems, while also improving brain power.

The theory is that lecithin breaks up and disperses cholesterol in the blood so it cannot become attached to the artery walls. There is no medical evidence to back up this belief, however. The body manufactures its own lecithin, and there is no reason to believe that any additional quantities of this natural emulsifier are necessary or helpful. Heart specialists have expressed concern that people buying lecithin in capsules, chewable wafers, tablets and oil solutions are deluding themselves—while sometimes continuing to smoke and omitting exercise and proper diet, practices which *have* been linked with higher probabilities of heart disease.

Some foods, such as honey and brown rice, have "magical" properties: *Yes or No*.

From time to time throughout history, the wonders of a certain food have been proclaimed, and eager listeners have tried it. One of the leading "miracle foods" today is honey. A health-food-store owner says, "I recommend honey for ulcers and cancers and for the prevention of both." Advocates of brown rice claim that it is a perfect food. Seawater is advertised as "nature's cleanser," and escarole is said to promote healthier complexion. Some of these fads may prove harmless. Others—particularly the macrobiotic diet's recommendation of the *exclusive* use of brown rice—can prove (and have proven) fatal.

Fascination with miracle foods—and other types of food myths—will probably always be with us. The most rational concept of a healthy diet still seems to be one which is based on the nutritional facts that scientists have spent years accumulating and verifying.

A Vital Ingredient May Be Missing in Your Diet

by Lawrence Galton

SOMETHING may be missing from the American diet—sufficient fiber, or roughage. Until a few years ago, its importance was regarded as just an old wives' tale, but mounting evidence suggests that the lack of this ingredient may be a contributing factor in a number of diseases, including appendicitis, intestinal polyps (a type of benign growth), diverticular disease, cancer of the colon and rectum, and heart disease.

Medical attention began to focus on the problem as the result of the brilliant detective work of a distinguished British surgeon, Dr. Denis Burkitt, who first became interested in the subject through research done by a naval surgeon, Capt. Thomas L. Cleave. Today, cancer of the colon and rectum (colo-rectal cancer) is the most common major malignancy in the United States, striking 114,000 Americans each year and killing more than 50,000. It is now second only to lung cancer as a cause of death from malignancy. Yet, in the underdeveloped countries of Africa, where Dr. Burkitt spent 20 years as a surgeon, colo-rectal cancer is a relative rarity. In Kampala, Uganda, for example, its incidence was 3.5 per 100,000 population, 1/13 that in the United States. Dr. Burkitt asked: why?

Many clues pointed to diet—among them, the way American blacks have been affected. Their ancestors came from African villages where colo-rectal cancer is rare. Fifty years ago, when there were still differences in the menus of black and white Americans, colo-rectal cancer struck two whites for every black. Now, with diets more uniform, blacks in America are as often affected as whites.

Dr. Burkitt found that colo-rectal cancer and certain other bowel diseases seem to be associated. All have been increasing among Africans moving from native villages to urban areas and Westernized diets. "In Uganda," Burkitt says, "you did not get appendicitis if you didn't speak English."

That diet could be involved in colo-rectal cancer has not escaped other investigators' attention. Some have viewed increased beef and fat consumption with suspicion. Countries such as Scotland, Denmark, Argentina, Uruguay and New Zealand, enjoying high beef consumption, have high rates of colo-rectal cancer. But Dr. Burkitt and a number of others suspect that the blame may be placed elsewhere: in the heavy consumption of cereals which have had most of their fibers refined right out of them.

Rural Africans, largely free of these bowel diseases, eat coarsely ground grains and only lightly processed cereals such as maize and millet, high in fiber content. Additionally, they eat such fiber-rich foods as sweet potatoes and plantain. They take in about 25 grams of fiber daily—until they adopt Westernized diets.

Americans do eat more fat now than 65 years ago, evidence suggests, and the consumption of whole-grain cereals has declined.

"We have assumed," says Burkitt, "that the unabsorbable fiber from our food doesn't matter because it lacks nourishment."

Why is fiber important? Burkitt, until 1976 with the British Medical Research Council, and other investigators working with him from all over the world, particularly Dr. Alexander R. P. Walker in South Africa, carried out studies showing the possible reasons. The investigators had subjects swallow radiopaque plastic pellets that could be detected in stools by X ray. They found that it took less than 30 hours for the majority of African villagers to pass 80 percent of the pellets. It took over three days for most boys attending an English boarding school. So the transit time needed for food to pass through the intestinal tract is markedly speeded by fiber and slowed without it. African villagers on unrefined diets also had much larger stools (average weight over 250 grams) than Westerners. For Englishmen on refined diets it was usually under 110 grams.

Moreover, some bacteria are able to act on the bile salts in the intestinal tract and convert them into deoxycholic acid, a potential carcinogen, or cancer-producing agent. Such bacteria are 100 times more prevalent among peoples on refined diets than among African villagers.

The activity of certain bacteria, small stools and longer transit times are associated with an increased risk of colo-rectal cancer. Where the stool is small, the carcinogens produced by the bacteria will be present in it in more concentrated form. Where the transit time is slow, they will be held against the bowel lining for a longer time. But with a high-fiber diet, there are fewer undesirable bacteria; the larger stool dilutes the concentration of any carcinogens they produce; and the faster transit time allows less opportunity for carcinogens to act on the bowel lining.

Other factors, including eating more fat, doubtless influence development of bowel cancer. But it seems clear that lack of fiber must be taken seriously as a major factor in colo-rectal cancer—and in a number of other common diseases as well.

Diverticular disease is one. Within the span of 75 years, from being almost unknown, it has become the most common affliction of the colon in many Western countries. In the United States, according to Dr. Lauren V. Ackerman of the State University of New York at Stony Brook, "Practically every adult has diverticula, colon outpouchings which, if they become inflamed, may lead to diverticulitis, a serious disease." Yet in rural Africa, diverticular disease is virtually unknown.

Investigators have been able to produce diverticula in animals fed low-fiber diets for prolonged periods. Conversely, in a test in England involving 70 patients, Dr. N. S. Painter was able to relieve 85 percent of the symptoms of the disease by giving bran. And, in a study at the Western General Hospital, Edinburgh, Scotland, the addition of bran to the diets of patients who had already undergone surgery for diverticular disease was found helpful in preventing recurrences.

Why should appendicitis, also virtually unknown among African villagers, be influenced by lack of dietary fiber? Without fiber, constipation is frequent. And with constipation, the entrance to the appendix becomes blocked, causing abnormal pressure. This damages the lining, which is then invaded by bacteria, producing appendicitis.

The close association between colo-rectal cancer and polyps in the colon suggests they may result from the same cause—lack of fiber. In the United States 10 to 15 percent of adults (about 25 percent of those over 70) have polyps, but in Africa they are almost unknown.

Can lack of dietary fiber be a factor in such heart diseases as angina pectoris and myocardial infarction? There is evidence for it. Studies indicate that incidence of ischemic heart disease (IHD)—caused by deficiency of blood oxygen—is exceedingly rare in all African tribal groups, but rising in urban areas, among Africans who adopt Westernized diets.

Dr. Hugh Trowell also found a curious situation in Great Britain. There, IHD mortality had been increasing up to 1939. Then wartime rationing led to use of wheat flour with greater fiber content, and the trend was arrested. The mortality resumed its rise after the war.

The studies also showed blood-cholesterol levels to be lower among rural Africans. Laboratory tests, probing this correlation, demonstrated that when chicks, rabbits and rats are fed high-cholesterol diets to which fiber is added, their blood-cholesterol levels somehow stay down.

Studies with human volunteers have shown the same apparent cholesterol-lowering effect. In one study, addition of butter to the diet increased cholesterol levels, but when fiber was also added the cholesterol levels fell 20 percent. In another, men given 140 grams a day of rolled oats, rich in fiber, experienced a 33-point drop in cholesterol level.

It is also possible that the consumption of unrefined instead of refined carbohydrates could combat obesity. Carbohydrates are supposed to be fattening. Yet many primitive peoples, who rarely are obese, eat much more carbohydrate than we do—for example, 580 grams per day in rural Bantustan. But they eat unrefined carbohydrates still loaded with fiber, which is not itself absorbed by the body, so does not add to weight. One study has indicated that of the calories in whole-meal bread, only 86 percent are absorbed, while 97 percent of the calories in white bread are.

If what Dr. Burkitt and others contend is true, is it practical to add more fiber to our diets? Yes, and apparently not much is needed. At an English boarding school, a study was carried out in which adolescent boys and faculty members received two heaped teaspoonfuls of bran and two slices of whole-meal bread daily instead of their usual white bread.

After three weeks on the new diet, intestinal transit times decreased by about a third, and stool weights were up by a quarter—suggesting that a return of only about two to three grams of crude fiber to the daily diet "might significantly alter bowel behavior toward that which is characteristic of communities free from non-infective bowel diseases."

At the University of Bristol, England, Dr. Kenneth W Heaton and associates found that in a group of patients given bran, those with a slow intestinal transit time found that this was speeded, whereas a fast transit time was slowed down. Says Dr. Heaton, the result "suggests that bran in some way 'normalizes' colonic behavior."

Not all the proof is in, but the simple expedient of making fiber a part of our regular diet might well do more to "keep the doctor away" than the proverbial apple.

How to Add Fiber to Your Diet

Many vegetables and fruits have high fiber content. Among them: broccoli, Brussels sprouts, cabbage, cauliflower, beets, carrots, sweet potatoes, berries, tomatoes, eggplant and summer squash.

However, cereal fiber appears to be most effective. Cereal fiber is found in whole grains and bran. Bran is the fiber-rich outer coat of the seed of cereal grain, which is largely removed in refining processes. In whole grain, the bran remains.

Commercial 100-percent whole-wheat breads are good sources of fiber. So are homemade whole-grain wheat-flour breads, whole-grain flour pancakes, muffins made with whole-ground cornmeal or with a combination of whole-wheat flour and bran cereal. Other sources include oatmeal, brown rice and buckwheat groats. But there is little in white rice, or the cake and pastry flours used in white breads and baked goods.

In breakfast cereals the largest amount of fiber are found in those with "bran" in their names. In some cases the fiber content is indicated on the package.

Bran itself is the most concentrated form of fiber. Two heaped soupspoonfuls of bran provide about two grams of fiber. And research indicates that it may take restoration of only about two to three grams of cereal fiber in the daily diet to improve bowel functioning and health.

To Reduce
Your Chances of Cancer

by Jane E. Brody

MRS. M gives her family only "organically grown" and "natural" foods because she is convinced that preservatives and pesticides cause cancer. Mrs. Y, who is always on a diet, is distressed over the finding that saccharin produced bladder cancers in laboratory animals. Mr. S daily gulps down large doses of vitamins, hoping they will keep him free from cancer, which seems to run in his family.

It is fashionable these days to look to diet as the cause, or preventive, of the major ills of modern man, including cancer. But in the excitement generated by the discovery that an occasional food additive or contaminant may cause cancer in animals—or that deficiencies in certain "micronutrients" (such as vitamin A, riboflavin, iodine and the trace minerals molybdenum and selenium) may set the stage for the disease—many people may be missing the most important point. A growing body of evidence suggests that principal concern should focus on the major, not the minor, components of the diet. According to Dr. David P. Rose, cancer specialist at the University of Wisconsin, the "new concept is that foods themselves—rather than preservatives or contaminants—may be involved in the cause of some of the most common cancers in the United States." Consider these findings:

• An international diet survey showed that those who developed cancer of the colon and rectum ate more meat than comparable persons free of those cancers.

• Mormons and Seventh-Day Adventists, who eat little or no

meat, have much lower rates of cancers of the colon, rectum, breast and uterus than comparable groups of Americans who eat meat. The Mormon and Adventist diets contain mostly vegetable, rather than animal, protein, and thus are high in fiber, or roughage.

• Most countries where deaths from cancer of the colon and breast are uncommon have diets low in animal and dairy fats.

• In Japan, where the traditional diet contains little meat and almost no dairy products, cancers of the colon and breast are uncommon. However, when Japanese migrate to this country and gradually adopt a Western diet, their risk of developing cancer of the colon and breast increases dramatically. In a few generations it equals the American rate.

• Obese persons have a higher than normal risk of developing cancer—particularly cancers of the breast, endometrium (lining of the uterus) and gall bladder—compared with people of normal weight. Even with overweight mice, the risk of cancer increases. Mice whose calorie and protein intake is restricted have a significantly reduced risk of developing cancer.

Based on this and related evidence, some authorities (for example, Gio B. Gori of the National Cancer Institute and David M. Hegsted of the Harvard School of Public Health) have urged a significant change in the typical American diet. And it is a change they believe would likely reduce the chances of developing heart disease as well as cancer. Here's what the experts recommend:

• Eat less high-fat beef, lamb and pork—more fish and poultry.

• When you do eat meat, select lean cuts and trim off all visible fat before cooking. Drain off all fat that cooks out.

• Avoid deep-fat frying. Instead, bake, boil, broil, roast or stew. In making a stew or soup, cook it ahead and chill it. Then, before reheating, discard the fat that congeals at the top.

• Substitute skimmed or low-fat milk and cheeses for whole milk and cheese. Substitute soft margarine for butter; use only liquid vegetable oils (preferably corn or soybean oil); keep egg consumption down to two or three eggs a week.

• Eat more vegetables, beans and whole grains, and fruits, instead of sugar-sweetened foods. Switch to a more vegetarian diet, experts say, and you are likely to have less artery-clogging cholesterol in your blood, less difficulty controlling your weight (which in turn helps to keep your blood pressure low), and possibly less risk of getting cancer.

In fact, in 1977 the Senate Select Committee on Nutrition and Human Needs urged precisely such a change in the American diet. It recommended a 25-percent reduction in the consumption of fats, and a 25-percent increase in carbohydrates (particularly in the form of whole grains, fruits and vegetables). The committee cited the relationship between the current fat-rich, fiber-deficient American diet and a high risk of cancer as well as heart ailments and other diseases.

Dr. Ernst Wynder, president of the American Health Foundation, which does extensive research on preventing illness, emphasizes that making such dietary changes "cannot hurt—it can only help." Cancer of the colon and rectum is the leading life threatening cancer among Americans of both sexes, and breast cancer is the leading cancer killer of American women. Widespread adoption of these dietary recommendations could in theory greatly reduce these deaths, and deaths from heart disease.

Alcohol also has been shown to increase the chances of developing cancer, particularly cancers of the esophagus, mouth, throat, larynx and liver. The risk of developing esophageal cancer is many times greater for heavy drinkers than for non-drinkers. And the greatest cancer risk is faced by persons who both smoke and drink heavily.

Good nutrition by itself is not adequate therapy against cancer. Nor does current research support the theory that cancer can be cured by eating this or that food item or food supplement. The evidence gathered so far on the effects of diet on cancer *prevention*, though, is encouraging. It's worth paying attention to, now.

THE BREATH OF LIFE

Take a Deep Breath

by Helen Durham

BREATHE to be healthy. Breathe to be handsome. Breathe to stand well, talk well, *be* well. On this point everyone agrees, faddist and physician alike.

"To breathe properly is to live properly," says the old yogi philosopher. "Breath is the stuff of which voice is made," says the voice expert. The posture expert's first command is to fill your lungs. The honest beauty specialist admits that increased circulation brought about by good breathing will do more for your complexion than a lifetime of massage. The psychologist will tell you that an inferiority complex may spring from something as simple as scant breath. As for the doctor, he will tell you that breathing is the first vital process of life. His business is to keep you breathing, from the time he thumps you on the back to get you going until he produces the oxygen to keep you from stopping. Most of us take in enough to sustain life but not enough to live it vigorously. We are like a car chugging along on only half its cylinders. If some of us actually filled our lungs with a great blast of air, we would have an oxygen jag, a lightheaded feeling—that is a physical fact. If you don't believe it try it sometime.

We are so accustomed to using only the tops of our lungs that we get the idea they end at the bust line. But they don't. On either side of the ribs they extend down to the waistline. Unless you constantly make use of this important lower-lung section in your breathing, you are a poor risk for the insurance company and a flop in the beauty contest.

Vida Sutton, whose job it was to train the tones of NBC radio announcers, used to say: you never talk better than you breathe. Without an ample column of air your voice lacks color and richness. The voice of the shallow breather is shallow, thin and squeaky. The person who breathes lazily has a lazy, drawling voice.

The radio announcer knows the value of deep breathing. Go into any broadcasting studio and see the announcer before his microphone, waiting to be flashed on the air, one eye on the clock. The back of his coat is rising and falling. He is tuning up his instrument.

The psychologist says it is quite possible to control your mood by your breathing. If you are nervous, excited, angry—breathe deeply. The calming effect is a miracle.

Deep breathing is the actor's first aid against stage fright. Even a seasoned star like Helen Hayes declared she could never face a first-night audience without screwing up her courage by a few deep breaths.

"It was Mary Garden," says Miss Hayes, "who first made me aware of the importance of breath. I was introduced to her as 'little Miss Hayes, the actress.' Miss Garden's response was to give me a vigorous thump just above the belt. 'Actress?' she said. 'You can't act, my child. You haven't the diaphragm of a baby.'

"For years I could play only ingénue rôles because I had only a fluffy little flapper's breath. I could never have played Coquette without the power and poise I acquired from learning how to breathe."

Many people stand badly because they breathe badly. When chests are concave and torsos slump, the first point of attack is the breath. Properly inflated lungs right the body just as proper ballast rights the ship.

Now if you're curious as to whether or not you breathe correctly, unbuckle your belt and slip it up a few inches, halfway between waistline and bust line. Exhale and pull your belt in as tight as you can until you're empty as a pricked balloon. Now take a whopper of a breath and see how many notches you can expand. It is here that chest expansion should be measured, instead of under the armpits as your old gym teacher believed.

Don't try to expand by swelling out in front, by abdominal breathing alone. Expansion should come across the back and sides as well. To see how much rear expansion you get, put your hands at the small of your back, thumbs forward, middle fingers touching behind. Give yourself a tight squeeze, exhaling as much as you can. Then inhale and see how far you can force your hands apart. Your ribs are a flexible cage that protects your lungs. As your lungs expand, the bony cage should expand all around. One way to learn how to breathe deeply is to get the sensation of packing your breath well in against the back of your ribs.

"Ordinarily breathing should be unconscious," says Dr. Eugene Lyman Fisk, "but every day deep-breathing exercises should be employed. People who are shut in all day may partly compensate for the evils of indoor living by stepping out of doors and taking a dozen deep breaths whenever the opportunity presents itself."

Without the help of your diaphragm you can never breathe as you should. The diaphragm is the floor of the chest. It is a dome-shaped muscle, with the dome inverted. As we inhale, the dome drops downward, increasing the chest cavity for the air to rush in. As we exhale, the dome flattens upward, forcing the air out. Without the help of this important muscle you cannot make a sound. You cannot pant, sigh, cough, grunt or clear your throat. A man's diaphragm is placed lower than a woman's, which gives his chest more room; and his more active habits of life have made this muscle stronger. Women, with a few exceptions, are shallow breathers, apt to neglect this muscle.

Happily, nature taught us how to use the diaphragm. Infants breathe correctly; so do sleeping persons. When we grow up or wake up we allow inhibitions to restrict free diaphragmatic action. A good way to re-educate your diaphragm, once it has gone wrong, is to lie flat on your back, discard the cares of the world and let the great muscle work naturally. If you do this until it becomes a habit you will breathe this way on your feet. The spectacular Maria Jeritza, whose operatic performances usually had a touch of the acrobatic in them, made it a point from time to time to sing a favorite aria lying on her back. She said she learned to sing in that position.

The only purpose of breathing is to get oxygen into our systems, for without oxygen we should quickly die. Every vital process in the body is dependent on oxygen for its performance. The more oxygen you have, the brighter will be your color, the more pep you will have; the smarter you'll be. If you're low in body, sunk in mind, awkward, ugly, rasping—even if you're a little bit crazy—"breathe!" is the advice for you.

Your Lungs

by J.D. Ratcliff

WE CRAMP them with poor posture and subject them to smog, dust and industrial fumes. We inflate them half a *billion* times in an average lifetime—wear and tear that would destroy any man-made material. Despite such punishment these remarkable organs—our lungs—give most of us long and trouble-free service.

Wherever we live—frigid north, arid desert, sooty city—our lungs require air much like that found in a tropical swamp: hot, moist, dirt-free. If the smoke and dust we breathe ever reached the lungs' minute air passages, they would be clogged within hours. If bacteria gained admittance freely, we would die of flaming infections. To guard against such disasters, nature has devised an incredibly complex air-conditioning system.

Its wonders begin with the nose whose special construction is a measure of its importance. Made mostly of pliable cartilage, it can be mashed and pummeled and still continue to function. Hairs in the lining of the nose screen out large dust particles, and its passages help warm the air. Most of this warming task, however, is accomplished in deeper nasal passages, where the bones are covered by tissues with an enormously rich blood supply. Air passing over these tissues is warmed like air passing over a radiator. On cold days the blood vessels dilate to produce more heat; on warm days they shrink.

As part of the elaborate humidifying system, glands leak fluid into the nasal passages—as much as a quart a day. Added moisture comes from tears that constantly bathe the eyes and spill over into the nasal passages through tear ducts. Here, too, the war on bacteria, which we breathe by the millions each day, gets under way. A remarkable enzyme called lysozyme, one of the most powerful bacteria-destroyers known, turns up in tears and mucus secretions.

The inspired air still contains a potentially lethal burden of dust particles. To help get rid of them, airways are lined with glands which secrete a sticky film of mucus It acts much like flypaper in trapping dust particles. This "flypaper" would be hopelessly clogged with dirt in a short time but for another remarkable mechanism: air passages have their own sweeping system. Microscopic cilia—hairs—cover the entire route, and flail back and forth 12 times a second. Moving faster in one direction than the other, they sweep debris *upward*—toward the throat. Swallowed, it will be harmless in the digestive tract.

The incredible energy of the cilia can be demonstrated by snipping a bit of tissue from a frog's throat. If placed on a table, the cilia will "walk" the tissue off the table. If placed in a bottle, the tissue will climb out!

At times we tax the capacity of these cleaning mechanisms—for example, when we smoke too much. In a futile effort to trap countless millions of smoke particles, the throat secretes excess mucus. The mucus itself becomes an irritant and must be coughed up. In a cough, air is trapped in the lungs by the glottis, the valve at the upper end of the windpipe, or trachea, which carries air to the lungs. When the valve opens suddenly, air rushes out with explosive force. Thus the cough, which we may consider a nuisance, is actually essential to life—as an emergency cleaning measure.

Normally we take 14 to 18 breaths a minute, using only about one eighth of our lung capacity. With each breath we inhale about a pint of air. Since resting lungs hold six pints, only a sixth of the air is changed at a time. During violent exercise, when cells are hungry for oxygen, deeper and more rapid breathing can bring into the lungs ten or more times the oxygen supplied during rest.

The lungs are not simply inflatable bladders; they are among the most complex structures in the body. Cut through, they look something like the cross section of a rubber bath sponge. Each lung has its own duct from the windpipe; it enters near the top and starts branching like a tree. The branches are the bronchial tubes. Their job: to deliver air to the *functioning* part of the lung, those 750 million microscopic air sacs called alveoli. All together they have a surface area 25 times that of the skin; spread flat, they would cover 600 square feet.

Each alveolus has a cobwebby covering of capillaries, so tiny that red blood cells must pass through them single file. Through their gossamer walls the blood gives up waste carbon dioxide and takes on refreshing oxygen. Every few minutes the body's entire supply of blood must pass through these minute blood vessels—*in* one end a dark blue-black, *out* the other a bright cherry-red. Day and night this all-important work must proceed without interruption. A pause of only six minutes would starve brain cells of vital oxygen, do irreparable damage.

Breathing itself is an intricate process. The lungs hang loosely in the chest, each in a separate compartment. (The heart is between them, in its own compartment.) Around them is a partial vacuum. Therefore, when the chest is enlarged, the vacuum tugs the lungs outward, thus sucking in air. Expansion of the chest is brought about by either—or both—of two methods. The diaphragm, the sheet of muscular tissue which divides chest from abdomen, may drop downward. Or the ribs, which are hinged to the spine, may swing outward. Expiration is simply a recoil mechanism.

Until the 1930s the chest was generally taboo territory for the surgeon, for once it was opened the lungs, no longer in a partial vacuum, would collapse and breathing would cease. Then came improvements in anesthesiology—chiefly the increased use of tubes which can be slipped down the windpipe so the anesthetist can rhythmically force air and oxygen into the lungs. With this innovation a brilliant new day dawned for chest surgery.

One of surgery's most stirring moments occurred in Barnes Hospital, St. Louis, on April 5, 1933. On the operating table before Dr. Evarts A. Graham, famed chest surgeon, lay his friend, James L. Gilmore, a Pittsburgh obstetrician. Three weeks earlier, Graham had detected cancer in Gilmore's left lung. Once the chest was opened it was apparent the entire lung would have to be removed—something never before done successfully. Graham hesitated, then remembered the directions his patient had given: "I want to be well, or I don't want to get off the table."

Dr. Graham proceeded with the drastic pioneer operation.

It worked: his friend and patient survived. But 24 years later Graham himself developed lung cancer. Since both lungs were involved, his life could not be saved by the operation he pioneered.

A generation ago most lung ailments were severely crippling or potentially lethal. Now, thanks to medical progress, virtually all lung diseases respond to some extent to surgical or medical treatment.

To begin with, better diagnostic procedures have become widely available. The specialist can slip a slender bronchoscope down the windpipe and into larger bronchi within the lungs to *see* conditions that prevail and to snip suspicious tissue for microscopic examination. Iodized substances introduced into lungs clearly outline bronchial passages on X-ray films. Through a battery of tests the specialist can measure the mechanical efficiency of breathing, even determine gaseous diffusion through the walls of microscopic air sacs within the lung.

Look at today's handling of some of the more common lung ailments. In asthma, muscles in bronchial tubes are in spasm, and passageways are frequently inflamed and filled with mucus. Air wheezes through the choked passageways; breathing is labored. A variety of new drugs can relieve these distressing conditions. Relaxants reduce tension in bronchial muscles; special detergents (sniffed as mists) break up mucus accumulations; corticosteroid hormones reduce inflammation. Result: the asthmatic no longer has to face a life of semi-invalidism.

In bronchial pneumonia, bacteria attack bronchial tubes. In lobar pneumonia they attack the vital air sacs as well. Intracellular fluid pours out; gaseous exchange halts. If lung involvement is great enough the victim drowns, in effect, in his own tissue juices. Now these pneumonias have, to a great extent, been controlled by antibiotics.

Physicians estimate that some two million people in the United States have emphysema—it is far more common than tuberculosis or lung cancer. There are many apparent causes: tumors, infection, asthma, smoking. In emphysema, minute air sacs in the lungs become distended, lose elasticity. Instead of collapsing and forcing air out after each breath, they permit it to stagnate. The victim's breathing is labored and painful. Treatment consists in attacking the underlying condition: with antibiotics if there is infection, with hormones if asthma is present. In more serious cases, removal of the involved portion of the lung may be necessary.

Step back a generation to realize how fortunate we are today. Tuberculosis, once "captain of the men of death," has been demoted to the rear ranks. Pneumonia death rates are only one sixth as high as a few years ago. Lung cancer is still a grim reaper, but no longer kills 100 percent of its victims. Other ailments of our faithful and hard-working lungs will, in the years ahead, almost surely yield to medical progress.

Do You Really Know How to Breathe?

by W. P. Knowles

NORMALLY we breathe without apparent effort—16 times a minute, 960 times an hour, 23,040 times a day. Because breathing is unconscious and automatic, like the heartbeat, we assume we do it properly and can leave it to nature. No assumption could be more subtly removed from the facts in an era of sedentary living.

The breaths we ordinarily take are shallow breaths. That means lots of stagnant air is left in the lungs—gases that fill the spaces and cheat the tissues out of oxygen. Lungs will hold six pints of air, yet with each breath a desk worker inhales only about a pint. So five sixths of the lung capacity lies idle. But when we restore the lungs to fuller use, we feel better, have more energy, suffer less from fatigue, sleep better, wake up faster. (And with better aeration we smoke less or not at all. Smoking—inhaling and exhaling—is one substitute for breathing; that's why it gets such a grip on people.)

Suitable posture is a first step. The average person goes around with his shoulder blades wide apart. By drawing the shoulder blades close together he does far more than just square his shoulders: he frees the whole abdominal region of unnecessary weight and pressure. This allows the diaphragm to rise and fall in rhythm, and so prompts him to breathe deeply.

I have a theory that famous work songs, ranging from those of the Volga boatmen to the cadent melodies of the black slave, offered more than just a rhythmic beat to help in hauling that barge or toting that bale. It's my belief the songs encouraged men to *breathe out* while they worked, to release air from the lungs in a moderate and orderly manner. You can't sing without exhaling gradually, and when you exhale you expel impurities and empty the lungs for a fresh and involuntary intake of air.

Real breath control means learning to control the way we *exhale*, not the way we *inhale*. Energy is best renewed by the orderly release of breath, not by strenuously pumping the lungs full of air. Thus in sustained physical exertion—carrying a heavy bag, walking rapidly, wielding a shovel—your power is enhanced when you concentrate on the slow expulsion of air from the lungs.

Speakers, singers, swimmers and runners know this. The rest of us can find it out by simple tests. When you step into a cold shower, for example, the tendency is to gasp and tense the muscles. This only increases the torture. If, instead, you try breathing out in a steady purring breath you will be amazed at how slightly the temperature of the water affects you. Exhaling helps the body accommodate itself to change.

In the same way, careful breath control, with emphasis on exhaling, helps us to relax under any kind of tension or stress. Most of us are only half-breathers: we breathe in because we can't help it, but we fail to breathe out completely. The result is we sigh a lot—a sign of our need to exhale. The sigh is nature's way of deflating the lungs when we have neglected the breathing apparatus long enough. The sensible thing is to learn to sigh in a systematic and organized fashion. We know that any interference with breathing causes acute distress. It follows, as common sense and science show, that any improvement in our breathing can bring exhilaration to mind and body.

The more air we exhale, the more we can breathe in. The amount we take in, which can be measured by a watch-size instrument called a spirometer, is known as our vital capacity.

To increase our vital capacity is the object of all breath discipline. Thus consciousness of breathing out becomes the most important factor of all.

But the main thing is to cultivate the habit. Breathe out before you begin any task. The chore of climbing a long flight of stairs can be minimized by breathing in on two steps and out on two steps. But expulsion of the air from the lungs must come before the first step. Half a dozen long outbreaths will bolster you and fortify your resistance when you lean against a bitter wintry wind. By breathing out slowly in any tedious or tense situation—whether it be at a meeting where you are bored, or at an interview when you are on tenterhooks from expectancy—you recharge your system and follow the pattern nature intended.

One of the best exercises to establish the habit of proper exhaling involves reading aloud. From a newspaper, read aloud on one breath as many words as you can without effort. Now count the number of words you covered. Tomorrow try again. See how much you can increase the length of your exhalation.

Practice with some favorite passage of literature you have memorized, such as the first Psalm. You probably won't get beyond "the seat of the scornful" on the first attempt, but after a dozen daily efforts you may get through the whole Psalm on one breath.

Another effective way to practice controlled outbreathing is counting. Sit down comfortably in an upright position, breathe in gently and steadily to the count of 4. Pause a second and then breathe out to the count of 12. Next time breathe in to the count of 5 and out to the count of 15. Continue this practice until you see notable progress. By the time you are able to breathe out to the count of 21 you will find that humming helps immensely to limit the amount of air you release. Humming as you breathe gives you your own form of work song.

Many are the by-products of breathing out consistently, but the greatest of these is awareness. It introduces a sharp change in our regular habits and, in a sense, makes us repossess our bodies. Conscious breathing brings with it a consciousness of posture. You begin to realize that you cannot sit all hunched up and breathe well, either in or out. But with shoulder blades pulled as nearly together as possible, you feel your lungs fill and empty with smoothness and ease.

By practice we can happily make our breathing involuntarily good just as it is likely now to be involuntarily bad. The body responds to wise treatment, and a consistent effort to enlarge vital capacity by learning to breathe out will pay off. Good habits will take over and in turn become second nature.

EMOTIONS COUNT

Your Mind Can Keep You Well

by John A. Schindler, M.D.

WHAT ONE THING contributes more than anything else to unhappiness? As a doctor I can answer that: a long period of illness. It is a little frightening, when you think of it, because there are a thousand different ailments this human clay is heir to, and one of them is as common as the other 999 put together. Fifty percent of all the people going to doctors in the United States today are victims of this one disease. Many would put the figure higher. At the Ochsner Clinic in New Orleans a report was published reviewing 500 consecutive admissions to that institution: 386 people—or 77 percent—were sick with this one disease. Persons of any age, in any walk of life, can contract it. Furthermore it is a terrifically expensive disease to diagnose and treat.

I hesitate to give you its name because immediately you will get a lot of misconceptions. The first will be that it is not a real disease. But don't kid yourself. It used to be called psychoneurosis. Now it is known as psychosomatic illness. And it is *not* a disease in which the patient just *thinks* he is sick. The pain you get is often just as severe as the pain you get with a gall-bladder colic.

Psychosomatic illness isn't produced by a bacterium, or by a virus, or by a new growth. It is produced by the circumstances of daily living. I have tried to find one word for it, but it takes three, each one them meaning about the same thing but in different degrees. They are: *cares, difficulties, troubles*. Whenever one has such a thick, impenetrable layer of c.d.t. that he can't get up above it into a realm of joy and pleasure occasionally, he gets a psychosomatic illness.

There are three general groupings of people who suffer from c.d.t. In the first group are the habitually crabby. A friend of mine has a beautiful farm. I drove past his farm one summer day and I thought to myself, "Those oats ought to make Sam happy." So I drove in, and I said, "Sam, that's a wonderful field of oats," and Sam said, "Yes, but the wind will blow it down before I get it cut." He got it cut all right, he got it threshed, and he got a good price for it. Well, I saw him one day and I said, "Sam, how did the oats turn out?" And he said, "Oh, it was a good crop, and I guess the price was all right, but you know a crop like that sure takes a lot out of the soil."

People like Sam invariably get a psychosomatic illness, and when they get it they get it hard. As a rule they are invalids for the rest of their lives. There is nothing you can do about it.

The second group, where most of us belong, are the people who all day long manage to be concerned, anxious, worrying about something. If there's nothing around home or the business, they worry about Mrs. Smith down the street. Why doesn't she get her daughter in before 1 A.M.? Something is going to happen to that girl!

The third group is made up of those who have an acute case of c.d.t. Maybe they have gotten themselves into some kind of mess—financial ruin or domestic trouble, perhaps. They are usually easier to treat than those in the second group. (Who are certainly easier to treat than those in the first group.)

How does this c.d.t. bring on illness? Thinking, we ordinarily suppose, is something that goes on solely in the brain. But that is quite wrong. Thinking involves the entire body in a series of correlated nerve impulses that center in the brain. Particularly is this true when an emotion colors our thinking. The psychologist William James gave us the best definition we have of emotion when he said it is the state of mind that manifests itself by a perceptible change in the body.

You don't have to be told when a man is angry. His face either gets white or it gets red; his eyes widen; his muscles tighten up so he trembles. That is the state of mind manifesting itself by a perceptible change in the body. Or take a person who blushes. In his case embarrassment produces a dilation of the blood vessels in the face. A third example is the man or woman who vomits or faints at the sight of blood.

Now, how does all this bring about a disease? Very simply. Most of our disagreeable emotions produce muscle tightness. Suppose all day long your thinking is acutely disagreeable. You are tightening up muscles. Take your fist and hold it loosely; it doesn't hurt; but hold it tight for a long time and it begins to hurt. The squeeze produces pain.

One of the first places to show tension is the group of muscles at the back of the neck. Another group that come into play very early are the muscles at the upper end of the esophagus. When they squeeze down you feel a lump. It is difficult to swallow. If the muscles in the lower esophagus contract, then it's more serious. Much more commonly the stomach is involved. And when the muscles of the stomach begin to squeeze down you are conscious of a heavy, disagreeable pressure inside. When the muscles squeeze down hard, then it hurts. And it hurts just as bad as any ulcer. In our town we had a grocer who had a pain exactly like that of an ulcer. He had plenty of trouble—a competitive business, a nagging wife, a wayward son—and he had this pain most of the time. Doctors assured him he had no ulcer. He finally began to believe them when he noticed that every time he went fishing the pain disappeared.

This same kind of muscle spasm can occur in any part of the colon. Many persons who complain of a pain exactly like gall-bladder pain don't have gall-bladder trouble at all. They're dissatisfied, and the upper colon is squeezing down. And believe me, their suffering is real. If the pain happens to be lower down in the colon, it will seem just like appendicitis. And then it takes a very smart doctor not to open that abdomen.

Other muscles besides those in the intestinal tract respond to emotional stimuli, particularly the muscles of the blood vessels. A good many of the people who have a headache severe enough to cause them to go to a doctor have that headache because some blood vessel inside or outside the skull is squeezing down so hard from nervous excitation that it produces pain.

And a third of all skin diseases treated by dermatologists are produced by blood vessels in the skin reacting to anxiety, worry, disgust, and so on. Each time certain individuals become upset or irritated or peeved, serum is actually squeezed out through the wall of the blood vessel and into the skin. The tissue becomes thickened with serum. Finally the serum is pushed up through the surface of the skin where it becomes scaly, crusty and itchy, and the patient has a neurodermatitis.

One favorite place for nervous tension is the muscles in the upper left part of the thorax. People rarely come to see us doctors because they have a pain on the right side. It's almost always on the left. If it's on the right—pshaw!—it doesn't amount to anything. If it's on the left—ah!—could be heart trouble! Then they start watching for it. And merely watching for it can bring the pain on.

Muscle tension is just one way symptoms are produced in a psychosomatic illness. One of the other ways is the effect the emotion has on the endocrine system. Most of you have driven down a street in an automobile too fast when suddenly somebody backed out from a side road. You started to breathe deeply, your heart started to pound and you got a little faint. Acute fear in your mind produces these bodily changes. An impulse is sent to the adrenal glands, which squeeze adrenalin into the blood stream. When that adrenalin hits the heart, the heart starts to thump. When it hits the respiratory center in the brain, you start to gasp. When it hits the blood vessels going into the brain, they narrow down and you feel woozy.

There are other organic effects of psychosomatic illness. If it happens to be the blood vessels on your heart that squeeze down every time you get excited or angry, it is serious. John Hunter, the English physiologist, had that kind of heart, and he always said, "The first scoundrel that gets me angry will kill me." And that's exactly what happened. He got up in a medical meeting one time to refute something he didn't like, and anger produced such a contraction of the blood vessels on his heart that he fell dead.

Many victims of psychosomatic illness are up and around. Many are in hospitals. Thousands have been in bed at home for years. To avoid psychosomatic illness, you must learn to think right. There ought to be in every university a course called "The Art of Human Living." It should teach us how to make our attitude and thinking as pleasant and cheerful as possible. It would be idiotic for me to tell you you can be pleasant and cheerful all the time. Of course you can't. But I can offer certain suggestions which will help you to think right about yourself.

First, quit looking for a knock in your motor. Don't be analyzing your feelings all the time, looking for trouble.

Second, learn to like to work. To get any place in this world you've got to work. One of the things you will escape, if you learn to like to work, is the tension that comes to those who look upon work as something to be got over with.

Third, have a hobby. A hobby is an important element in getting your mind off work tension. During the day when you are hurrying and worrying, just relax for 30 seconds by thinking briefly about that thing you're making in the basement, that community project you're interested in, or that fishing trip you're taking next weekend.

Fourth, learn to like people. Carrying a grudge or dislike can have disastrous bodily effects. We had a man in the hospital who got there because he had to work in an office with a man he didn't like. He said, "I don't like the way he combs his hair; I don't like the way he whistles through his teeth: I don't like the way he always starts a sentence with 'Listen!'" On questioning the patient I found he never liked anybody—his mother or his father or any member of his family. But you have to meet people. You've got to live with them, so learn to like them.

Fifth, learn to be satisfied when the situation is such you can't easily change it. A young lady was in a hospital with a psychosomatic illness because she had become dissatisfied with her life. She had been a secretary in Washington. There she married an Army captain. Before long she found herself living in a trailer, raising three children. She didn't like to live in a trailer, didn't like to raise children in a trailer, wasn't sure she liked to live with her husband in a trailer. She wanted to be a secretary back in Washington. I didn't tell her what her trouble was. I just advised her to send to the library and get the four Pollyanna books and read them. She did, and returned to live in the trailer and like it. She had learned that it is just as easy under most conditions to be satisfied as to be dissatisfied, and it is much more pleasurable.

Sixth, learn to accept adversity. In this life you're going to meet some adversity. You may meet a lot, but don't let it bowl you over. I had a patient who hadn't worked for a year. Then his wife died. A month later his son was killed. And he sat around thinking "How unfortunate I am—why did this have to happen to *me!*" He became very sick. He hadn't learned to accept adversity. A lot of people start a psychosomatic illness after an adversity.

Seventh, learn to say the cheerful, humorous thing. Never

say the mean thing, even if you feel like doing so. In the morning, look at your wife or your husband and, even if it isn't so, say, "My dear, you look good this morning." It will make her (or him) feel better, and it will make you feel better.

Finally, learn to meet your problems with decision. About the worst thing to do is have a problem and to mull it over and over in your mind. If you have a problem, decide what you are going to do about it and then quit thinking about it.

There are some of the things you have to learn if you want to escape the most common disease of all. The key is: *I'm going to keep my attitude and my thinking as pleasant and cheerful as possible*. There isn't any better definition for happiness.

How Much Change Can You Take?

DR. THOMAS H. HOLMES, professor of psychiatry at the University of Washington, devised a scale assigning point value to changes, good and bad, that often affect us. When enough changes occur during one year to add up to 300, a danger point has been reached. In the population he studied, 80 percent of the people who exceeded 300 became seriously depressed, had heart attacks or suffered other serious illnesses.

LIFE CHANGE	POINTS
Death of spouse	100
Divorce	73
Marital separation	65
Jail term	63
Death of close family member	63
Personal injury or illness	53
Marriage	50
Fired from job	47
Marital reconciliation	45
Retirement	45
Change in health of family member	44
Pregnancy	40
Sex difficulties	39
Gain of new family member	39
Change in financial status	38
Death of close friend	37
Change to different kind of work	36

LIFE CHANGE	POINTS
Change in number of arguments with spouse	35
Foreclosure of mortgage or loan	30
Change in work responsibilities	29
Son or daughter leaving home	29
Trouble with in-laws	29
Outstanding personal achievement	28
Wife beginning or stopping work	26
Beginning or ending school	26
Revision of personal habits	24
Trouble with boss	23
Change in residence	20
Change in schools	20
Vacation	13
Minor violations of law	11

To Beat Stress: Do Your Own Thing

An interview with **Hans Selye**, *the pre-eminent researcher in this field*

Q. Dr. Selye, is it true there is more stress in today's society than in years past?
A. People sometimes compare our lives with that of the cave man, who didn't have to worry about the stock market or the atomic bomb. They forget that the cave man worried about being eaten by a bear or dying of hunger—things few people worry about today. It's not that people suffer more stress today; it's just that they think they do.
Q. Then stress is a normal state?
A. Yes, and it's important that people understand this. Whenever people experience something unpleasant, for lack of a better word they say they are under stress. Yet there is such a thing as pleasant stress—as in the case of the Olympic winner at the moment of his glory. He secretes all the stress hormones just as he would if he had heard of a death in the family. We call the pleasant or healthy kind "eustress," the unpleasant or unhealthy kind "distress."
Q. Are men and women equally subject to stress?
A. Certainly. But let me add that the more the women's movement permits women to take what have usually been considered male jobs, the more women are subject to so-called male diseases—often related to stress—such as cardiac infarctions, gastric ulcers and hypertension.

Q. Exactly what is stress?

A. I define stress as the nonspecific response of the body to any demand. Stress is the state you are in, not the agent which produces it, which is called a "stressor." Cold and heat, for example, are stressors. In man, with his highly developed central nervous system, emotional stressors are the most frequent and most important. All the demands you make—whether on your brain or your liver or your muscles or your bones—cause stress.

Q. What happens under stress?

A. In all mammals, including man, the endocrine glands produce a hormone which in turn stimulates the adrenal glands. When this happens, the usual responses are an increase in pulse rate and an increased tendency to sweat. You will also become more irritable and will sometimes suffer insomnia, even long after the stressor is gone. You will usually become less capable of concentrating, and will have an increased desire to move about.

Q. What are the more frequent causes of stress?

A. They differ in various civilizations and historical periods. At the moment, I would say the most frequent causes of distress in man are psychological—lack of adaptability, not having a code of behavior. One reason for this is that the satisfaction of religious codes has diminished in importance. So has the idea of being loyal to your monarch or leader. One of the main problems for our youngsters is they have no motivation. They don't believe what they are taught in school. They are very energetic, but they haven't anything to run for. This problem was defined by Montaigne, who said, "No wind blows in favor of the ship that has no port of destination."

Q. Is stress basically bad for you?

A. Not necessarily. It's the same as saying, "John is running a temperature." Well, who isn't? What you mean is that John is running too high a temperature. This brings us to two important words—"hyperstress," or too much stress, and "hypostress," or not enough. Both words are relative. For me, it may not be enough; for you, it may be too much. But it is inconceivable that anyone should have no stress at all. Most people who are ambitious and want to accomplish something live on stress. They need it.

If you take a turtle and force it to run as fast as a race horse, you will kill it. So it's useless to say to a turtle-type human that he must accomplish something big to match his famous father. If he hasn't got it, leave him alone. You can't make a race horse out of a turtle. But the reverse is also true. If you are the race-horse type, and are told not to do something, you come under terrible distress.

Q. Is excessive stress harmful?

A. By all means. For instance, you can be bothered by your mother-in-law or your boss to the point where you suffer continuously. When people say, "It gives me an ulcer" or "a pain in the neck" or "a migraine headache" to do certain things, it's not just a way of talking. It actually happens. Worse, chronic exposure to stress over a long time may cause more serious diseases. Among these are hypertension, cardiovascular disease, heart accidents, mental breakdowns.

Q. Then stress can actually shorten your life?

A. Very much so. What we call aging is nothing more than the sum total of all the scars left by the stress of life. These scars are, in the medical sense, not only lines in your skin; they can be chemical or mental, and do irreparable damage.

Q. How can people cope with stress?

A. The secret is not to avoid stress but to "do your own thing"—an expression to which I fully subscribe. It implies doing what you like to do and were made to do, at your own rate. For most people, it is really a matter of learning how to live, how to behave in various situations, to decide: "Do I really want to take over my father's business? Or would I rather be a musician?" If you really want to be a musician, then be one.

The most important thing is to have a code of life, to know how to live. Find yourself a port of destination—and practice what I call altruistic egoism. You may argue that an egoist can't be altruistic. But people forget that egoism is natural—you can't fight it. And so is altruism. The port of destination for me is to acquire as much goodwill and as many friends as possible. After all, if you are desired, if you feel necessary, then you are safe.

Q. If you can't handle a stressful situation by yourself, whom should you consult?

A. That's the $64 question, and the main reason why I started the International Institute of Stress in Montreal. There are a few physicians specializing in stress diseases, but most of them are not well trained. Specialists must be developed who can deal with the stress of being a boss, or an employe, or a wife.

What's the use of healing your gastric ulcer with the usual antacids if you remain exposed to constant stress? You will only come back with another ulcer. So we need people trained to deal with stress.

Q. If you had to give one piece of advice to people about stress, what would you say to them?

A. I would offer the wisdom of the Bible translated into terms a scientist can easily accept today: "Earn thy neighbor's love."

But Hard Work Isn't Bad for You

by Hans Selye, M.D.

WHEN I got into medical school, somewhat prematurely at the age of 18, I was so fascinated by the possibilities of research that I used to get up at 4 a.m. and study, with very few interruptions, until about 6 p.m. I still remember my mother telling me that this sort of thing could not be kept up for long, and would undoubtedly precipitate a nervous breakdown. Now in 1973 as I write this I am 66. I still get up at 4 a.m. and work until 6 p.m. Yet I am perfectly happy leading this kind of life. No regrets.

"There is more to life than just work," many say today. Or, "You should work to live, not live to work." And the Western world is racked by the insatiable demand for less work, more pay. Work is seen as something that wears you down, that produces stress—and stress is known to take a heavy toll.

It is true that biologic stress is involved in many common diseases such as ulcers, high blood pressure, cardiac accidents, allergies, mental derangements, even aging. But does this mean we should avoid stress whenever possible? That we should avoid hard work because it is stressful? Certainly not. *Stress is the spice of life.* It is associated with all types of activity, and we could avoid it only by never doing anything. Who would enjoy a life of "no runs, no hits, no errors"? Besides, certain types of activities actually have a curative effect, helping to keep the stress mechanism in good shape, as exercise of your muscles keeps you physically fit.

Work, to define it, is what we have to do; play is what we like to do. Even reading the best prose, fishing, gardening, playing tennis or golf is work when you do it for a living—though the literary critic may play golf to relax, and the professional athlete may read.

To function normally, man *needs* work as much as he needs air, food, sleep, social contacts or sex. To look forward to total automation is as senseless as looking forward to the day of test-tube babies, making sex superfluous. As philosopher Henri Bergson pointed out, it is more appropriate to call our species *homo faber* (making man) than *homo sapiens* (knowing man). For man's characteristic feature is not his wisdom but his constant urge to improve his environment and himself.

Our aim, therefore, should not be to avoid work but to find the kind that suits us best. The best way to avoid undue stress is to select an environment (wife, boss, social group) in line with our innate preferences, and an activity we like and respect, which is within our talents. Only thus can we eliminate the need for constant adaptation which is the major cause of harmful stress.

Work wears you out mainly through the frustration of failure. Each period of stress, especially if it results from unsuccessful struggles, leaves some irreversible chemical scars (think of them as insoluble precipitates of living matter), which accumulate to constitute the signs of tissue aging. Successful activity, no matter how intense, leaves virtually no such scars. Instead, it provides you with the exhilarating feeling of youthful strength, even at very advanced age.

The most successful among the hard workers in almost any field often live to a very advanced age. Think of Pablo Casals, Winston Churchill, Albert Schweitzer, Toscanini, Konrad Adenauer, Charles de Gaulle, Pablo Picasso. All continued to be successful well into their 70s, 80s or even 90s. Of course, in their many years of intense activity, these people never "worked": they lived a life of "leisure" by working at what they liked to do.

Admittedly, few people belong to their elite category. But I believe anyone can live long and happily by working hard along more modest lines, as long as he loves his activity and is reasonably successful at it. A carpenter building a well-made table can have the same satisfaction of success and fulfillment. The art is to find a job that you like and that people honor. Man must have recognition; he cannot tolerate constant censure.

Short hours are a boon only for those underprivileged who are not good at anything, have no particular taste for anything, and no hunger for achievement. These are the true paupers of mankind.

The Relaxation Response

by Herbert Benson, M.D., with Miriam Z. Klipper

IN 1968, SIX of us doctors at Harvard Medical School were studying the effects of mental stress on the blood pressure of monkeys. In the midst of our study, a group of transcendental meditators came to our laboratory and asked me if I'd study them too. "We think," one said, "that we can lower blood pressure through meditation." At first I turned them away with a polite no thank you. Why investigate anything so far out as meditation? But they persisted. And on reflection my initial no became a yes. What was there to lose?

Even in 1968, quite a few people had turned to Transcendental Meditation to counter the stresses of modern life. Meditation, they insisted, produced what they called an "altered state of consciousness." This feeling is hard to define but had been sought and reportedly experienced by meditators throughout history—through Yoga in India, Taoism in China, Buddhism in the Far East, and in Judaism and Christianity. St. Augustine wrote of it as a contemplation upon the unchangeable—that is, on God—achieved by a shutting off of the mind from external thoughts to produce a mental solitude. William James, one of the fathers of modern psychology, called it a "mystical feeling of enlargement, union and emancipation that has no specific intellectual content of its own." Emily Brontë, the 19th-century English poet and novelist, defined it rapturously when she wrote:

But, first, a hush of peace—a soundless calm descends;
The struggle of distress, and fierce impatience ends;
Mute music soothes my breast—unuttered harmony,
That I could never dream, till Earth was lost to me.

If meditation could do this to bring peace and calm, we wondered somewhat skeptically at Harvard, what might it do for high blood pressure? The answer was important because high blood pressure, which predisposes one to heart attacks and strokes, has become epidemic in America.

Over the next couple of years, we repeatedly monitored a number of volunteer meditators (initiates of Transcendental Meditation, as developed by guru Maharishi Mahesh Yogi) during their meditation. We found that meditation—or what we came to call the "Relaxation Response"—did indeed produce physiologic changes in the body. There were increases in intensity and frequency of alpha brain-wave patterns; a significant decrease in heart and breathing rates, oxygen consumption and muscle tension; and a marked decrease in blood lactate, a substance suspected of producing anxiety attacks. All these changes indicated a more relaxed condition. What we had here, then, was scientific validation of age-old wisdom: that meditation *can* improve one's physical well-being.

What did not change in these early experiments involving young, healthy subjects was blood pressure: it was low before, during and after. But perhaps they had low blood pressure because of their continued practice of meditation. If this was true, the possibility existed that people with hypertension *could* lower their blood pressures through such a practice.

In subsequent controlled experiments, made at Harvard's Thorndike Memorial Laboratory, we found that daily meditation did indeed lower blood pressure moderately in hypertensive people—enough possibly to be of great value, when more is known, in preventing or treating the disease. (It seems unlikely, however, that the regular elicitation of the Relaxation Response *by itself* will prove to be adequate therapy for severe high blood pressure. *In any case, those who suffer from any disease should practice the response only under the care and supervision of a physician.*)

We are continuing our studies of the Relaxation Response at the Beth Israel Hospital of Boston because we believe it is a way to deal with the tensions and emotional upsets caused by the pressures of everyday living. Even though it has been evoked in the religions of both East and West for most of recorded history, you don't have to engage in any rites or esoteric practices to bring it forth. It requires no special education or aptitude. Just as each of us experiences anger, contentment and excitement, each has the capacity to experience the Relaxation Response. It is an innate mechanism within us all.

Remember, there is no single method of meditating that is unique in eliciting the Relaxation Response. Though Transcendental Meditation is one of the most widely practiced techniques, our tests show that any one of a number of age-old or newly derived techniques produces the same result. Here is the simple technique our group has worked out:

1. Sit in a comfortable position so there is no undue muscle tension, and choose a quiet environment with few distractions. Avoid lying down; there is a tendency to fall asleep.

2. Close your eyes.

3. Deeply relax all your muscles, beginning at your feet and progressing up to your face. Keep them relaxed.

4. Breathe through your nose. Become aware of your breathing. As you breathe out, say the word "ONE," silently to yourself. For example, breathe IN . . . OUT, "ONE"; IN . . . OUT, "ONE," etc. Breathe easily and naturally. The repetition of "ONE" helps break the train of distracting thoughts; attention to the normal rhythm of breathing enhances the repetition.

5. Continue for 10 to 20 minutes. You may open your eyes to check the time, but do not use an alarm. When you finish, sit quietly for several minutes, at first with your eyes closed and later with your eyes opened.

6. Do not worry about whether you are successful in achieving a deep level of relaxation. Adopt a passive, "let-it-happen" attitude and permit relaxation to occur at its own pace. When distracting thoughts occur, try to ignore them and return to repeating "ONE." With practice, the response should come with little effort. Practice the technique once or twice daily, but not within two hours after any meal, since the digestive processes seem to interfere with it.

The feelings accompanying the Relaxation Response vary among individuals. The majority feel calm and relaxed. A small percentage immediately become ecstatic. Others describe feelings of pleasure, refreshment, well-being. Still others note relatively little change. But regardless of the subjective feelings described by our subjects, we have found that the physiologic changes, such as decreased oxygen consumption, are taking place.

How do you pick the right time to practice the Relaxation Response? It depends on individual preference. A businessman we know elicits it late in the morning for 15 minutes in his office; he feels it "clears the cobwebs" that have accumulated and gives him fresh perspective on business problems. A housewife meditates for 20 minutes after her husband and children have left for the day and again before her husband comes home; she no longer feels harassed while trying both to get dinner and to get the family organized for another day. A factory worker meditates on the subway going home from work—"unwinds," he says. A student meditates between classes; he feels he is more attentive in class, and even attributes better grades to it.

A word of caution: Many meditational organizations teach that if a little meditation is good, a lot is even better. Our observation, however, is that many people who meditate several hours every day for weeks at a time tend to hallucinate. But we have not noted any harmful side effects in people who bring forth the Relaxation Response once or twice daily for 10 to 20 minutes.

A second word: The benefits of meditation will last only as long as you regularly bring forth the response.

And let me make one further suggestion: In our society, we give little attention to the importance of relaxation. We have eliminated many of the traditional methods of evoking the Relaxation Response, such as prayer and meditation. We even view a person who takes time off as unproductive and lazy. Yet, in our ever-changing, quick-paced world, we need relaxation more than ever. Perhaps society should sanction time for meditation. Is it unreasonable to incorporate this inborn capacity into our daily lives by having a "Relaxation Response break" instead of a coffee break? All too few of us are making use of this remarkable and too-long-neglected asset.

Your Personality
May Be Killing You

by Patrick Young

• DO YOU fret that you are always falling behind in the things
you should or could do, and do you try to do more and more
things in less and less time?
• Do you become highly irritated when you aren't seated in
a restaurant immediately, or when your plane is delayed, or
when traffic holds you up?
• Are you so competitive that you get angry when a child
beats you at a game?
• Do you clench your jaws thinking and double your fists
during ordinary conversations?

If this sounds like the real you, research at Mount Zion
Hospital and Medical Center in San Francisco suggests you are
a heart attack waiting to happen. For many years, Dr. Meyer
Friedman of Mount Zion's Harold Brunn Institute and Dr. Ray
Rosenman, now of Stanford Research International, have studied the relationship between personality and heart attacks.
They've concluded that personality traits are a major factor in
heart attacks—more important than obesity, high blood pressure and even cigarette smoking.

The two cardiologists have dubbed people whose personality
traits put them at highest risk Type A, and those at lowest risk
Type B. Says Friedman, "At least 90 percent of all patients
having heart attacks under age 60, we've found, exhibit a Type
A behavior pattern." This means that heart disease involves
psychological, social and environmental factors that have been
inadequately explored. "The physician must look at the patient

as well as his cholesterol," say the two researchers.

Most Americans are a combination of Type A and Type B behavior patterns; the more Type A an individual is, the greater the risk. Friedman and Rosenman estimate that ten percent of urban males are severe Type A and ten percent pure Type B. Women until recently were more often Type B. "By custom they are not put in a socioeconomic milieu that encourages speed and aggression," Friedman explains. But as times change, so does the role of women in society, and women's liberation has produced a corresponding jump in heart attacks among women.

The idea that a life-style and its stresses can be a factor in heart disease is far from universally accepted. But it is winning converts as other researchers confirm these statistical and bio-chemical findings.

Friedman and Rosenman became interested in personality patterns in the late 1950s, while both were at Mount Zion doing research into the role of cholesterol as a factor in heart attacks. With the cooperation of a women's club. they tried to determine if higher coronary rates in men resulted because their diets were different from their wives'. The study showed the diets and blood cholesterols were basically the same. The club president then suggested the two doctors look at what was *really* killing off males—the way they drove themselves.

In 1960, the Mount Zion team screened 3524 male volunteers aged 39 to 59 and classified them by personality types. Some 3000 of the volunteers were studied for up to 8½ years. Among them, Type As were found to have at least twice as many heart attacks as Type Bs. Moreover, the researchers subsequently discovered that a Type A's coronary is twice as likely to be fatal; and As who survive their first heart attack have several times more risk of suffering a second. Even more surprising, Type As who never smoked cigarettes had nearly the same heart-attack rate as Type Bs who smoked.

The researchers use special interviews to aid them in classifying personality types. But they find that *how* questions are answered—the tone of voice, volume, physical movements and expressions—is a better indicator than the answers themselves. The classic Type A personality—the really high-risk individual—is habitually impatient, constantly under stress from an urgent, pressing feeling that he hasn't enough time. His body movements are brisk. He speaks in explosive, hurried speech, and his body seems always tense, never relaxed. He is often obsessed with numbers—of sales made, articles written, forms completed—and prone to vent hostility in verbal abuse, even on family or friends.

"The two characteristics of Type A behavior are 'hurry sickness' and 'free-floating hostility,'" say the researchers. Such individuals are in what they call a "chronic, continuous struggle." If this struggle is not abated, they suspect, it will do little good to alter one's diet, smoking or exercise habits. The behavior pattern is more a state of mind than station in life. "There are plenty of As among truck drivers," notes Friedman.

Type B people, by definition, have personalities that are the opposite of Type As. This doesn't mean Type B people are incapable of hard work, achievement, and advancing to lofty positions. In fact, they generally make better executives because they don't rush decisions, make snap judgments, or antagonize their subordinates. "The B type knows his capabilities and limitations," says Friedman. "The A doesn't, and doesn't wish to."

Type As abound among trial lawyers, TV performers, salesmen, auto racers and newspaper reporters. There seem to be more Type Bs among patent attorneys, government clerks and accountants.

The Mount Zion researchers can't say precisely what produces a Type A personality, but they suspect that parental and social expectations play a large role. Most parents want their children to succeed, so they encourage, even force, them to compete in school and outside. (Psychiatrists say some people spend their lifetimes trying to live up to impossible expectations instilled in them by their parents.) And Western society undeniably encourages Type A behavior by offering special rewards to those who can think, perform, communicate, and conduct their affairs more quickly and more aggressively than others.

"For many, the stress has become almost unbearable," says Dr. Friedman. "Everybody is selling his time for money and the 'good things' money can buy. Many parole officers tell me they have to acclimate long-term prisoners to this increased pace of society before they are released."

Type A behavior, then, is an outward expression of inner turmoil and desires. But the Mount Zion group has found that stress afflicting Type As apparently produces important physical changes as well, changes that may explain why Type As are far more susceptible to heart attacks. Type As have high cholesterol; increased norepinephrine, a vital chemical of the nervous system; increased ACTH, a hormone that stimulates the adrenal glands; and low levels of growth hormone. Also, their blood clots faster than normal, and autopsy studies show that Type As average twice as much hardening of the coronary arteries as Type Bs.

There is no scientific evidence as yet that changing a person's behavior will prolong his life, although clinical impressions suggest that people who do change lengthen and improve the quality of their lives. Friedman himself suffered mild heart attacks in 1966 and 1971 and another attack in 1974, necessitating surgery. The attacks left him pondering his future. With some effort, he says, he managed to change some of his Type A behavior through what he calls "re-engineering" and others call "behavior modification." He and Rosenman have written a book, titled *Type A Behavior and Your Heart*, in which they outline some steps to help those who also want to "re-engineer."

Curing "hurry sickness" is basic, and part of the cure lies in realizing that relaxation is not a luxury but a necessity. The Mount Zion doctors urge eliminating unnecessary events and activities; getting up 15 minutes early to give yourself more time to dress and talk with the family; slowing down your pace of eating and drinking; taking time alone to read, dream, and analyze your life. "As you sweat over something," they say, "ask yourself if it's really going to make a difference in your life five years from now."

The two researchers strongly urge doing one thing at a time. "Remember," they write, "that even Einstein, when tying his shoelaces, thought chiefly about the bow." Make an effort to pay attention to people. Focus on what they are saying; don't let your mind wander.

If you find something you are doing tends to induce tension—writing reports, balancing your checkbook, ironing—take short breaks. And if a particular individual constantly angers you, find ways to avoid him or her.

Perhaps the best thing to do about hostility is to keep reminding yourself you're hostile, Friedman says. This is a forewarned-is-forearmed approach. The thought will surface as your temper rises, and help you realize what's happening. Then you can check your outburst.

If all this sounds a bit like pop psychology, well, in a way it is. And if it seems rather hard to apply in real life, it is that, too. But the alternative, the doctors suggest, is even more unpleasant. "If you don't also change your Type A behavior pattern," says Rosenman, "other protective measures against heart attack—a healthy diet, exercise, no smoking—may be largely a waste of time."

CHECK IT OUT

What ECG Tells the Doctor About Your Heart

by J.D. Ratcliff

FOR MOST of us the squiggles on an electrocardiogram (ECG) are as mysterious as hieroglyphics on an Egyptian tomb. But to the skilled physician these messages from the heart are enormously revealing: at times they are reassuring signals, at other times calls for help.

The ECG may warn of approaching heart troubles, and sometimes it spots "silent" heart attacks that have taken place without our knowledge (10 to 20 percent of us have them). Forewarned, doctors can often take steps to prevent more serious trouble. The test indicates damage done to a heart muscle when its blood supply is cut off by a clot lodging in a heart artery, and suggests how rapidly healing is taking place. It indicates when artery hardening begins to threaten the heart's nourishment. And if the necessary balance between certain chemicals in the blood (calcium and potassium, for example) is not being maintained, it waves a red flag.

Because this remarkable test yields information instantaneously, it is of particular value to the anesthesiologist, who needs to know on a second-to-second basis how a patient's heart is standing the strain of anesthesia and major surgery. Wires from the patient's body are hooked to an oscilloscope, making the ECG pattern constantly visible on a TV-like screen. Any faltering or change in the pattern is at once apparent, and is promptly dealt with. In those cases where the heart is deliberately stopped for internal repair, the oscilloscope screen presents one of the most dramatic of all operating-room sights.

As chemicals are injected to stop the heart, the wavy ECG curve falters, then flattens into a straight line. This is death of the heart—but, in these cases, temporary death.

What is the ECG? Simply the measurement of the heart's electrical activity. Following the lead of earlier investigators who had demonstrated the electrical nature of heart activity by experiments with frogs, John Burdon-Sanderson and Augustus D. Waller, English physiologists working in the 1880s, were able to distinguish the electrical impulses of the human heart.

We now know that just before each beat the pacemaker, a node of specialized muscle and nerve tissue situated in the wall of the upper right chamber of the heart, shoots out a smidgen of electric current. This spreads through muscle fibers in the auricles, or upper chambers of the heart. The fibers contract, forcing blood into the ventricles, the lower chambers. The current passes through special conducting fibers to spread over thick ventricular walls, and these chambers, too, contract—the right ventricle forcing blood to the lungs for oxygen, the left pushing fresh blood through the rest of the body. Simple as it may sound, this electrical activity is infinitely more complex than anything that takes place in the most sophisticated computing machine. In sum, the ECG is a test of the heart's ignition system, telling how smoothly and efficiently the system is working.

Willem Einthoven, a gifted Dutch professor of physiology, was the first to devise, in 1903, a galvanometer capable of measuring the wisps of electricity produced in the heart—a breakthrough important enough to win for him, in 1924, a Nobel Prize. He badgered students, colleagues, friends into letting him strap electrodes to their bodies while he recorded, on moving strips of paper, the wavy electrical patterns so familiar to the world today.

Yet neither Einthoven nor anyone else knew the full meaning of the electrical changes in the beating heart which these patterns represented. To a large extent this knowledge was gained on the autopsy table. Doctors studied electrocardiograms made during life, then examined wrecked hearts after death, and related the two. They found characteristic patterns for a variety of heart ailments. For example, when a clot plugs a heart artery in coronary thrombosis (the commonest form of heart attack), the portion of the heart normally fed by the plugged artery dies and is eventually replaced by scar tissue.

This leaves an "electrical hole," for, unlike heart muscle, the scar tissue generates no electricity and is usually detected by the ECG. Indeed, the test may enable physicians not only to check the size of the damaged area but to pinpoint its location with astonishing exactitude.

A generation ago, physicians sometimes had difficulty differentiating between appendicitis, gallbladder disease, severe indigestion and heart attack. Outward symptoms of all can be more or less alike. Today, as technology has improved electrocardiograph machines and as interpretative skills have grown, the ECG has virtually banished such doubts, diagnosing heart attack with almost unerring accuracy.

Step into a doctor's examination room to see what happens when an ECG is taken. The test is quick, painless. A doctor or technician attaches electrodes to the body with rubber straps after rubbing the skin vigorously with a jelly containing salt and pumice to provide good electrical contact. The electrodes are applied in a succession of different "leads" or patterns.

With electrodes in place, the machine is turned on, and the heart's minute electric currents are picked up and amplified thousands of times, to guide a stylus over a moving strip of paper. The resulting curve has three major components: the "P wave" tells how the auricles are electrically stimulated; the "QRS segment" how the electrical wave sweeps over the ventricles; the "T wave" how the ventricles are recharged.

Each heart has its own characteristic ECG pattern. What looks like an abnormal deflection (or wave), signaling trouble for one person, may be quite normal for another. In borderline cases, expert diagnosis plus other tests must be relied on to give a final answer. But 80 percent of the time the ECG follows conventional patterns readily recognized by a cardiologist.

How often should one have this test? Most physicians advise it as part of the annual physical checkup after age 40, if not before. All electrocardiograms should be filed for future reference; examined serially, they may tell a graphic story as to whether disease is stationary or progressing.

Perhaps the most impressive thing the ECG tells us is how much wear and tear our hearts can withstand and still permit us to enjoy relatively good health and long life. We tend to think of the heart as a delicate, fragile thing. Actually, it's a pretty tough muscle. It gets sick, then heals itself, and it alters its functioning to meet varying conditions. Accustomed to variable performance from other body organs (breathing quickens during exercise, slows at night; glands step up activity enormously to meet stressful situations, etc.), we still somehow expect constancy from the heart. We shouldn't. In some cases, hearts have speeded up from a normal 60–70 beats a minute to over 100 and continued at this rate for long periods, without harm. Skipped beats are widely feared; actually, there is little evidence they in themselves are dangerous. If danger does exist, the ECG will usually give warning.

Heart murmurs—the sound of blood passing through the heart—were once considered a sure sign of difficulty. Many children were put to bed as invalids because of them. It is now known that more than 50 percent of young children have murmurs, but in many cases these are harmless and disappear during adolescence. The ECG has aided physicians in distinguishing harmless or "functional" murmurs from those which indicate that disease or heart defect is present. A reassuring follow-up study of 96 persons who had heart murmurs 20 years earlier showed that in 80 percent the murmurs had disappeared; only two had heart disease related to the childhood murmur.

Another valuable development is the taking of ECGs during exercise. (See the article that follows.)

... And the "Stress Test" ECG

by Arlene and Howard Eisenberg

THE 38-year-old Wall Street executive looked embarrassed as, electrode leads trailing from his chest, he stepped onto the exercise treadmill. "I'm only doing this to get my wife off my back," he told the physiologist. "Those pains I've been having are just from a pinched nerve."

Indeed, electrocardiograms taken while the man was lying down had revealed no sign of heart disease over the previous four years. But after observing him for ten minutes on the treadmill, alerted by abnormalities on the ECG monitor, cardiologist Dr. Abner J. Delman, medical director of Cardio-Metrics, Inc., of New York City, stopped the test. He recommended to the patient's doctor follow-up angiocardiography—X rays employing a special contrast dye injected into the coronary blood vessels to precisely outline damage. The film revealed atherosclerosis so advanced the patient required immediate triple bypass heart surgery. The stress test may well have saved his life.

The 118 passengers and crewmen of a British European Airways jet were not so fortunate. Their plane crashed shortly after takeoff from London's Heathrow Airport in June 1972, killing all aboard. A court of inquiry established that the 51-year-old captain had a coronary attack just after getting into the air. His condition, said the report, "must have been developing for 30 years or more," yet the inexorable narrowing of his coronary arteries had gone undetected in routine ECGs the previous two years.

More than one million Americans annually are felled by heart attacks—many within weeks or even days after passing standard "resting" ECGs. Says Dr. Irving M. Levitas, director of the Cardiac Stress Laboratory at Hackensack (N.J.) Hospital, "Lots of people with coronary disease show normal resting ECGs. You have to test the heart the way you do a car—take it out on the highway and let it ping."

How do you safely test your heart in action? For many years, the only answer was the Masters Two-Step Test, which has the patient step on and off a two-level platform for a three-minute period. But this test put too much stress on some, too little on others. Many physicians resisted using it because of the remote possibility a patient might drop dead in the office.

The new "exercise" ECGs are performed on a stationary bicycle or treadmill, while a cardiologist monitors your heart continuously and stops you if an abnormal ECG or blood-pressure reading warns of danger ahead.

"What we get," says physiologist William S. Gualtiere, "is an indirect image of the extent that atherosclerosis has narrowed the individual's coronary vessels." Adds Dr. Samuel M. Fox III, past president of the American College of Cardiology, "The evidence is very strong that exercise stress testing is a powerful predictor of future coronary disease."

Stress testing also detects latent stroke dangers such as development of excessively high blood pressure. A woman patient registered normal pressure at rest; but, shortly after her treadmill test began, it soared to 200, too high for the low level of exercise.

Exercise testing is equally valuable in *ruling out* suspected coronary artery disease. An engineer was referred to Washington Hospital Center after three different emergency admissions with severe chest pains to a hospital coronary-care unit—none of which appeared to be a heart problem. "He had become a psychic cripple," recalls Dr. Fox, "afraid to do anything for fear of a recurrence. We stress tested him slowly and carefully, up to 190 heartbeats per minute, without any indications of heart disease. He left with apprehensions erased and a new outlook on life. He has been fine ever since."

Symptoms that might lead your doctor to conclude that you need a stress test include shortness of breath, an occasional squeezing sense of pressure in walking up stairs or during stress, and extra heartbeats or palpitations. Particularly recommended for testing are adults with one or more of the risk factors spelled out by the American Heart Association: a history of heart disease in the family, high blood pressure, diabetes, high serum lipid levels (fat components in the blood), overweight, high-pressure life style, smoking. Stress testing also makes sense for any inactive person who plans to take up tennis, jogging or other strenuous exercise, to make certain he or she can safely meet the increased demands.

"Unfortunately," says Dr. L. Loring Brock, director of the Heart-Lung Center in Denver, "testing is often the end rather than the beginning of treatment. Many doctors do not include in the report specific advice for exercise programs to improve cardiovascular health." Adds Dr. Herman K. Hellerstein, of Case Western Reserve University School of Medicine: "Exercise to strengthen the heart should be prescribed with the same precision as any other powerful therapeutic procedure," with "specific periods, frequencies and intensities" spelled out. In addition, patients should be urged to reduce other risk factors—obesity, a high cholesterol level and smoking.

Such centers as Cardio-Metrics, the many affiliated offices of Cardiac Treatment Centers, Inc., of Camp Hill, Pa., and the Cooper Clinic in Dallas, Texas, do just that. A program is prescribed for each patient, built around a preferred activity—swimming, bicycling, walk-jog-running, etc.

Stress testing is available in most medical centers and large hospitals. If you would like to be tested, the easiest way to find the cardiovascular exercise lab nearest you is to ask your physician, or to contact your local hospital.

Many doctors feel that within a few years stress testing will become a routine part of every thorough physical exam. It is, as Dr. Brock puts it, "probably the most dependable predictor of the potential heart-attack victim of all the tests available to us."

New Light on a Hidden Killer

by Lawrence Galton

BILL PETERS is a successful 40-year-old executive. Big and brawny, he looks well and feels fine. Nonetheless, his company requires him to have regular medical checkups. At his latest, the doctor took his blood pressure twice, then said, "Slightly above normal, Bill. Not much, but we're still going to do something about it."

Today, more and more doctors are taking even the mildest hypertension such as Bill's seriously. For they have gained important new insights on this often-neglected, yet vicious disease. High blood pressure affects at least 34 million Americans and is a factor in the deaths of three quarters of a million annually. Yet, only about 15 percent of these 34 million victims are receiving the treatment they need.

Bill Peters is one of the lucky ones. Because steps were taken to control his slightly elevated pressure, his chances of being felled by stroke or heart disease have been dramatically reduced.

Most people with hypertension are unaware of the fact. For the ailment is stealthy. Most often it produces no symptoms at all. The Michigan Heart Association reports that a screening program at a large factory uncovered hypertension in 919 employees—78 percent of whom did not know they had it. Even when symptoms occur—such as headaches, dizziness, fatigue or weakness—they may not be recognized for what they are since they are common to so many other disorders. Moreover, in 85 to 90 percent of diagnosed hypertensive patients the specific cause of the condition cannot be pinpointed.

Blood pressure is simply the force exerted by the flowing blood against the walls of the arteries. Each time the heart beats, this pressure increases; each time the heart relaxes, the pressure decreases. When a physician checks pressure, he makes two measurements and writes them fraction-style, say, as 130/80. The first and larger figure, 130 millimeters (the pressure exerted by a column of mercury 130 mm. or 5.1 inches high), is the systolic pressure—the maximum pressure in the arteries when the heart pumps; the second is diastolic pressure—as the heart rests between contractions.

Normal pressure may fluctuate widely, decreasing during sleep, increasing during physical exertion or emotional excitement, even during the visit to the doctor. That's why many physicians measure blood pressure several times in one visit. And there is a wide range of normal: 100 to 140 for systolic, and 60 to 90 for diastolic. Nor does an isolated reading above 140/90 mean abnormal pressure. Only when elevation is continuous does a person have hypertension.

Hypertension does its harm in several ways. In one, excessive pressure makes the heart muscle pump harder, and after a time the heart enlarges; then it may weaken and fail to pump effectively.

Or, as many investigations show, hypertension may accelerate the progression of atherosclerosis, involved in coronary heart attacks which kill some 800,000 Americans every year. In a 14-year study of 5100 people, ages 30 to 60, in Framingham, Mass., it was found that coronary heart disease, with its heart attacks, was three to five times more common in people with high blood pressure. Adding to the indictment, a study by the Health Insurance Plan of Greater New York of first heart attacks showed that—compared with those male victims who had normal pressure—twice as many men with pre-existing hypertension died within a month. Moreover, the hypertensive men who survived the first attack had twice the risk of recurrence, and five times the risk of heart death during the next 4½ years.

High blood pressure may contribute to artery-clogging atherosclerosis by damaging blood-vessel walls, allowing cholesterol and other materials to nest in the damaged areas. As these deposits build up, arteries narrow, and their blood-carrying capacity is reduced, sometimes even completely blocked.

When this happens to an artery feeding the brain, stroke results—each year, nearly 200,000 of us die this way.

During the 14 years of the Framingham study, stroke hit 65 of the men, 70 of the women. The risk proved to be four times as high among those who had hypertension—though they had no symptoms—as among those with normal pressure.

The study brought to light an altogether surprising fact, too. It had long been assumed that only diastolic-pressure elevation is critical, since that indicates stress when the heart is supposed to be relaxing. In fact, some elevation of the systolic had been regarded as an innocuous consequence of aging. "Contrary to popular belief," says the Framingham report, "systolic blood-pressure elevations proved no less important as a risk factor in stroke." Indeed, the findings indicate clearly that hypertension, even of mild degree, *at any age,* in either sex, whether systolic or diastolic, is the most common and most potent precursor to strokes.

Fortunately, there is a positive side to the discoveries. It had been known for years that treatment of extremely severe hypertension has dramatic effect on most patients. Now there is also clear evidence of the efficacy of treatment in less severe cases. Working with 17 hospitals across the country, the Veterans Administration Cooperative Study Group, led by Edward D. Freis, spent six years gathering it.

The group reported in 1970 on 380 male patients with mild and moderate hypertension—diastolic pressures 90 to 114, just above the up-to-90 normal range. Some were given medication, others only symptomatic treatment and placebo pills. In the actively treated group, the risk of developing heart failure or a stroke was *reduced by two thirds..* (Twenty untreated patients had to be placed on stronger anti-hypertensive drugs because of severely elevated blood pressures; this did not occur in any of the treated men.)

Say Dr. Freis and his colleagues: "There is little doubt that anti-hypertensive treatment proved beneficial."

The ideal is to bring pressure down to normal levels and keep it there. When medication is needed, the physician adjusts the patient's regimen until he finds a drug or combination of drugs that will control pressure effectively with minimal side effects. Often modification of diet to eliminate extra pounds, and mild exercise to ease emotional tension, prove beneficial. Some patients bring pressure down simply by reducing the salt in their diets.

To assure adequacy of treatment, Dr. Irvine H. Page of the Cleveland Clinic has his patients take their own readings at home—a practice easily learned, and now recommended more and more often. Patients record their pressure, usually when they get up and again at bedtime, and submit the readings once a month to the physician. Says Dr. Page, "At first I worried this might make neurotics of some patients, but that has proved to be exceptionally rare."

Clearly hypertension stacks up as a vast health problem—but also as a momentous opportunity for preventive medicine. "The good news is that we have found many ways to treat it," says Dr. Page. "And it has been definitely established that if blood pressure *is* kept within relatively normal limits, stroke, heart failure and heart attacks are sharply reduced."

What does all this mean for *you?* Simply:

If you have mild hypertension but have ignored it, ask your physician to recheck you, then follow his advice on bringing pressure down.

If hypertension has never been diagnosed, recognize that no one is immune, and pressure may go up at any time *without* warning symptoms. An annual checkup is therefore all the more important. Making certain your blood pressure is in line—and stays there—is one thing you can do with reasonable ease to reduce your chances of being crippled or wiped out by a couple of major killers.

THE RIGHT DIET FOR YOU

Think Before You Diet

by Robert O'Brien

ARE YOU thinking about going on a diet? If so, maybe you'd better think twice. You may be a person for whom diet is almost impossible. Indeed, you could be one of the Americans who, many authorities now agree, are better off overweight.

Doctors and psychiatrists, studying the problem of obesity, are increasingly asking why so many of us eat beyond our needs. And in case after case they find we are depending on food not just as a source of energy but as a means of getting through the tensions of everyday living. Eating is at once a pleasure, a solace, and an escape from the disagreeable situations of life.

For some the urge to eat follows clash and conflict. Not long ago when I kept an appointment with a small-town manufacturer, he met me at the office door and led me down the street to a coffee shop. "I just went through a terrific hassle with the shop grievance committee," he said, as he sipped a double chocolate malted milk shake. "My wife tells me I'm too fat. But if I didn't eat when I'm all keyed up, I'd blow my top."

Others put on weight when an event looms as formidable or filled with uncertainty—an approaching marriage, a new job, impending surgery, a big business deal. Many overeat when they feel bored, or sorry for themselves and entitled to consolation.

Again, an overabundance of food may represent security. I once knew a newspaperman who blew two thirds of every paycheck at the supermarket. "When I was a kid," he explained, "there were times when there wasn't enough food in the house to go around. That's never going to happen with my family if I can help it." He looked proudly at his two chubby sons and plump wife.

Some people have to eat "when they feel blue, angry, apprehensive or ashamed," Dr. Walter W. Hamburger of the University of Rochester told the American Dietetic Association. "It is as if eating protected them from feeling too much."

This anthology of stress, typical of the variety of factors involved in overeating, suggests the overwhelming case against the assumption that *anyone* can diet, that "all it takes is will power." Actually, your success in dieting will depend largely on how stable you are emotionally.

Cornell's Graduate School of Nutrition completed a study of the performance of 116 dieters, all referred to the clinic by doctors, and all of whom *wanted* to diet. They were first classified into three groups: those whose emotional stability appeared to be above average; those of average stability, with some underlying tensions or anxiety; those of below-average stability, who appeared to have deep psychological troubles.

Of the 32 dieters in the first group, 16 got "excellent" results. The remaining 16 experienced "moderate success": they lost weight, but at a slowly diminishing rate. The reasons for their overweight were relatively simple: some were victims of today's sedentary, mechanized living; some were middle-aged persons whose physical activity had fallen off but whose food intake hadn't; some just liked good food and didn't know how much their bodies required.

Of 44 dieters with average emotional stability, only six came out "excellent." Twelve experienced "moderate success," while 22 finished with "small success" and four were total failures. This "average" group probably represents the large majority of the nation's overweights; like my manufacturer friend, they need food to help combat strain and stress. Dr. Charlotte M. Young, professor of medical nutrition at Cornell and co-director of the experiment, called them the greatest challenge. "They require insight into the way they eat to relieve anxieties and tensions," she said. "They need to be helped to find other means of relief."

Of 40 dieters in the third group—those with serious psychological problems—only one achieved an "excellent." Four had "moderate success." Eight won "small success." Twenty-seven failed completely. Dr. Young and her associates felt that in general these subjects must have psychiatric help with their inner conflicts before they can hope for success in dieting. "What is worse," she said, "dieting may be harmful, since guilt and frustration because of their failure at it are added to their problems."

Many doctors hesitate before prescribing diets to overweights if they are happy, functioning well socially and professionally, and otherwise appear in good health. A minister's wife was a pleasant, cheerful person when she first arrived in her husband's new parish. She was a tireless worker, filled with patience and understanding and a genuine liking for people—and she was 20 pounds overweight. To be slim like the fashionable young wives of the parish, she undertook a crash diet. She dropped from size 18 to size 14 in three months. But instead of finding life happier, she could no longer cope with her parish duties, and her peevishness distressed her, her husband and everyone around her.

"Some people are better off overweight," said her doctor. "You are one of them." Now she's her plump self again, and once more the delight of the parish.

At best, dieting should never be undertaken in times of stress—by people worried about money, domestic affairs or their job. Psychiatrists at the Mayo Clinic have listed others whose life circumstances might make dieting a serious risk: those who are lonely and deprived of companionship; women "obviously already tense and anxious around middle life"; men in their late 50s, with retirement imminent (they would be wise to defer dieting until they are adapted to their new, more restricted life).

One national authority warns doctors to proceed with gravest caution in recommending dieting to *any* middle-aged overweight. "Many of them," he says, "are hard-working men and women who unfortunately receive relatively little satisfaction from their family or their job." Enjoyment of food—eating what they want and as much as they want—may be the safety valve that keeps them functioning.

Before these overweights can diet successfully they require a constructive substitute for the gratifications of overeating; another form of diversion. Pressure-ridden commuters have been helped to victory over the urge to eat by a new interest in rose growing or a half-hour of archery in the back yard every evening. High-powered executives may need more dynamic substitutes: golf, sailing, hunting, riding.

In spite of the dangers and difficulties, many people can and should reduce. They know that weight has a direct bearing on their mental well-being, efficiency and general good health. Here are some suggestions which may help toward success:

1. Ask yourself: *Why* do I overeat? What is my pattern of overeating? Between meals? All day long? Just before going to bed? Do I feel guilty about it? The answers may hold valuable clues as to how to deal with the compulsion.

2. Set a modest and immediate goal—the loss of, say, a pound or two a week. Make yourself answerable to someone or something, if only a bathroom chart, at regular intervals—once a week, if possible.

3. Allow for an occasional relapse—a splurge on a special occasion when it would be unseemly or tactless to stick to a diet.

4. Settle on a *moderate* diet—one that supplies adequate nutrition for your daily energy requirements.

5. Make time for regular exercise that is pleasant, mild and easily adapted to your home environment.

Dieting is more than mechanical control of food intake. It is basic training in the classic virtue of moderation. It is a long and essentially lonely process of learning constructive ways of handling problems that one now handles by overeating.

Nibble That Fat Away

by Stanley L. Englebardt

HOW OFTEN have you seen a cow that was much fatter than the rest of the herd? A sea gull too fat to fly? An obese giraffe?

These aren't facetious questions. They help explain a remarkably simple concept of dieting that can benefit nearly everyone who wants to lose weight.

Scientists have known for a long time that most animals in the wild, left to their own natural eating patterns, rarely get fat. Scientists have also long been aware that changing animals over to meal-feeding has a dramatic effect on their weight. In fact, 90 years ago a German nutritionist reported experiments with pigeons and chicks in which he found that those animals fed only at intervals had greater weight gains than those fed the same amounts *ad libitum* (not controlled by a fixed schedule).

In more recent studies with laboratory animals, reported in 1974, professors Gilbert A. Leveille and Dale R. Romsos, of Michigan State University, found that rats and pigs fed only one or two large meals a day, instead of being allowed to follow a pattern of *ad libitum* feeding, or what some call a "nibbling diet," develop an increased capacity to store energy as fat cells. If the animal stays on a meal-eating regimen long enough, these accumulated grams of excess body fat will eventually add up to obesity.

But did such knowledge about animals have applicability to human weight-control problems? Serious investigation to find the answer began to get under way in the 1950s.

Among the first to demonstrate the unusual effects of a nibbling diet was the late Dr. Clarence Cohn of Michael Reese Hospital in Chicago. In one experiment, he divided some 1500 white rats into two groups, each one receiving the same amount of food. One set was force-fed all its rations twice daily; the other was allowed to nibble at will. After 41 days, a significant difference was noted between the two groups: while both groups of rats weighed about the same, the meal-fed animals had more body fat than the control group of nibblers. Post-mortem measurements and subsequent experiments confirmed that the meal-eaters had almost twice as much fatty tissue and an unhealthy increase in serum cholesterol.

In 1961, Dr. Cohn reported his long-term observation of a patient who suffered from an excess of lipids, or fatty substances, in his bloodstream. He had the man change his eating pattern to several small meals a day, without altering the content or overall calorie intake. Over a seven-month period, the man's serum-lipid count dropped to an almost normal level.

Investigations by other scientists were turning up similar results. Dr. Pavel Fábry and his colleagues at the Institute for Clinical and Experimental Medicine in Prague, Czechoslovakia, studied 89 healthy men between the ages of 30 and 50, and another group of 440 men aged 60 to 64, to observe their eating patterns. It was found that, compared with those who consumed three or fewer meals a day, those who ate five or six meals weighed less and had less body fat. Moreover, they exhibited two major medical benefits: They had a significantly lower blood cholesterol (the substance implicated as one of the prime risk factors in heart attacks), and the 60 to 64 age group showed increased glucose tolerance—the ability of the body to handle a sudden influx of sugars.

This latter finding did not come as a complete surprise—doctors have been putting diabetic patients on nibbling diets for a long time. By taking food in multiple small amounts, the body is spared the job of having to cope with a sudden large amount of blood sugar. In this way, thousands of diabetics have been able to reduce their daily need for insulin. The fact that many diabetics lose weight on this diet indicates that it may also serve as a treatment for obesity.

Still, nobody understood why scattering the same amount of calories over multiple small meals should produce such differences. Then Michigan State researchers Leveille and

Romsos dissected their rats, and discovered several anatomical changes. The stomach and small intestine of the meal-eaters had expanded about 40 percent in order to cope with the greater load of food. This meant the meal-eaters were processing and storing almost twice as much fat and sugars in the period following the meal.

"What this suggests," says Dr. Leveille, "is that physicians and dietitians might pay attention to the timing of food consumption as well as to its quantity and quality. By adhering to mealtimes, man may have become the architect of his own obesity."

Prof. Dorothy J. Pringle, of the nutritional-sciences department at the University of Wisconsin-Madison, conducted a study with six women students, ages 18 to 20, who were at least 23 percent above their ideal weight. The diet contained 1300 calories, which were divided among six small meals. "We concentrated on foods that would stand up well without refrigeration," says Professor Pringle. Wrapped in clear plastic, items such as turkey sandwiches, apples, oranges and cold vegetables were then tucked into shoulder bags or purses.

"It's as easy to eat a sandwich and fruit between classes as it is to munch on a candy bar," said one student. As for results, the young women agreed they had "more energy," a feeling of satiety and a weight loss of from two to five pounds per week. Studies done by Fábry and others have shown that humans who nibble throughout the day instead of eating one or two large meals can more easily maintain their normal weight on the *same calorie input*.

My own experience with a nibbling diet shows it is not difficult to dovetail such an eating schedule into a busy day. Two months after a medical examination revealed an elevated blood-cholesterol count, I tried nibbling to lower my serum lipids and to lose a few extra pounds. The diet contains about 1350 calories, which are distributed among six or seven meals.

At first, I thought the frequency of the meals would be a nuisance. But it took less than a week to adjust to the schedule. The only in-between meals came at 10 a.m. and 3 p.m.—times I usually take a coffee break anyway. In addition to coffee, I now eat crackers, a sandwich, fruit or a cold vegetable.

Results came quickly. In less than a month I'd lost seven pounds, and in eight weeks my blood cholesterol was in the normal range. I am still on a nibbling regimen, although my caloric intake is up to what it was when I started the program.

There are, of course, ground rules for a successful nibbling diet:

• To lose weight, you must cut daily calories below previous levels. Once a target weight has been reached, you can adjust upward until you're on a maintenance program. The type of food must be nutritionally adequate for long-term use.

• Your goal is to stabilize and maintain your desired weight. This can't happen if you switch back and forth between frequent small meals and occasional big meals. You must be prepared to stay on the nibbling regimen over a long term.

• Don't expect any dramatic weight loss. It is never as easy to take off weight as it is to put it on. When nibbling rats are switched to meal-eating, it takes less than nine days before they start producing the increased amounts of fats that will eventually add measurable layers of adipose tissue. But when they return to *ad libitum* feeding, it requires at least six weeks before the body is able to stop producing large amounts of fat. The same pattern might be true in humans.

• Finally, don't interpret the freedom of a nibbling diet as a license to tank up on junk foods. Although treats are allowed, their caloric content must be added to the daily total. Thus, injudicious consumption of cream puffs, pizzas and candy could play havoc with the overall program.

THIS NIBBLING DIET has been prepared by Prof. Dorothy J. Pringle. It is designed to effect a weight loss of about one to two pounds per week for a short sedentary woman, or two to three pounds per week for a tall active man. Distribute 1300 calories over each day until a target weight has been reached.

Use any items in the food groups on pages 151–53, as specified in the diet below. Thus, a typical lunch might include 1 slice of bread (starch group) with 2 tablespoons of peanut butter (meat group), cold, cooked broccoli (free vegetable) with 1 teaspoon of mayonnaise (fat group) and a tangerine (fruit group); a sample midafternoon meal might consist of 6 round crackers (starch group) with a teaspoon of margarine (fat group), one ounce of cheese (meat group), a fresh tomato (free vegetable) and ½ cup of orange juice (fruit group). Foods in the free foods group may be eaten at any time, and you can have one "treat" each day.

Distribution of food during the day

Breakfast:
½ SERVING FROM MILK GROUP
1 FROM MEAT GROUP
2 FROM STARCH GROUP
1 FROM FRUIT GROUP

Midmorning Meal:
1 MILK
1 STARCH
1 FRUIT

Lunch:
1 MEAT
2 STARCHES
1 FRUIT
1 FAT
FREE VEGETABLE

Midafternoon Meal:
1 MEAT
1 STARCH
1 FRUIT
1 FAT
FREE VEGETABLE

Supper:
2 MEATS
2 STARCHES
1 FRUIT
FREE VEGETABLE

Bedtime Meal:
1 MILK
2 STARCHES
1 FAT

Food Groups

Milk Group: sources of carbohydrate and protein
 1 c. (cup) skim milk or buttermilk
 1 c. plain skim-milk yogurt

Meat Group: sources of protein and fat
 2 tbs. (tablespoons) peanut butter
 ¼ c. cottage cheese
 1 oz. hard cheese
 1 egg
 1 thin slice of cold cuts
 1 frankfurter
 ¼ c. canned fish
 1 oz. cooked meat, poultry or fish (about ¼ cup)

Starch Group: sources of carbohydrate and protein
 ½ slice of bread (whole grain or enriched)

¼ c. cooked cereal (whole grain or enriched)

½ c. dry cereal (whole grain or enriched)

1 graham cracker

5 saltines

6 crackers (1½ inch diameter)

¼ c. rice, noodles or macaroni

¼ c. dried beans or peas

¼ c. corn

⅓ c. parsnips

½ c. carrots, beets, green peas or winter squash

2 medium onions

½ small potato

Fruit Group: sources of carbohydrate

½ c. fruit juice

1 apple, 1 pear, *1 orange, *1 tangerine, 1 peach

*½ grapefruit

*¼ cantaloupe

½ banana

½ c. applesauce

½ c. fresh pineapple

2 tbs. raisins

Fat Group:

1 tsp. (teaspoon) butter, margarine or oil

1 tbs. cream cheese

1 tsp. mayonnaise

1 tbs. French dressing

2 tbs. light cream

1 slice of bacon

Free Foods Group: having few calories; some contain many nutrients

asparagus

broccoli

cabbage or sauerkraut

cauliflower

salad vegetables

eggplant

greens (*e.g.*, spinach)

mushrooms

okra
green beans
summer squash
seasonings
tomato
vinegar
black coffee or tea
low-calorie soft drinks
low-calorie sweetener

Treats: sources of sugar
2 tsp. sugar
1 tsp. honey or syrup
1 tsp. jelly or jam
1 heaping tsp. chocolate beverage mix

*These fruits are rich in vitamin C, and you should eat at least one serving a day.

Your Best Weapon Against Overweight

by Curtis Mitchell

ALMOST everyone fights fat at one time or another. Reducing fads come and go; dieters hopefully cut their calories for a week—or a month—and then, in droves, fall off their diets. Dr. Claude H. Miller of New York has found that only two out of every 100 patients who reduce on clinically supervised programs are ordinarily able to attain a good weight and then retain it for as long as one year. Only two out of 100!

Well, there's good news tonight. There's a device on the market that can help you not only take off weight but also *keep* it off. Last year, more than four million Americans bought and used it.

It is called a scale. If you use it faithfully, three things can happen.

First, it can tell you how much flab you need to lose to improve your health—and your looks. Second, it can motivate you to get a sensible reducing diet from your doctor, and then stick to it. Third, when you are proud or pretty again because your weight is what it ought to be, it will help you stay there.

Medical specialists in the field of weight reduction agree on the importance of a regular weighing-in program. When I asked Dr. Max Novich, of Perth Amboy, N.J., a team physician for the 1972 Olympic boxing squad, if weight fluctuation is really important for non-athletes as well as athletes, he said, "It's crucial. I weigh every day." Dr. Kenneth H. Cooper, author of *Aerobics,* says, "My office scale is one of the busiest pieces of equipment I own." Dr. Irwin Maxwell Stillman, author of *The Doctor's Quick Weight Loss Diet*, recommends that you make it a habit to get on your bathroom scale, unclothed, first thing every morning, without fail. Any time you're up three pounds, he says, you should consider it more serious than if your thermometer showed three degrees above normal.

According to Dr. Robert C. Atkins, a New York specialist in carbohydrate metabolism and author of *Dr. Atkins' Diet Revolution*, "Using your scale daily makes you aware of your problem, which is essential to action. Knowing what you weigh, you can file a mental plan as to what you can eat. Then carry out the plan each day."

How can you establish your best weight? Everyone should keep a year-to-year record of his weight. If you haven't done this, try to recall your weight during your 25th year—your 22nd, if you are a woman. By that age your skeleton had stopped growing; your weight then, according to Dr. Jean Mayer, the noted nutritionist who is now president of Tufts University, is the weight you should maintain as long as you live. This applies to everyone except a relatively few individuals who, because of malfunctioning glands or heredity, are special cases and must seek professional advice.

Attaining your ideal weight is a three-step project.

1. Get a bathroom scale—either the flat-on-the-floor, spring-tension type, or the upright type, on which you move a counterweight until the scale is in balance. The advantages of the latter are that it is easier to read and measures more precisely, though it costs more. Whatever type you choose, be sure to try it out in the store. Can you read the figure clearly when you step on the scale? Manufacturers point out that their scales work best on a hard, level surface, and may be inaccurate when placed on a slope or carpet.

Don't go scale-hopping. The scale at your pharmacy or at the gymnasium or at your neighbor's house probably varies from the one you have at home. Stick to your own.

2. Keep a chart and a tape measure handy. In addition to regularly recording on the chart your nude weigh-in figure (always weigh at the same time!), try registering your key dimensions as indicated by the tape measure. The male field of battle is the midriff, just below the navel. Women usually measure their hips and thighs.

Use all the psychological gimmicks you can to make the

chart and tape measure help you. To salute success and effectively reinforce sagging resolution, it may help to hang your chart where it will be seen by others. When an obese oilman in Oklahoma City installed a giant chart on his office wall, and recorded his daily loss in king-size figures, his office staff became so interested that he dared not backslide—which was the way he'd planned it. A New York couple posted their chart on the most frequently passed wall in their home, and were shamed into staying on the straight and narrow by the hazing of their small fry.

3. Hang in there and fight. When the needle on your scale seems to be sticking, don't give up. Physiologists know that pounds rarely vanish in a straight downward line. Rather, they drop step by step, with some steps bigger than others. One doctor says, "I always warn my patients they are likely to hit a plateau somewhere along the line. Otherwise, they may get discouraged and tie into a steak-and-potato binge."

Eternal vigilance is the price of slimming, says Hilde Bruch, psychiatrist and author of *The Importance of Overweight*. So, make your scale a daily confidant. Trust it, and take its advice. You may lose a few battles, but you will win your war.

Stay Slim—For Good

by E. Ann Sutherland and Zalman Amit

DIETS don't work—at least, not for the vast majority of people who are overweight. Why? Because excessive weight is not so much a result of *what* you eat as of *how* you eat, and what your *attitudes* toward food are. Diets, which substitute a rigid, often highly abnormal eating pattern for the existing abnormal pattern, cause only a temporary change in eating behavior. The only way to prevent the recurrence of overweight is to make a *permanent* change.

At the New Clinic for Behavior Therapy and Research, in Montreal, we have developed a program for precisely this purpose. Of the hundreds of overweight men and women who have completed the program, three quarters have successfully stayed with it for at least two years, keeping their weight at a healthy and attractive level. We believe our approach can be of help to every overweight individual.

The best way to learn any new pattern of behavior is to break it down into small, manageable parts and work through them step by step—as you would learn to drive a car. You'll have to monitor your eating constantly. This may be a bit tedious, but if you want the program to work for you, you must take the steps seriously. Remember: This is not a *diet*, to be used, discarded, taken up again.

1. Write it down. First, keep a full account of *everything* you put into your mouth—every slice of bacon, every drink, every stick of gum. (Only exceptions: clear tea, black coffee, water.) The question is not how many calories you consume, but how you pattern your eating.

Also record these details: When do you eat? How early in the day do you start? How late at night do you finish? How often do you snack in between? Where do you eat? At the table, or on the move? With whom do you eat? Do you eat more when you eat alone? Do your recording within 15 minutes after you eat, every time you eat.

You'll probably be surprised, even shocked, by how much and how often you eat. But don't attempt to eat less by skipping meals: Increasing your body's need for food makes you become more susceptible to the temptation of quickly eaten foods, such as sweets.

Master the record-keeping. Only when you have done it without major error for at least seven consecutive days should you move on to the next phase. And then you must continue your recording in the weeks ahead, adding more information.

2. Regulate your eating times. You *must* eat three full meals and two snacks every day, without fail. No more, no less. Start your meals within specified times: breakfast between 7 and 9:30 a.m., lunch between noon and 2 p.m., dinner between 6 and 8:30 p.m. Eat anything you like, as long as it's at one sitting. You may take your snacks in the morning, afternoon or evening. But decide which two of these snack times you'll use, and stick to them. (A snack is one beverage plus one item of food—a piece of toast or fruit.)

Constant snacking is a major cause of overweight. Avoid it. Don't taste food while cooking it. Do without even "diet" drinks, except as part of a scheduled meal or snack. They encourage you to drink for taste rather than thirst, and in our experience can play a major role in sustaining a problem eating pattern.

If you're accustomed to a cocktail before dinner, continue, but it must be consumed as part of a meal at the table. Remember that alcohol is food, and must be controlled along with everything else. At parties, stick to one drink and one item of food only, as your evening snack.

Nearly all our patients express incredulity when asked to eat three meals and two snacks daily. "I'm overweight already," moaned 165-pound housewife Marsha S. "I'll swell up like a balloon." But she took our word for it—and came out, eventually, 40 pounds slimmer.

Make no exceptions, and don't tailor your eating to other people's demands. *You* are the one with the problem. Explain the program to your family, and let them adapt to *you*. Don't skip lunch. Don't delay your own dinner if your husband or wife is going to be home late. Continue complete records of what, when, where and with whom you eat, and how well you have kept to schedule. Continue on to phase three only after you have proved yourself able to stay on schedule for *seven consecutive days*.

3. Regulate your shopping and storage. You now have to control the kinds of food you buy and the way you store it. Do you usually shop from a list? If not, start doing so. Once in the store, you may have to make substitutions—a cut of meat on sale, another kind of cheese—but don't add anything. If you've forgotten to list it, do without. And always shop on a full stomach. (If *you* don't do the shopping, pass these ground rules to the person who does.)

If you often buy snack or convenience foods, you're making it very easy to stay overweight. Buy only foods that require preparation—unsliced bread, wedges of cheese, whole salami. Dispense with junk food such as potato chips, chocolate bars, salted nuts.

Finally, organize yourself so you do *all* your weekly shopping in *one* trip. If you plan carefully, there should be no need to keep going back. If you must buy an item that will not keep for a week, send someone else to buy it. Studies have shown that overweight people tend to eat not so much in response to hunger as to purely external cues such as the sight, smell and sheer availability of food. Avoid the extra exposure and extra risk of starting an "eating binge."

How you store your food is almost as important as what you buy. You don't want to be faced with an array of appetizing leftovers and potential snacks every time you open your refrigerator or cupboard. To avoid temptation, no foods should be exposed to view. Pack them in nontransparent plastic containers, brown paper or aluminum foil. The point is to build in a delay between your first feeling of "wanting" food and the actual getting of it, and to give yourself a chance to decide if it fits into your new pattern. Again, continue to keep accurate records. Go on to the next phase only after mastering this one.

4. Be aware of the act of eating. One of the typical features of a problem eating pattern is the tendency to eat almost unconsciously. To counter that tendency:

- *Sit down to eat*. Cut out completely any "eating on the

run"—while standing beside the refrigerator, walking, riding in the car. If you make yourself sit down at a table every time you eat, you'll become more aware of what you're doing.

• *Always set a full place for yourself.* No matter how small the snack, set out knife, fork and spoon.

• *Cut out distractions.* You must no longer work, listen to the radio, watch TV, smoke or read while you eat. Allow yourself no distraction from the act of eating—except to talk to another person at the table.

• *Before every meal, drink a glass of water.* Not tea or coffee, just plain water—a full, eight-ounce glass. This will stop you from rushing at your food. When you eat, there is, on average, a 20-minute delay before the food activates your satiety mechanism. Typically, overweight eaters rush at their food and finish it all within that 20-minute period, before they can even begin to feel full. Drinking water before your meal will take the edge off your hunger.

Once you successfully master these tasks, you have passed the halfway point in your program. You should soon begin to lose weight, if you have not already. You should also realize by now that you have considerable self-discipline. You have what it takes to finish successfully.

5. Learn to eat slowly. Put your fork or spoon down after every mouthful, taking it up again only when your mouth is empty. When you eat with your hands, put the sandwich, or fruit or whatever, down after each mouthful.

This, like the water-drinking, will give your stomach more time to register its reactions. The slower rate of eating, combined with your gains in awareness, will make you feel full before you can finish your customary portion. You should immediately see the results in lowered food intake—and weight loss.

6. Leave something on your plate. At every meal (not snacks), let some portion of each item of food go uneaten, even if it's only one bite of meat, one teaspoon of potato, one string bean.

If you are a typical problem eater, you were probably taught to clean your plate for the sake of starving children in India, or wherever. You may still feel guilt when you don't finish your food, and this emotion can enforce an addictive eating pattern. For it's really only a small step from feeling that you *must* clean your plate to devouring a whole box of chocolates, or a whole packet of cookies.

Learn to estimate how hungry you are, and to put on the plate as much of each item as you think you'll need. Then add an extra spoonful so you can leave that extra bit on your plate. When the meal is over, scrape that leftover food into the garbage. Under no circumstances offer it to anyone else.

This may seem wasteful—but the waste is small compared with the amount of food you have been wasting simply by eating more every day than you really need. Ruining your health won't help starving children anywhere. If you feel strongly about the latter, send them the money you ultimately save on food bills.

7. Speed up your weight loss. These final tasks—*optional* accelerators for weight loss—should be undertaken only if you are still 15 pounds or more over your target weight, even though you have mastered all phases of the program to date. (If already less than 15 pounds over, simply continue with the program as outlined to date, opting for a slow and steady one-pound-a-week loss.) While maintaining the program:

Cut out all desserts except fresh fruit. Your craving for sweets has probably begun to diminish in any case, and after you reach your ideal weight, you will be able to eat some desserts. But for now, no cookies, cakes, canned fruit, etc.

Don't take any second helpings. This again is a temporary measure, but it's a habit you might profitably maintain as a useful guideline later.

Eliminate your favorite dishes. You still tend to eat more of them than you would of any other meal. If you drop them, you will eat less—until you develop other favorites.

Use a salad plate. Serve yourself a little less food at mealtimes, and on a smaller plate than a dinner plate. This is a perceptual trick to make less food seem more satisfying.

You have now accomplished everything necessary to build up a new, healthy eating pattern. But continue to record your performance every day for three more weeks. You need that time to consolidate the progress you've made, and to make the pattern almost second nature to you.

Officially, the program ends here. The rest is up to you. If, as time goes by, you find yourself slipping seriously, go back to record-keeping for a two- or three-week booster session. Remember, if you want to *keep* your weight under control, you must be faithful to the new eating pattern you have learned.

The Fastest Diet—
Is It for You?

by Michael Goodwin

SANDRA SCOTT of Brooklyn, Ohio, a suburb of Cleveland, remembers what she had for dinner on March 21, 1976: "Soup, broiled fish, tossed salad, a roll and butter, applesauce cake and a cup of tea." Recalling a meal eaten so long ago is something most people cannot do, but Sandra Scott has a special reason—she did not eat again for 178 days.

At 34, standing only five feet two inches tall and weighing more than 230 pounds, Sandy Scott had wanted to lose weight for a long time. She tried most of the popular diets, but sooner or later they, or she, always failed. Then she tried the most radical diet of all—fasting. Under the supervision of doctors at a Cleveland hospital, her weight dropped to 131 pounds. During the six-month period in which she subsisted on water, tea, diet soda and a protein supplement, she dreamed that, for the first time in her adult life, she would not be overweight. A year later, at age 35, she was a new person—and determined to stay that way.

Though under attack for endangering health and having a high incidence of weight return, fasting is becoming increasingly popular as a method of treating the massively obese, especially in cases of medical necessity. Several books have appeared hailing it as the easiest, quickest and most natural way to shed even a few unwanted pounds, and resorts where people pay substantial fees not to be fed have sprung up around the country. Supporters assert that not eating is easier than eating a tantalizing little, and that fasting purifies the body, rests the central nervous system, slows the aging process, saves money and improves sex.

There are well-qualified, respected doctors who believe that fasting, when used properly, can be a valid and medically sound treatment for obesity. And while this latter group represents only a fraction of the American medical establishment, they are convinced that for many obese people fasting may be the only way to lose large amounts of weight.

On the other hand, Dr. Philip L. White, director of the American Medical Association's Department of Foods and Nutrition, warns that the "Madison Avenue" promotion of total fasting could result in dangerous misuse by "casual dieters," and that for some people fasting could be lethal. Adds noted nutritionist Dr. Jean Mayer: "I would no sooner ride in a car driven by someone who hadn't eaten in three days than I would with someone who just had three martinis."

Just what *are* the facts behind fasting?

The world may be plagued by undernutrition and starvation, but obesity is still the major nutritional affliction in this country. Although being too fat is considered ugly and known to be harmful—it can lead to and aggravate heart disease, arthritis, diabetes, hypertension and gallstones, and generally tends to shorten life—the problem is getting worse.

Fasting, the most dramatic way to attack the problem, is being studied at a few centers across the country. Started in 1971, the program that Sandy Scott belonged to at the Mt. Sinai Hospital of Cleveland has used modified or protein-supplemented fasts. As of 1977 it had 800 patients actively enrolled and another 2000 on the waiting list, all of them trying to lose at least 100 pounds. Those accepted spent the first week and the last several days of their fasts in the hospital so their mental and physical reactions could be closely monitored. In between, they came in once a week for a checkup and an interview with a doctor and to pick up a supply of powdered protein supplement. After reaching a target weight, each patient was given an individually tailored diet based on life style and caloric needs.

Despite the fact that she was always a "frustrated, compulsive eater," Sandy found it not difficult to give up eating. She maintained her daily life and held down two jobs as a social worker. She exercised daily, including jumping rope, and had only minimal experience with such common side effects of fasting as dizziness, nausea, headaches and difficulty in keeping warm. The hardest thing, she said, was "finding clothes that could withstand constant alterations" and learning "how to deal with success and all the compliments."

The idea behind a fast is basically the same as that behind all diets—give the body fewer calories than it needs and it will burn up stored fat, thus literally eating itself. Normally the body converts food to fuel, the primary source of which is glucose, a carbohydrate essential to the brain. During fasting, or starvation, the body begins to burn up the glucose stored in the liver, but the liver's supply is not enough to last even one day. Since glucose cannot be synthesized from fat, the body then begins to break down protein in the muscles to get it, a process which eliminates considerable salt and water— and shows up on the scales as a big weight loss.

As the fast and the breakdown of body tissues progress, fat travels to the liver where it is broken down into incompletely burned fat compounds called ketones. When enough of these ketones get into the bloodstream, enzymes in the brain begin to oxidize them. This process generally starts after about one week of fasting and gradually replaces glucose catabolism as the body's major source of energy. In fact, without increasing ketone production and a correspondingly decreasing need for glucose, protein breakdown would eat away large amounts of the heart, respiratory and skeletal muscles in a matter of two or three weeks and death would result.

The brain, however, can never do entirely without glucose. And because even minimal losses of protein can be dangerous for pregnant women, children and those with heart, liver or blood diseases, doctors recommend a medical checkup for anyone planning to fast for more than a day or two.

In order to minimize protein loss during extended fasts, Dr. Victor Vertes, then director of the Mt. Sinai program, required his patients to take a protein supplement five times a day. The supplement provided the patient with most of the protein required by the brain, thus sparing the muscles and other vital tissues.

Dr. Vertes reported that 80 percent of those who began the program were able to reach their target weights. One man, sustained by his own fat and the supplement, fasted for one year and shed 321 of his 565 pounds. Dr. Ernst J. Drenick of the Veterans Administration Hospital in Los Angeles reported weight losses of up to 11 pounds in one day for some of the 200 massively obese people he has seen through fasts.

Most people who have fasted say that, after the second or third day, hunger pangs tend to disappear. Some doctors believe this happens because the high ketone level somehow suppresses the appetite, while others say that going "cold turkey" breaks the obese person's addiction to unnecessary food. At any rate, Sandy Scott's discovery that she was not "dying" for something to eat seems typical of obese people who have fasted for more than a few days.

Indeed, after her fast, Sandy found it difficult to eat her first meal at all. "I was scared," she says. "It took me two hours to decide to cook it and then I sat there for another hour before I ate it." For the next month, Sandy gradually got back into meat, salad and fruits, and thereafter was able to eat anything, as long as it all added up to less than 9800 calories a week.

In addition to programs of extended fasting, programs of short-term fasting are also available. At the Grady Memorial Hospital in Atlanta, Dr. John K. Davidson supervised the fasts of nearly 3000 obese diabetics for periods ranging up to two weeks, and he reported that 90 percent experienced significant drops in blood-sugar levels afterward. Many other diseases related to obesity are positively affected by large weight losses. Several doctors report that hypertension, arthritis and, in some situations, even schizophrenia either disappear or become more controllable through fasting.

Fasting, however, is not an unmixed blessing. Besides protein loss, the catabolism of the body's tissues can result in a dangerous buildup of uric acid, which can crystallize as stones in the kidneys and bladder (a reason why doctors usually recommend that anyone fasting drink about two quarts of water a day), and a serious depletion of minerals, vitamins, salts and fluids.

"Too much is unknown about what happens on a fast," says Dr. Theodore Van Itallie, an obesity expert from St. Luke's Hospital in New York. "The problem with fasting is that some people can tolerate it and some can't."

Another problem is the recidivism rate: When carbohydrates are reintroduced into the body, salt and water begin to be retained again. Studies indicate that as many as 70 percent of patients eventually regain their weight. Critics contend the failure rate is so high because the root causes of obesity can be conquered only through a permanent change in eating habits and life-style.

Thus fasting by itself is not a cure. At best, the quick weight loss can awaken within the obese person the desire and confidence to halt his own self-destruction. At worst, fasting can complicate what already may be a perilous health condition, cause irreparable damage to organs or even death. As with any therapeutic measure, the advantages must be weighed against the risks on a case-by-case basis.

Nonetheless, fasting has helped thousands of people, many of whom had given up hope of ever leading normal lives. As more data from the handful of programs now under way are collected and published, and as new programs evolve, fasting, in some form or another, is certain to gain increasing approval within the medical establishment. Meanwhile, the Sandy Scotts of the world have been drawing their own conclusions. "I've never felt better about myself in my whole life," she said.

LIVING LONGER

When Do You Hit Your Prime?

by Jill Newman

*The happy times, the best years of your life, can come
in carefree childhood, in romance and early parenthood,
in social and career high points, in the well-earned relaxation of retirement. Often these peak years come when
you least expect them, but many psychologists maintain
that certain periods in your life are more conducive to
success and happiness than others. Herewith, some of
their findings:*

When are you smartest? You are probably sharper during
your teens and 20s. You can accumulate and absorb facts more
easily then. The ability to apply these facts—to think and reason—seems, however, to improve with age. "Your mathematical I.Q. drops as you get older," says Dr. Aaron Beck,
professor of psychiatry at the University of Pennsylvania Medical School, "but your verbal I.Q. registers higher."

Many psychologists believe, moreover, that your mental
capacity and functions are as great in middle age as they are
at 25 and, if sufficiently exercised, they may even improve
with time.

When are you most creative? Between the ages of 30 and
39, according to an estimate of psychologist Harvey C. Lehman
in *Age and Achievement*. Much depends, however, on such
variables as the field of endeavor and the age at which creative
work is begun. Most creative people maintain a high level of

productivity throughout their lives. Lehman's study of the career of Thomas Edison, for instance, reveals that, while the inventor's highest peak of discovery came at the age of 35, he remained active and creative into his 80s.

When are you healthiest? For men, 15–25; for women, 15–30. "It is during this time that your muscles are in best shape, your weight is at its ideal, you are least likely to get various illnesses and there are fewer hospitalizations," says Dr. Shepard G. Aronson of the New York County Medical Society.

With the exception of periods of pregnancy, women are decidedly ahead of the game. They remain at the peak of health longer than men. The highest incidence of sickness begins at an earlier age for men (60–70 years) than for women (65 and on). Even male life expectancy—69.5 years, according to U.S. Public Health Service statistics—is considerably shorter than for females (77.2).

When are you most sexually responsive? "Both male and female sexual drives usually reach high plateaus in late adolescence," according to experts Masters and Johnson, "and continue relatively unabated throughout the remainder of their lives. There may be some falling off of sexual interest beyond the age of 60, but that loss is not of significant level."

When will you earn the most? During your 40s and early 50s. According to University of Wisconsin (Madison) economist Robert J. Lampman, professions that require much schooling, such as law and medicine, may not "pay off" until the 60s, whereas less highly educated salary earners (such as public-school teachers) may hit their stride in the 50s and nonskilled laborers in the late 30s and 40s.

When does your personality change the most? Most psychologists agree the basic structure of your personality is pretty well set by the age of five. Your personality continues to grow, expand and develop, however, particularly during the 40s, when, according to Gilbert Voyat, professor of psychology at City University of New York, "people begin to re-evaluate their lives in terms of what they are, as opposed to what they might have wished to become." For many, this time can turn out to be an acutely painful moment of truth.

Contrary to myth, however, people do not become more embittered and irritable as they grow older. "You get nicer, more mellow," says psychologist Joyce Brothers. "You begin to sort out what's important and don't get so upset at minor things."

When are your best years? According to psychologist Voyat, the years 30–45: "One has a realistic sense of one's limitations, yet one is in full plenitude of one's potential." The loosest yet perhaps the best formulation comes from Dr. Albert Ellis of New York's Institute for Rational Living. "The best years of your life," he says, "are the ones in which you decide your problems are your own. You don't blame them on your mother, your environment, the ecology or the President. You realize that you control your own destiny."

Add Years to Your Life

by C. P. Gilmore

You go in for a physical examination. "You're in pretty good shape," says the doctor, "but you ought to take better care of yourself. Stop smoking, drop a few pounds, exercise, and taper off on your drinking."

"Sure," you say. But deep down you know you won't do all those things.

Sound familiar? Unfortunately, it's by far the most common pattern. Now, however, doctors are beginning to use a more effective technique to get us patients to act in our own interest. It's called the health-hazard appraisal.

Here's how it works. You begin your visit to the doctor by filling out a detailed medical form—age, weight, history of personal and family illnesses, etc. The form also inquires about your smoking, drinking and exercise habits. It even asks how many miles a year you drive and how often you wear a seat belt. It asks women questions aimed at determining their risk of breast and cervical cancer. And finally, it asks for your serum-cholesterol and blood-pressure levels.

Next, your answers are analyzed, by the doctor himself or by a group that provides computer analysis.

The doctor is now ready to give you specific—and sometimes startling—information. "Your chronological age is 49," he begins, referring to a three-page form. "Unfortunately, your way of living has given you the same chance of dying in the next ten years as a person of 57. So your 'risk age,' as we call it, is 57.

"Now the good news," he continues. "You can get back years you might be losing and even add a few. If you put into effect a series of steps I'm going to tell you about, you can, in effect, reverse the aging process and make yourself younger than your chronological age, as far as risk is concerned. The calculations here show that your target age—the effective risk age you can reasonably expect to attain—is 44.

"And this printout," he says, pulling out another sheet, "shows what is causing your excess health risk. Here's how you can reduce it. Stop smoking and you'll gain back two years. Getting your blood cholesterol down from 280 to 210 will give you another two years. Lowering your blood pressure will add three more years." And so on.

The basis of the statistical tables that enable a doctor, or a computer, to calculate your "risk age" is complex. (See end of article.) But, as the following example shows, application of the tables is simple.

Several years ago, data concerning a 37-year-old woman was fed into the health-hazard computer at Methodist Hospital in Indianapolis, where the appraisal technique was developed. While the report showed that her risk age was an alarming 50.3 years, the analysis revealed she could reduce it to 33.5. If she stopped her heavy drinking, she would lower the chances of death from car accidents, cirrhosis and pneumonia, reducing her risk age by 11.8 years. If she stopped smoking, she would decrease the risk of heart disease, lung cancer, emphysema, pneumonia and stroke, subtracting two years from her effective risk age. Lowering her slightly elevated blood pressure could subtract another 1.3 years. A variety of other steps—including regular Pap smears and breast self-examination—would further reduce her risk age by 1.7 years.

Scenes like this are becoming more common in hospitals, clinics, and doctors' offices around the country. The reason, doctors point out, is simple: "The appraisal is the best tool I have for getting somebody's attention," says Dr. Charles Ross of Interhealth, a San Diego company that computes risk analysis for many health institutions. "Everybody knows smoking is bad, for example, but this gives you the numbers and you can't hide anymore."

The analysis doesn't always produce bad news, of course. When doctors at Ames Research Center in California applied health-hazard appraisal to one 40-year-old man, they found he had a risk age of 36. Further, if he would use a seat belt and exercise more often, he could drop his risk age to 33.

The appraisal technique is too new for doctors to know precisely how effective it is in motivating patients. Nevertheless, the evidence that does exist is positive. For example, doctors at the Ames center used health hazard appraisal on 488 patients and then picked 107 at random a year later for follow-up tests. The risk ages, the researchers found, had been reduced on the average by 1.4 years. Furthermore, 20 percent had made important life-style changes, such as losing weight or giving up smoking.

"I remember one man in particular," says the center's Dr. John Sherwood. "He was overweight, diabetic, hypertensive and rather accepting of the situation. His true age was 51. But his risk age was 66. When we showed him his appraisal, he took his situation a lot more seriously. He dropped 35 pounds, and began taking medicine for hypertension and doing something about his diabetes. His risk age is still a few years higher than his actual age, because of the diabetes. But he looks and feels better, and he's accomplished something his family doctor had been trying to get him to do for years. I just gave him the numbers and he responded."

Dr. Cornelius K. Blesius, an internist in El Paso, Texas, says that fewer and fewer of his patients are having heart attacks since he began using health-hazard analysis. "Now, it's not just the doctor talking. The patient understands for himself what is at stake," he says. "So we have two people—the patient and the physician—working toward the same goal."

With health-hazard appraisal, the doctor can give the specifics and the patient knows exactly what should be done to lower his risk and add to his life. Chances are he will also understand a more subtle point. True preventive medicine is up to him.

How Your "Risk Age" Is Computed

The health-hazard appraisal is based on statistical tables collected and developed over 20 years by Dr. Lewis C. Robbins of Health Hazard Appraisal, Inc., in Indianapolis, and Dr. Jack H. Hall of Methodist Hospital in Indianapolis.

From the now-famous Framingham study, which involved monitoring the health and life-styles of 5200 residents of that Boston suburb, and from other long-term studies, they have rated the importance of each major health risk. Analysis of the results showed, for example, that a man with a serum-cholesterol reading of 240 is three times as likely to have a heart attack as one with a reading below 200, and that someone with a systolic blood pressure of 160 runs four times the risk of one below 120.

Next, from national mortality statistics, the doctors obtained the specific probability of death at each age. For every 100,000 men of age 40, for example, 5560 will die of all causes over the next ten years. To put it another way, the risk of dying in the next ten years for an average 40-year-old man is 5.56 percent. Finally, from other studies, they gathered facts on the average person's weight, blood pressure, cholesterol, smoking habits and so on.

Using data from all these sources, the doctors could now compute a person's life expectancy—based not just on his age, but also on the health risks present in his life-style. Consider a man of 40 who has high cholesterol, is overweight, had one parent who died young of heart disease, and displays several other factors known to increase the risk of dying. The doctors would first figure just how great his risk is, then compare it with the average risk for that age. Suppose such calculations show a 14.3-percent chance of death in the next ten years. The tables show this is the risk of an average man of age 50. Thus, the 40-year-old man, through a combination of factors, has become, in terms of health hazards, a 50-year-old. Of course, the analysis also shows how the subject could improve his odds and thus add years to his life.

Clues to Living Longer, Staying Younger

by Patrick M. McGrady, Jr.

Does marital status make a difference in aging or length of life?

Yes. As a rule, single men and women have shorter lives than married men and women. Studies show that those who have been widowed, especially men, have a longer life expectancy if they remarry soon. Both men and women seem to have a greater resistance to disease and death when their marriage is intact.

Do women live longer than men?

Yes. Mortality rates for women are lower at all ages; only after age 65 does their rate begin to approach that of men. But relatively little is known about the process of female aging. One reason is that most of the long-term studies of aging—like those begun on military personnel during World War II—have been limited to men. Another is that the menstrual cycle adds to the complexity of charting women's physiology.

Does sexual activity help keep you youthful?

"Yes," says Richard Passwater, former director of research at the American Gerontological Research Laboratory. "So much of staying young is mental. Long-lived people tend to live for today and tomorrow. They continue their sexual enjoyments as long as they can."

Does childbearing affect a woman's longevity?

Yes. According to a 1960 study, women who have borne three children have the lowest mortality rates. Those who have borne four or more have the highest. Childless women and those with only one child generally don't live as long as mothers of two or three, according to University of Chicago sociologists Evelyn M. Kitagawa and Philip M. Hauser.

Do sleeping habits make a difference?

Yes, but it's impossible to say how much sleep is ideal. Some people thrive on five hours a night, others seem to require eight or nine. Scientists agree that consistency in sleeping pattern is more significant: it's better to get six hours' sleep every night than ten hours one night and three the next.

Does alcohol affect longevity?

Yes and no. Dr. Carl Eisdorfer, chairman of the department of psychiatry and behavioral sciences at the University of Washington School of Medicine, found that small amounts of alcohol have no significant effect on longevity. Dr. Alexander Leaf, chief of medicine at Massachusetts General Hospital, did a study of people alleged to be the world's oldest, and noted the prevalence of moderate wine drinking among them. Excessive drinking, on the other hand, clearly does shorten life.

Do thin people live longer?

Not necessarily. While it's true that very few old people are fat, this does not mean that every pound you gain is going to shorten your life. In fact, a study in Framingham, Mass., showed that during at least 30 years of middle life, leanness was a higher factor for mortality than obesity! In the opinion of some scientists, preliminary evidence from other sources indicates that our on-again, off-again dieting endeavors are a life-shortening stress, that it is healthier to keep your weight steady at ten pounds above normal than to keep going up and down.

What *is* known is that weight extremes in either direction are definitely unhealthy. Weighing 20 percent more or less than you should weigh can, in certain cases, be a life-shortener.

Will exercise help keep your body youthful?

Yes—the benefits of regular exercise are indisputable. A study of 6351 longshoremen published in the *New England Journal of Medicine* found that "repeated bursts of high energy output established a plateau of protection against coronary mortality." In other words, men engaged in rigorous and persistent physical labor have fewer heart attacks. But many researchers believe that exercise need not be strenuous to keep you in shape. A study of British postal employes, for example, found that mail carriers plodding the streets had fewer heart attacks and lived longer than their fellow employes in desk jobs.

Do social factors affect longevity?

Yes. Those who live the longest generally have high intelligence, reasonable financial security, good health and an intact marriage, according to Dr. Eric Pfeiffer, director of geriatric psychiatry, University of South Florida College of Medicine. One reason, of course, is that affluent people are generally better nourished and have better medical care.

Apparently, the greater the success, the longer the life-span. According to statistical studies in the United States, the so-called captains of industry live remarkably longer than the general population, and significantly longer than other business executives. Why? Gerontologists theorize that, while some people are overcome by stress, successful people have a knack for converting tensions and stresses into life-enriching challenges. Other experts point out that success need not be financial; an optimistic attitude and general satisfaction with life are more important.

Can you prevent skin from aging?

Some wrinkling is inevitable, but wrinkling caused by behavior reactions (such as smiling, frowning, squinting from smoke or bright light) can be controlled. Avoid expressions that disturb the placidity of your face—they tend to make it age faster. Give up smoking; one California study indicated that smokers tend to have significantly more wrinkling than non-smokers.

What do the really long-lived people have in common?

Only one in every 35,000 Americans reaches the age of 100, but unconfirmed statistics show pockets of longevity in at least three other parts of the world: Vilcabamba in Ecuador, the Soviet Caucasus, and Hunza in Pakistani-controlled Kashmir. All three areas are mountainous agricultural regions in which hard work and vigorous daily walking are necessary for survival. The people eat a low-fat, low-protein, natural diet free of additives and preservatives. And they live in a psychological climate marked by virtual non-retirement, respect for old age, strong family ties and a minimum of emotional stress. Although recent studies have invalidated the extreme age claims of many of the areas' "centenarians," researchers do note a marked vigor and health among the elderly inhabitants.

The first principle of any life-extension program, then, is to savor every moment of the life you have—whether it lasts one more year or a hundred. As the philosopher Jean Jacques Rousseau put it: "Teach him to live rather than to avoid death: Life is not breath but action, the use of our senses, mind, faculties, every part of ourselves which makes us conscious of our being."

In other words, enjoying life is one of the best ways to lengthen it.

MUSCLES IN MOTION

Get Fit and Stay Fit, With Aerobics

by Kenneth H. Cooper, M.D.

AFTER one of my lectures to a group of physicians a few years ago, a listener stopped me in the corridor. "I always tell my inactive patients they should get more exercise," he said. "And I usually suggest something mild, like walking, to get them started. But when they ask me *how much* or *how long*, I'm stumped. I don't know how much is enough. Do you?"

I didn't, but the problem had bothered me too. I had specialized in exercise physiology after graduating from medical school, and the more I thought about it the more I felt that what we needed was a catalogue of all the popular forms of activity, reduced to measurable amounts, so one could pick and choose among them and know that *this* much exercise would produce exactly *that* amount of benefit.

It was the U.S. Air Force that finally gave me the opportunity to solve this problem. After entering the service, I was assigned to do research on exercise, especially as it affects pilots and astronauts. I had at my disposal the most modern and sophisticated testing equipment, including some inherited from space-age technology. I also had an almost unlimited supply of the most priceless research commodity of all, the human body.

Four years later, by 1968, we had evaluated more than 5000 subjects—officers and airmen, the active and inactive, the well and unwell, men and women—both in the field and in the laboratory. The information about exercise we collected may be the most extensive in medical history. The breakthroughs made in these tests, and the refinements in existing data, have immeasurably increased our knowledge about the ways in which exercise—or the lack of it—affects the body.

In our program, all popular exercises have been scientifically measured for the amount of energy it costs the body to perform them. These amounts have been translated into points, and it has been firmly established that, to produce and maintain the essential health of your body, a basic minimum of 30 such points each week is necessary. Earn those 30 points by whatever assortment of exercises you like, and you will have answered the question, "How much?"

The best kind of fitness is what we call endurance fitness: the ability to do prolonged work without fatigue. It has to do with the body's *overall* health—health of the heart, lungs and entire cardiovascular system, and other organs, as well as muscles. And the key to the whole thing is oxygen.

In simplest terms, any activity—breathing, digesting, even the beating of the heart—requires energy. The body produces this energy by burning foodstuffs, and the burning agent is oxygen. The body can store food at each meal, using what it wants now and saving some of the rest for later. *But it can't store oxygen.* We breathe every minute of our lives to keep the supply coming in, for if it were suddenly cut off, the brain, the heart, everything would cease functioning.

But, you might argue, if we need more oxygen we can just breathe more, so what's the problem? The problem is to get enough oxygen, which is carried in the blood, to *all the areas* in the human body—the small, hidden, almost infinite number of areas—where food is stored. Only then can the two combine to produce energy as required.

Most of us can produce enough energy to perform ordinary daily activities. As the activity becomes more vigorous, however, some of us can't keep up. This is because in some bodies *the means for the delivery of oxygen* is limited. This is what separates the men from the boys, the fit from the unfit.

The best kind of exercise therefore is that which demands oxygen and forces your body to process and deliver it. *Even if you've been inactive or sick, these exercises may be good therapy—but you must have your doctor's permission.* If you follow the point system and get enough of the right kind of exercise, our Air Force studies have shown, many wonderful changes will take place in your body. I call these changes the "training effect." Some highlights:

• The lungs will process more air with less effort.

• The heart grows stronger, pumps more blood with each stroke, reducing the number of strokes necessary. Thus a conditioned man may have a resting heart rate 20 beats per minute slower than a deconditioned man, saving as many as 10,000 beats in one night's sleep—or up to 30,000 beats every day of a man's life.

• The number and size of the blood vessels that carry the blood to the body tissue are increased. So is the total blood volume, by as much as a quart in some men!

• The tone of muscles and blood vessels is improved, and blood pressure is often reduced.

Now, let's get to the exercises. The best ones are running, swimming, cycling, walking, stationary running, handball, basketball and squash—in just about that order. Isometrics, weight lifting and most calisthenics don't even make the list. Why? Consider the three basic categories of exercise:

Isometric exercises generally tense one set of muscles against another, or against an immovable object. Examples: pushing against opposite sides of a doorjamb, or pulling up on the chair you're sitting on. Such exercises can increase the strength of skeletal muscles, but cause no appreciable increase in oxygen consumption. Consequently they have no significant effect on lungs, heart or blood system, or on overall health.

Isotonic exercises contract muscles to produce movement, but again without demanding much oxygen. Popular examples are calisthenics and weight lifting, and some of the mild participant sports like archery, bowling and horseshoes. These too are aimed almost entirely at the skeletal muscles, and cannot qualify as primary conditioners.

I get some arguments, of course, especially about calisthenics. There are a few all-muscle calisthenics that will make your chest heave, your heart pound and your blood race. But the huffing and puffing end too soon to do you much good. (A notable exception is running-in-place, if kept up nonstop for a considerable length of time.) I do calisthenics myself, but I earn my points elsewhere.

Aerobic ("with oxygen") exercises are the foundation on which any exercise program should be built. These are exercises which demand oxygen and which you keep up long enough to start producing those wonderful training-effect changes in your body.

How much is "long enough"? When do the benefits actually begin?

Our research indicates that if the exercise is vigorous enough to produce a sustained heart rate of 150 beats per minute, the training-effect benefits begin about five minutes after the exercise starts and continue as long as it is performed. If the exercise is not that vigorous it must be continued considerably longer.

But how in the world can any man figure out his heart rate while in the act of exercising? That is the beauty of the point system: we've done all the figuring for you. We selected exercises that demand oxygen, measured them for the exact amounts they require, then translated these amounts into points. The only principles laid down are that you must maintain a minimum of 30 points a week, and exercise at least four times a week, or every other day. The benefits start dropping off if you fall below either minimum. Don't, for instance, try to earn 30 points in one day and then forget exercise for the next six. But the choice of how you earn the points is yours. Find the point value of each exercise you plan to do, and do enough to earn 30 points.

Before you start, however, you may want to know what kind of shape you're in now.

To determine this, in our Air Force tests we rely mainly on the power treadmill. The treadmill, combined with oxygen-measuring equipment, is the ultimate at this state of the art in measuring total fitness. It permits accurate measurement of a subject's maximum oxygen consumption, and correlates it with his heart rate and blood pressure. It also enables us to determine how many milliliters (ml.'s) of oxygen a body consumes per kilogram of body weight per minute of exercise—and this is the figure we have translated into points.

Scientific and thorough, the treadmill test is also expensive and time-consuming. So what we have done is translate it into a simple 12-minute run/walk test. All you need is a place where you can run a measured distance of up to two miles. (*If you are over 35 years of age or have any medical condition, you must get your doctor's permission before you try the test.*) Your local high school or YMCA may have track facilities. If not,

1. Running Program

CATEGORY I	II	III	DISTANCE (miles)	TIME (mins.)	TIMES a wk.	PTS. a wk.
	1st	...	1	13:30	5	10
2nd	...	...	1	13	5	10
3rd	2nd	1st	1	12:45	5	10
4th	3rd	...	1	11:45	5	15
5th	4th	2nd	1	11	5	15
6th	5th	3rd	1	10:30	5	15
7th	6th	...	1	9:45	5	20
8th	...	4th	1	9:30	5	20
9th	7th	5th	1	9:15	5	20
10th	8th	...	1, 1½	9, 16	3, 2	21
11th	9th	6th	1, 1½	8:45, 15	3, 2	21
12th	...	7th	1, 1½	8:30, 14	3, 2	24
13th	10th	...	1, 1½	8:15, 13:30	3, 2	24
14th	11th	8th	1, 1½	7:55, 13	3, 2	27
15th	12th	9th	1, 1½, 2	7:45, 12:30, 18	2, 2, 1	30
16th	13th	10th	1½, 2	11:55, 17	2, 2	31
To maintain fitness after completion of conditioning program, follow any one of these alternatives:			1	8	6	30
			1	6:30	5	30
			1½	12	4	30
			2	16	3	30

To use this and other charts: Find your category (as determined by the 12-minute test) in one of the three columns at left. Under the category, find the appropriate week, then read across to see what you should do that week.

Note: Start program by walking. Then walk/run, or run, as necessary, to meet the changing time goals.

use a nearby park or a quiet stretch of ro
distance by using the odometer in your ca
to run, dress in loose clothing and bring a
second hand. The idea is to get as far as yo
in 12 minutes. Many men enlist their wives a
along in the car and toot the horn when time

Try to run the whole time, at a pace yo
without excess strain. If your breath gets sh
while until it comes back, then run some more. I
for the full 12 minutes. Then check your distance

Distance Covered		Fitness
Less than 1 mile	I.	Ve
1 to 1¼ miles	II.	Poo
1¼ to 1½ miles	III.	Fair
1½ to 1¾ miles	IV.	Good
1¾ miles or more	V.	Excell

*For men over 35, 1.4 miles is Good; for women, 1.3.

If you fall into one of the first three categories, you fail
test. But don't be too discouraged; about 80 percent of
American population rates there, too.

The categories are important because they place you in different conditioning programs—a 16-week program for Category I, 13 weeks for Category II, 10 weeks for Category III.
If test results place you in Categories IV or V, you're already
fit. Keep up a 30-point week and you'll stay that way. (If you
prefer to omit the test, simply put yourself in Category I and
take the full course.)

For the conditioning period we've worked out six different,
progressive courses, based on a variety of activities. (See charts
on the following pages.) Select whichever activity you prefer
and start in.

The running program (Chart I), without equivocation, is the
best. It's quick, sure and inexpensive. I can recommend it to
anyone of any age, assuming there is no physical impairment.
It exercises the arms and legs and has a firming effect on muscle
groups throughout the body, notably the abdomen. Running
can be done alone or in groups, indoors or out, at any time of
day.

Swimming (Chart 2) is a close second. Swimming exercises most of the large muscle masses, especially the arms and legs, although not in the same way as running. You can't expect the same firming effect on the abdominal muscles.

The disadvantages with cycling (Chart 3) are that you need a bike, and that weather—icy streets, wind—can play havoc.

2. Swimming Program

I	CATEGORY II	III	DISTANCE (yards)	TIME (mins.)	TIMES a wk.	PTS. a wk.
	WEEKS					
1st	1st	...	100	2:30	5	6
2nd	...	...	150	3	5	7½
3rd	2nd	1st	200	4	5	7½
4th	3rd	...	250	5:30	5	10
5th	4th	2nd	250	5	5	10
6th	5th	3rd	300	6	5	12½
7th	6th	...	300	6	5	12½
8th	...	4th	400	8:30	5	17½
9th	7th	5th	400	8:30	5	17½
10th	8th	...	{ 400, 500	8 10:30	2 } 3 }	19
11th	9th	6th	{ 400, 600	8 12:30	2 } 3 }	22
12th	...	7th	{ 500, 700	10:30 15:30	3 } 2 }	24
13th	10th	...	{ 600, 800	12:30 16:30	3 } 2 }	25
14th	11th	8th	{ 600, 800	12:30 16	2 } 3 }	29½
15th	12th	9th	700	15	5	30
16th	13th	10th	1000	20:30	4	34

To maintain fitness after completion of conditioning program, follow any one of these alternatives:			500	8–12	8	32
			600	10–15	6	30
			800	13–20	5	32
			1000	17–25	4	34

Points here are calculated for the overhand crawl. The breaststroke is less demanding, and so is the backstroke. The butterfly is considerably more demanding.

Also, cycling doesn't benefit the muscles of the upper body as much as running and, especially, swimming; it does toughen up the legs and hips more. However, the aerobic benefits—the training effect—for the internal organs are identical to those of running and swimming.

3. Cycling Program

I	CATEGORY II	III	DISTANCE (miles)	TIME (mins.)	TIMES a wk.	PTS. a wk.
	WEEKS					
1st	1st	...	2	7:45	5	10
2nd	...	...	2	6:45	5	10
3rd	2nd	1st	2	6:15	5	10
4th	3rd	...	3	11	5	15
5th	4th	2nd	3	10	5	15
6th	5th	3rd	3	9:15	5	15
7th	6th	...	4	15	5	20
8th	...	4th	4	13:30	5	20
9th	7th	5th	4	12:30	5	20
10th	8th	...	{ 4, 5	12:30 16:30	4 } 1 }	21
11th	9th	6th	{ 4, 5	12:30 16	3 } 2 }	22
12th	...	7th	{ 4, 6	12:15 19	3 } 2 }	24
13th	10th	...	{ 4, 6	12:05 18:30	3 } 2 }	24
14th	11th	8th	{ 5, 6	15:30 18:30	3 } 2 }	27
15th	12th	9th	6	19	5	30
16th	13th	10th	8	25:30	4	32
To maintain fitness after completion of conditioning program, follow any one of these alternatives:			5	15–20	6	30
			6	18–24	5	30
			8	24–32	4	32
			10	30–40	3	30

Points are based on use of an American single-speed bike, following a course that is equally uphill and downhill, equal time with and against the wind. For a course that is constantly against a wind of 5 m.p.h. or more, add 1/2 point per mile. If using a racing bicycle, stay in highest gear as much as possible and deduct 1/2 point per mile.

Walking (Chart 4) is the bottom half of running. It consumes more time, but it's quite valid. Its overwhelming advantage is that it can be done by anyone, anytime, anywhere—and it doesn't even look like exercise. Don't underestimate stationary running (Chart 6). It can be substituted for other exercises on rainy or cold days when you can't get outdoors. You can do it while watching the morning news on television; then shower, and you're through exercising for the day.

4. Walking Program

I	CATEGORY II	III	DISTANCE (miles)	TIME (mins.)	TIMES a wk.	PTS. a wk.
	WEEKS					
1st	1st	…	1	15	5	5
2nd	…	…	1	14	5	10
3rd	2nd	1st	1	13:45	5	10
4th	3rd	…	1½	21:30	5	15
5th	4th	2nd	1½	21	5	15
6th	5th	3rd	1½	20:30	5	15
7th	6th	…	2	28	5	20
8th	…	4th	2	27:45	5	20
9th	7th	5th	2	27:30	5	20
10th	8th	…	{ 2, { 2½	27:30 33:45	3 } 2 }	22
11th	9th	6th	{ 2, { 2½	27:30 33:30	3 } 2 }	22
12th	…	7th	{ 2½ { 3	33:15 41:30	4 } 1 }	26
13th	10th	…	{ 2½, { 3	33:15 41:15	3 } 2 }	27
14th	11th	8th	{ 2½, { 3	33 40	3 } 2 }	27
15th	12th	9th	3	41	5	30
16th	13th	10th	4	55	4	32

To maintain fitness after completion of con-			2	24–29	8	32
ditioning program, follow any one of these			3	36–43	5	30
alternatives:			4	48–58	4	32
			5	60–72	3	30

Handball, basketball and squash (Chart 5) are almost identical in their benefits. They have the advantage of competition.

With all the basic conditioning courses, be prepared for sore muscles. This soreness is temporary, and only indicates that you're beginning to use muscle groups which have been dormant too long. Nevertheless, do not plunge headlong into a program convinced that you can speed up the process. The running program, for instance, starts with walking. To try to get going faster is likely to lead to trouble with the feet, the

5. Handball, Basketball, Squash Program

	CATEGORY		DURATION	TIMES	POINTS
I	II	III	(mins.)	a week	a week
	WEEKS				
1st	1st	. . .	10	5	7½
2nd	. . .	. . .	15	5	11¼
3rd	2nd	1st	15	5	11¼
4th	3rd	. . .	20	5	15
5th	4th	2nd	20	5	15
6th	5th	3rd	20	5	15
7th	6th	. . .	30	5	22½
8th	. . .	4th	30	5	22½
9th	7th	5th	30	5	22½
10th	8th	. . .	35	5	26¼
11th	9th	6th	35	5	26¼
12th	. . .	7th	{ 35, 40	{ 3 2	27¼
13th	10th	. . .	{ 35, 40	{ 3 2	27¼
14th	11th	8th	{ 30, 45	{ 2 3	29¼
15th	12th	9th	40	5	30
16th	13th	10th	50	4	30
To maintain fitness after completion of conditioning program, follow any one of these alternatives:			40	5	30
			50	4	30
			70	3	30

"Duration" refers to time spent in continuous exercise. Do not include breaks or time-outs.

ankles and other joints. Stick to the charts verbatim. They've been tested and retested, and are safe as well as sure.

Once you've worked your way back into condition, the idea is to stay there. And the way to do it is with a 30-point weekly program consisting of any combination of aerobic exercises. As long as you get 30 points a week, you can be assured that you are getting a scientifically measured minimum to keep in active and productive health. But 30 points is the *minimum* for any age above 10. The 90-year-old shouldn't earn fewer, but the 19-year-old should earn more. In fact, for teen-agers I recommend as many as 50. Fat people, too, should get more than the 30-point minimum. And they should diet.

For anyone who is serious about athletics, I'd recommend a bare minimum of 50 points per week during the off season. For those involved in endurance sports such as boxing, basketball or soccer, the minimum should be as high as 100. Distance runners score up to 500 points a week. Think of them if you're ever tempted to complain about your weekly 30. And what about women? Women used to cite as their argument for not exercising the fact that they outlive men. However, heart disease is increasing among the weaker sex, and inactivity probably shares the responsibility.

Some of the Women's Air Force contingent participated in our research program. Before training, only 20 percent made it into the Good category. Afterward, 45 percent made it. They showed that women can cope with the point system as easily as men—they need between 25 and 30 points a week—and receive identical training effects. What pleased them most was the way they changed fat weight to lean weight, and lost inches off their waistlines, all the while improving their health.

Any discussion of the benefits of aerobic exercise must deal with the most important muscle in the human body—the heart—and its ills. Ironically, the heart usually works faster and less efficiently when you give it less to do. A conditioned man who exercises regularly will have a resting heart rate of about 60 beats per minute or less; the average office worker, about 80.

What's your rate? Sit still for five minutes, then take your pulse and count the beats per minute. If you're 80 beats or above, you are not in top condition. The thing to do is to get up off that chair and get to work exercising. You might save your heart some of those 20,000 to 30,000 extra beats you've forced on it every day.

6. Stationary
Running Program

| | CATEGORY | | DURATION | STEPS per | TIMES | POINTS |
I	II	III	(mins.)	min.	a wk.	a wk.
	WEEKS					
1st	1st	...	2:30	70–80	5	4
2nd	...	...	2:30	70–80	5	4
3rd	2nd	1st	5	70–80	5	10
4th	3rd	...	5	70–80	5	10
5th	4th	2nd	7:30	70–80	5	11¼
6th	5th	3rd	7:30	70–80	5	11¼
7th	6th	...	10	70–80	5	15
8th	...	4th	10	70–80	5	15
9th	7th	5th	12:30	70–80	5	18¾
10th	8th	...	12:30	70–80	5	18¾
11th	9th	6th	15	70–80	5	22½
12th	...	7th	10 (in a.m.), 10 (in p.m.), 15	70–80 70–80 70–80	2 3	25½
13th	10th	...	12:30 (in a.m.), 12:30 (in p.m.), 15	70–80 70–80 70–80	2 3	28½
14th	11th	8th	12:30 (in a.m.), 12:30 (in p.m.), 15	70–80 70–80 70–80	2 3	28½
15th	12th	9th	20	70–80	5	30
15th	13th	10th	20	80–90	4	32

To maintain fitness after completion of conditioning program, follow any one of these alternatives:	10 (in a.m.), 10 (in p.m.), 15 15 20	70–80 70–80 70–80 80–90 80–90	5 7 5 4	30 30 30 32	

In counting number of steps, count only when left foot hits the floor.
Feet must be brought at least 8 inches from the floor.

As your heart grows stronger in response to training, more exertion is necessary to tire it. This will be quite noticeable. During the first few weeks or months of regular exercising you are likely to feel tired each time. But eventually you will be getting all the exercise you need (30 points) without feeling it.

One of the most remarkable effects of aerobic conditioning is vascularization: more blood vessels open up in the muscle tissues, creating new routes for delivering more oxygen. This vascularization is a vital factor in the health of the heart. When its tissue is saturated with healthy blood vessels, this considerably reduces the chance of cardiac failure. And even if such a failure should occur, the extra vessels can "go around" the stricken area, outflanking it to keep the surrounding tissue healthy and improving the chances of a speedy recovery. So if you haven't done anything for your heart lately, start now. Exercise it.

Point Values for Other Activities

			POINTS*
Golf	18	holes	3
Rope Skipping	5	minutes	1½
Skating (ice or roller)	15	minutes	1
Skiing (snow or water)	30	minutes	3
Tennis	1	set	1½
Volleyball	15	minutes	1
Football	30	minutes	3

* Based on caloric requirements.

A few final tips to remember:

Any time of the day is fine for exercise. But spend a few minutes with warm-up calisthenics first, and then don't sit down or stand motionless immediately after strenuous exercise. Give the body a chance to unwind by walking around slowly for three to five minutes.

Don't exercise right after a meal. Wait at least two hours. (On the other hand, exercising just before a light meal is a good way to combine exercise with diet.)

Be prepared for "going stale"—for a period when you begin

to wonder why you ever started a training program. It happens to everyone. Just sweat it out. Go through the motions. Your enthusiasm wiil return. *Don't quit.*

As a doctor who has specialized in physical fitness, I'd like to see my country become again a nation of doers instead of spectators.

Run Your Way to Happiness

by James F. Fixx

ONE DAY a decade ago, something crucial occurred while I was playing tennis with a friend. I was in my mid-30s and worked at a big magazine in Manhattan. One of my more pleasant duties was to entertain authors at lunches and dinners, and what with too many martinis and too little exercise my weight had climbed from the 170 it had been during my teens to a beefy 214.

Nonetheless, I still prided myself on a respectable, if roly-poly, game of tennis. Which is why I was so irrationally irritated when I felt a ripping sensation in my right calf. The injury was not serious, and even though I limped painfully for a week or two I never bothered to see a doctor.

What was striking was the way I felt about the damage. My body had betrayed me, and I was angry. I still thought of myself—secretly, at least—as an athlete. Someone who all his life had played tennis, touch football and Saturday-afternoon softball shouldn't be thus laid low.

As soon as the pain had eased, I decided to do some running to strengthen my legs. Three or four times a week I would shuffle a half-mile or so, seldom more. Eventually I moved from New York to suburban Connecticut, where running was pleasanter. I stopped smoking—the Surgeon General's report scared me—and I began to run somewhat farther. Then one day I decided to enter a local five-mile race.

At the starting line there must have been 200 runners, most of them young and lean. But there were also a good many men in their 40s, 50s and even 60s, and a scattering of women and children. With luck, I thought, I might not do so badly. Instead, I came in last. Mystified, I asked why.

I went to the local library and hunted up some books on running. A friend loaned me some copies of a runner's magazine. I began to learn what training was, and found myself thinking about running more and more. I forced myself to lose weight in order to do better at it, and I began to run every day. Friends started to tell me I looked wonderful. No one had said *that* for a long time. Finally, two years after I had taken my first running steps, I even managed to win a minor championship—the Connecticut 10,000-meter title in my age category.

But what I found even more interesting were the changes that had begun to take place in my mind. I was calmer and less anxious. I could concentrate more easily and for longer periods. I felt more in control of my life, with a sense of quiet power. And if at any time I felt this power slipping away, I could instantly call it back by going out and running.

I began to ask other runners about their experiences. It turns out there is an almost invariable pattern of development. Typically, a person begins running in search of fitness. But after several months or years, he or she gradually begins to spend far more time running than the requirements of fitness alone would dictate. Finally, he or she realizes that something in running has a uniquely salutary effect on the human mind.

As I did research for this book, I traveled a great deal, talking with all sorts of runners. In almost every case I would start the discussion with a specific subject in mind—running following a heart attack, say, or racing tactics, or the types of muscle tissue involved in running—and for a while we would stick to that subject. But at some point the conversation would invariably slip off into a topic I had not even brought up: the psychology of running. Everyone, it seemed, was secretly interested in—and, in a surprising number of cases, obsessed by—what goes on in runners' minds and how the sport changes people. I found this such a curious phenomenon that I finally mentioned it to Joe Henderson, a leading authority on running. "I'm not surprised," he told me. "I think the mental aspects of running are going to be the next big field of investigation. That's where the breakthroughs will come."

The people I spoke with described their experiences in persuasive and even poetic terms. Nancy Novogrod, for example, is a young New York editor who runs six miles four or five times a week. She told me, "A good run makes you feel sort of holy."

Allan Ripp is in his early 20s. For years he was bothered by asthma. ("Every gasp was terrible," he said. "I couldn't think about anything else.") Then he took up running. Although he is careful not to claim that running cured his asthma, he does say it has been a principal factor in causing the attacks to stop. "Running is the greatest thing that ever happened to me," he affirms. "It gives my life a sense of rhythm. It's not just a game or a sport. It's an adjective—something that defines me."

The feelings that these runners describe have been scientifically documented. Psychologist Richard Driscoll used jogging successfully in an experiment to alleviate anxiety during exams among University of Colorado students. Dr. Michael B. Mock of the National Heart, Lung and Blood Institute told me: "In a society where, for many reasons, there is a tendency for a large majority of people to have depression, exercise has been found to counter depressed feelings by increasing one's sense of self-esteem and independence." I even came across one psychiatrist, Dr. John Greist of the University of Wisconsin, who, having assigned a group of abnormally depressed patients either to a ten-week running program or to ten weeks of traditional psychotherapy, found the running to be at least as effective.

While I was looking into the mental dimensions of running, I noticed that many writers have in fact been circling the subject for some time. Roger Bannister, the first person ever to run a mile in less than four minutes, once wrote:

> I can still remember quite vividly a time when as a child I ran barefoot along damp, firm sand by the seashore. The sound of breakers on the shore shut out all others, and I was startled and almost frightened by the tremendous excitement a few steps could create. It was an intense moment of discovery of a source of power and beauty that one previously hardly dreamt existed. . . . The sense of exercise is an extra sense, or perhaps a subtle combination of all the others.

Some runners even argue that running brings about mental states so remote from those of everyday life as to be unimaginable to most of us. Mike Spino, sports director of California's famed Esalen Institute, has written in *Beyond Jogging*: "Running can be a way of discovering our larger selves. Average people as well as superstars touch spiritual elements when they least expect it."

Thus there seems little doubt that running does enhance mental health. But does anyone know why? Not really, though there are some theories. One is that the brain, nourished by an unusually rich supply of oxygen because of running, responds by calling into play its self-correcting mechanisms. Another is that the body and the mind are so closely linked that when you help the body you help the mind as well.

The deeper pleasures of running are seldom experienced all at once, nor do they come to those who run only once in a while. To feel the profound changes that running can bring about, you need to run for 45 minutes or an hour at least four days a week. It takes that much running for its insistent, hypnotic rhythms to induce what some runners describe as a trancelike state, a mental plateau where they feel miraculously purified and at peace with themselves and the world.

As committed a partisan as I am, however, I am bound to admit that a few people simply seem not to be cut out for running. This has nothing to do with one's body structure; some large-boned people, though they have precisely the wrong build for running, thrive on it. What it does reflect, I believe, is a cast of mind that makes it difficult to tolerate running's enforced contemplativeness, its meditative aspects.

If you try running and find it worse than a trip to the dentist, perhaps you're one of the people whom nature never intended to run. But you should at least know that many runners don't begin to enjoy the sport until they have been at it for several weeks or even months. So give it a fair trial; if you don't, you could end up missing an extraordinary experience.

In the years ahead, much that is new will no doubt come from individual runners as they pay attention to what happens in their minds. This is the main reason why running, old as it is, is still such an adventure. There are frontiers in it for us all.

Tennis, Everyone?

by Carl T. Rowan and David M. Mazie

THE OLD line used to be, "Tennis, anyone?" These days, "Tennis, everyone!" would be more appropriate.

Signs are everywhere. At two o'clock in the morning you can find aficionados volleying on all-night courts in New York and Los Angeles. Any morning—outdoors in the summer, indoors in winter—courts overflow with housewives turned women-lobbers. Tennis villages have risen with as many as 50 courts surrounded by clusters of townhouses. Airlines offer tennis vacations. In Harlem, dozens of boys who used to shoot baskets on the playground now smash overheads on makeshift, middle-of-the-street courts. In suburbia the tennis court has replaced the swimming pool as a back-yard status symbol.

More than 15 million American men, women and children now play tennis. They shell out half a billion dollars a year for rackets, balls, lessons, clothing, membership dues, court construction and fees, ball-throwing machines and other trappings of the game. And that doesn't include doctor's bills for uncounted cases of tennis elbow.

The boom has produced striking changes in the sport that began a century ago in England. For decades tennis was a staid, snobbish game played mainly by whites dressed in white, using white balls on neatly manicured grass. Games were scored in a quaint language of "love-15-30-40," "advantage" and "deuce." Most of the top players came out of a handful of genteel Eastern clubs. As recently as the 1940s, most U.S. Lawn Tennis Association tourneys were played at clubs that didn't accept blacks or Jews.

Today tennis is an all-year, all-weather, all-hours, all-comers, all-colors sport. A growing number of America's best young players are products of public courts or community and junior tennis programs. White clothing has given way to blue, yellow and red. The new, simplified "tie-breaker" scoring system brings a quick and exciting end to once-interminable sets. Grass courts are being replaced by 90 different court surfaces and a rapidly increasing number of indoor courts. There were some 50 indoor facilities in the United States in 1965. Eight years later more than 700 clubs were operating 2500 courts, and an average of three new indoor-tennis emporiums were opening each week. In New York, where tennis is being played under plastic bubbles, atop piers and roofs, court fees range up to $50 an hour.

What brought tennis to the center court of the sports world? One factor, certainly, is America's physical-fitness kick. Adults are told that vigorous exercise is good for the heart. Kids are told they ought to be playing games instead of watching. Tennis offers an ideal answer, a fast-moving sport you can play without devoting half a day to it. And you can start at age six and still be playing after 60.

Another factor is the blooming of tennis as a spectator sport. For years pro players were second-class citizens. Their matches were often little more than exhibitions, played on wooden courts one night, on a tarpaulin or supermarket parking lot the next. In 1964 prize money totaled only $84,000 for the entire U.S. professional circuit.

Then in 1967 Lamar Hunt's World Championship Tennis (WCT) organization moved into the pro game, bringing cash and publicity, and incorporated open tennis, which put the top professionals and amateurs across a net from one another for the first time. Professional tennis attained glamour, drama, heroes—Stan Smith, Arthur Ashe, Ken Rosewall, Rod Laver; then heroines—Billie Jean King, Margaret Court, Chris Evert, Evonne Goolagong. Inevitably, television became interested. In 1971 Laver won $292,417, nearly $50,000 more than golf's leading money-winner, Jack Nicklaus; and Billie Jean King became the first woman in any sport to earn $100,000 in a year.

Tennis also has boomed because it's an ideal sport for relaxing. As Bus Whitehead, a Lincoln, Neb., businessman, says: "I used to play golf, but as I walked along the fairways,

I would still think about problems at the office. With tennis I don't have time for that. I'm thinking tennis the whole time." There are those who think tennis so much that it becomes an obsession. Says Washington tennis pro Allie Ritzenberg: "Some people get so all they want out of life is food, sex, clothes and a well-strung racket."

The real key to the popularity of tennis may well be its universal appeal. No one need be a tennis widow or orphan. It's estimated that about half the new tennis players are women and girls. The "racket bunny" has appeared—a gal who dons tennis togs in the morning and wears them the rest of the day— in the supermarket, at the beauty parlor, in the car pool. The owner of a tennis shop in Beverly Hills, Calif., says some customers spend $600 or more on clothes in a half-hour shopping spree.

As for the kids, they're flocking to the courts. Budding Davis Cuppers have their choice of some 500 summer tennis camps. There is, for example, Newk's Tennis Ranch (John Newcombe is one of the owners) in New Braunfels, Texas. Newk's runs 13 weeks of junior camps, drawing close to 2000 boys and girls. Thousands of inner-city children are getting a chance to play tennis these days, thanks to two privately financed programs. "Tennis in the Streets" sends out mobile vans with everything needed to set up temporary courts on a street or playground. The National Junior Tennis League uses "instant competition" and team play to introduce youngsters to tennis in the same informal way they discovered sandlot baseball and playground basketball.

Grownups have their tennis camps, too—places like John Gardiner's ranch in Arizona. This c e offers total-immersion tennis—strategy, techniques and strokes taught 3½ hours a day by talented young pros aided by ball-throwing machines, instant videotape replay, gourmet food and massages. At some tennis ranches, enthusiasts can choose from a three-day clinic for husbands and wives, a five-day clinic for women, a weekend for singles.

This sporting life does not come cheap. The camps, junior or senior version, cost from $200 to $1000 a week. Individual lessons are $15 to $30 an hour. Club memberships can run into four figures. The ultimate tennis luxury—a private court at home—costs from $10,000 to $30,000.

Tennis' rapid growth has brought problems, the most obvious of which is lack of facilities. (In California, players who finally get a court have been known to lock themselves in with a chain around the gate.) But that has done nothing to damp the popularity of the sport. Today, names like Borg, McEnroe, Austin and Navratilova are as recognized as the names of football, baseball and golf heroes. And for the millions—from celebrities to ghetto youngsters—tennis is proving truly a love game.

Hop, Skip and Jump

by Curtis Mitchell

To STAY healthy, a person must *use* his legs. The famed cardiologist Dr. Paul Dudley White spoke of legs as one's second heart. For exercise, medical and health authorities advise walking, striding, jogging, even cross-country running. All are effective. Many people, however, find them boring or too time-consuming.

Today, housewives, executives and schoolchildren are rediscovering another way to use their legs. For many, it is more fun. It can be done indoors or out. The only equipment required is a nine-foot length of cotton, hemp or nylon—a jump rope.

"For producing the greatest fitness in the least amount of time," says Dr. Kaare Rodahl, eminent head of the Institute of Work Physiology in Oslo, Norway, "nothing surpasses the simple jump rope." Says Paul Smith, director of general administration for the Shoreline School District in Seattle, Wash.: "Rope skipping approaches being a perfect all-around exercise. It is for people of all ages and physical conditions." Through Smith's efforts, scores of community and PTA skip-rope units have been formed, much like square-dance groups. Rope jumping is included in training programs at West Point, and it is used by a number of astronauts.

Consider some of its advantages. It can be especially effective in trimming legs, thighs and hips. The rhythmic turning of the rope exercises more of the upper body than jogging does. Jumping makes sturdier feet and ankles (for skiers), stronger wrists (for golfers); it improves balance, agility and coordination. Moreover, jumping increases energy.

Nobody knows where rope skipping first developed. People of all ages enjoyed it centuries ago in the Far East and Europe. Visitors in the Philippines have found small fry jumping joyously with lengths of split bamboo. As long as Americans can remember, schoolchildren have skipped, chanting "I love coffee, I love tea..." But, until recently, children and prizefighters were our only really dedicated skippers. Kids jumped for fun: boxers knew it helped their endurance.

A study conducted at the University of Illinois in 1957 was perhaps the first to demonstrate the considerable tangible benefits. Participants in the study were schoolboys, ages 9 to 11, whose only exercise was vigorous rope skipping. They developed more efficient hearts and improved endurance. Their chests deepened. Fat was reduced and muscular strength improved. Posture also improved. More agile, the boys could jump about four inches higher than before entering the program.

But what would skipping do for adults? Nobody really knew until 1961, when Dr. Rodahl, then director of research at Lankenau Hospital in Philadelphia, tested it. Seeking a way to counteract the midafternoon fatigue of his staff, he started a rope-skipping class for women workers, secretaries and research technicians, ages 19 to 24. They jumped rope for five minutes a day, during the lunch hour, five days a week. In one month, their physical-work capacity increased by an average of 25 percent.

At Temple University, a group of men, ages 19 to 43, went through a similar program, jumping rope ten minutes daily, five days a week, for two months. Average improvement in cardiovascular efficiency (a person's capacity to take up and utilize oxygen for the production of work) was 23 percent: some bettered themselves by 31 percent. Their hearts beat slower; they could handle harder, heavier work loads; and many developed a stronger hand grip.

At Arizona State University, researcher Jack Baker took 92 unfit students, put half in a 30-minutes-a-day jogging program, half in a 10-minutes-a-day rope-skipping program. When tested, the two groups shared almost identical improvement in cardiovascular efficiency. Baker's conclusion, reported in *Research Quarterly*, the physical educator's bible, was that, for the purpose in view, 10 minutes with the rope is equal to 30 on the road.

What's the magic behind rope skipping? We seem to be natural-born hoppers and jumpers, especially when under tension. Watch cheerleaders during a game: they bounce like yo-yos. Watch winning players after a crucial touchdown or basket: they leap about like kangaroos. Or staid matrons when they hit the jackpot on a TV money show. Physiologists know that even small jumps alternately contract and relax the muscles of calf and thigh, improving muscle tone, aiding the return of blood to the heart and improving peripheral circulation.

A number of schools are adding rope jumping to their physical-education programs. In 1964, a Florida educator, Ted Bleier, included rope skipping as part of a conditioning program in the Dade County curriculum, and his students enabled the state to win more Presidential Fitness Awards than any other except California. "Skipping is so much fun," says Frank Prentup, former baseball coach and professor of physical education at the University of Colorado, "that kids who ordinarily would cut physical-education classes now come out for it." After seeing a Prentup-coached group demonstrate the finer points of skipping—twirls, flips, flings, spins, rockers—Gladys Peck, a dancing teacher in the Atlanta, Ga., public schools, introduced rope skipping to her students as an art form.

Skipping can start early and last a lifetime—either as a complete training regimen or as a supplement to other workouts. Ben Bloom, formerly a research chemist at the National Institute for Arthritis and Metabolic Disease, in Washington, D.C., had been skipping rope for some 22 years when, in a 1967 article, he wrote: "I do my skipping in the living room and leave my rope on the couch. In this way, the sight of it encourages me to do a couple of extra rounds now and then. When I have company, the rope is a conversation piece, and frequently the whole place starts jumping!"

To Start Jumping*

Equipment: Sash cord, size 7 to 10, is eminently satisfactory. Get a piece long enough to reach from armpit to armpit while passing under the feet. Hardware stores carry it. Or you can buy a skip rope ready-made, with handles, at a sporting-goods store.

First Week: Warm up by jumping in place (on both feet together)

50 to 100 times, without the rope. Next, skip the rope 50 times, at whatever speed you like. (Beginners will find it easier at first to lift both feet off the ground at the same time.) On your first day, that's plenty. On the second, third, fourth and fifth days, add ten skips per day. By week's end (a five-day week is ample) you'll be doing 90 skips without stopping.

Second Week: Warm up without the rope by doing 50 slow hops. But note: this week, abandon that feet-together hop and step over the flying rope one foot at a time, left-right, left-right, as if jogging in place. Start with 100 such skips. Each day add ten more. Final day, 140.

Third Week: Warm up as usual. Skip 100 times without stopping. Rest 15 to 30 seconds. Skip another 100 times.

Fourth Week and Later: By now, improved endurance should enable you to skip with less effort. The object now is to skip fast enough or long enough to get a bit out of breath—the result of making the heart call for more oxygen. "Anything short of this," warns Dr. Rodahl, "does not result in any appreciable training effect."

Ultimate Goal: Skip and rest, skip and rest, until the day you can do 500 consecutive skips in five minutes. Continuing at this level, Dr. Rodahl believes, will maintain your fitness for many years.

Dos and Don'ts: When you skip, relax. Look straight ahead. Jump just high enough—about an inch—for the rope to pass under your feet. Wear sneakers or similar shoes, no heels. Land on the balls of your feet. Don't use much arm movement. The hands should describe a circle about eight to ten inches in diameter. Skip on a thick carpet or on a lawn, never on a hard surface.

---

*Individuals over 40: Consult your physician before embarking on a program.

The Pulse Test

by Laurence E. Morehouse

EVERY day, a 63-year-old retired Los Angeles assistant fire chief jogs a quarter of a mile, stops to check his pulse, then continues on, slowing down or speeding up depending on the rate of his heartbeat. By pulse taking he is able to tell whether his heart is getting too little, too much, or just the right amount of exercise to strengthen it. His exercise program—like that of thousands of people who are using the technique—is thus more effective, and safer, than many others being followed today.

Most exercise programs use distances run, miles cycled or weights lifted as a measure of how much work the body performs. This is fine, except that it tells you nothing about your *individual* exercise requirements. You may not be doing enough work to exercise your heart properly, or you may be doing too much and thus injuring it.

The new "heart-rated" program is different in that it uses a marvelous little computer within the chest of each of us—the heart itself—to provide the missing information. I started working it out about 20 years ago when Dr. Samuel M. Fox, then chief of the U.S. Public Health Service's Heart Disease Control Program, asked me to develop a simple, easy way for people to regulate their exercise. (I was a professor of physical education, and later the founding director of the Human Performance Laboratory at U.C.L.A.). I launched a pilot program with 22 southern California business and professional men.

Since then, the technique has monitored energy expended by astronauts on the moon, and it is recommended by many physicians to prevent heart attacks as well as to strengthen the heart muscle of patients who have recovered from coronaries. Here is how it works, in five basic steps:

1. See your doctor. It is imperative that you undergo a medical examination before you embark on *any* exercise program.

2. Learn to count your pulse. Locate the artery in your right wrist by placing the fingertips of your left hand in the little groove about two inches above the base of your thumb. Using the second hand of your watch, count the number of heartbeats in six seconds; convert this figure into beats-per-minute by adding a zero to the count.

3. Check your heart at various levels of activity. Learn what your heartbeat per minute is while sitting still, gardening, walking the dog or sweeping the front steps. It's one index of your heart's fitness. A normally healthy person will exhibit a sitting heart rate of 60 to 80, a standing rate of about 90 and a light-exercise rate of around 100.

4. Choose exercises befitting your age and condition.

To condition your heart, you need to do two things: pursue an activity that pushes your heart rate to 120 or higher, and maintain that activity and heartbeat for ten minutes or longer. Milder exercise is better than nothing but not sufficient to increase your heart's vigor. The activity chart on the next page will help you make your choice. If your doctor approves, aim to work up to an exercise heart rate equal to 200 minus your age. That is, if you are 40 years old, it should not be higher than 160. Don't be too eager. A heart rate above 160 is for healthy, well-conditioned young athletes. There are no added benefits to be derived from exhaustive exercise—unless you yearn to become a decathlon champ.

In choosing your exercise, avoid competition in sports that require a sudden burst of energy, such as tennis or singles handball. Instead, choose a *rhythmic* exercise: walking, jogging, swimming, stair-climbing, cycling, rowing.

5. Achieve your goal gradually. It is important that you reach your ultimate exercise plateau a little at a time. If you're out of shape, start with a plateau of 100 heartbeats a minute, increase it to 110 in the first month, 120 the second, 130 the third, and so on until you have achieved a level suitable to your age and condition.

Schedule daily workouts of at least 15 minutes—including two or three minutes of stretching and limbering exercises to warm up, ten minutes of exercise and a couple of minutes of walking around to taper off. While exercising, check your pulse at two-minute intervals, then either slow down or speed up according to the goal you have set for yourself.

Once you have gone through these five steps and achieved your new exercise plateau, work vigorously every other day for at least ten minutes. More than that is unnecessary. You cannot store up the benefits of exercise any more than you can store up sleep. Maintenance of fitness—once achieved—may require as little as 30 minutes of vigorous exercise per week.

Exercise is not a cure-all, but it has demonstrable side benefits. Many people find that they eat more sensibly, avoid stress situations and cut down on smoking. Fresh evidence suggests that vigorous exercise (at least 30 minutes a week at a heart rate of 120 or more) can also melt away excess pounds by burning up the body's fat. No matter how rundown a healthy person's physiological functions may be, they can be improved—at any age—by applying a "load" to the body in gradually increasing amounts.

Activities and Heartbeats—Choose the One for You

100–110
Car polishing
Bicycle riding (5 m.p.h)
Pitching horseshoes
Light calisthenics
Ironing

110–120
Walking (2½ m.p.h.)
Bowling
Archery
Softball
House painting

120–130
Golf (carry own bag)
Ballroom dancing
Exercycle
Canoeing (2 m.p.h.)
Sweeping, scrubbing

130–140
Climbing stairs
Table tennis
Pick-and-shovel work
Rowing
Swimming

140–150
Chopping, sawing wood
Tennis
Walking (4 m.p.h.)
Skating (figure)
Badminton

150–160
Skiing (downhill
Skating (speed)
Handball
Mountain climbing
Vigorous dancing

OVER 160
Running (fast, uphill)
Hockey
Rowing (peak effort)
Basketball
Skiing (cross country)

Striding—
The Most Natural Exercise

by William FitzGibbon

OUR ancestors were firm believers in the values of walking. Thomas Jefferson, for one, called it "the best of all exercises." Others, like Abraham Lincoln, were great walkers themselves. Yet they didn't know the *precise* physical effects of walking. Modern medicine does—and today doctors make assertions about the benefits of brisk walking that have a sound basis in medical fact.

It is not mere walking they are talking about—it is *brisk* walking, which brings the human stride into play. Says the American Medical Association's Committee on Exercise and Physical Fitness: "Walking briskly, not just strolling, is the simplest and also one of the best forms of exercise." To which heart specialist Dr. Paul Dudley White added: "It is the easiest exercise for most individuals, one that can be done without equipment except good shoes, in almost any terrain and weather and into very old age."

Sauntering, window-shopping, ambling—these do not bring the stride into action, and, slow though they are, they are often tiring. Each of us has his own stride—and hitting it, for one long distance or several short distances in the course of a day, brings to us the boons of this distance-eating, timesaving, untiring, pleasurable motion that is so natural to the human species.

No other creature plants down a heel, rolls on a sole to a springy big toe in a movement in which both feet are on the ground together only 25 percent of the time, knees articulating, muscles flexing easily, pelvic saddle swiveling in a marvel of simple engineering. Nowadays, for good reason, man has applied the term "hit your stride" to describe times in workaday or personal activities when things have meshed for him, when he has been in overdrive and operating smoothly, doing more work with less effort and fewer mistakes.

"I have two doctors," goes the old saw, "my left leg and my right." Dr. White backed this up, saying, "A vigorous five-mile walk will do more good for an unhappy but otherwise healthy adult than all the medicine and psychology in the world." Here's why:

Striding improves the blood circulation. All of the benefits from daily striding are closely keyed to the increased oxygen intake, greater heart exercise and better blood circulation that this natural exercise provides. The human muscular system acts as an auxiliary blood pump, returning blood to the heart. Since the leg muscles are the largest and most powerful muscles in the body, their work is enormously important. But if they are not being used much, at least with any vigor, then they are not squeezing the blood back toward the heart with any force.

Brisk walking is also important as it affects the human capillary system. There are 60,000 miles of blood vessels in the body, mostly capillaries—those minute vessels responsible for irrigating the flesh. Danish Nobel Prize-winning physiologist August Krogh first showed, in the 1920s, how capillaries open and close: only a few will open when a muscle is at rest; perhaps 50 times as many will open when the muscle is being exercised. In 1965, physiologist K. Lange Anersen, of the University of Bergen, Norway, reported that a sturdy daily activity such as striding will not only awaken dormant capillaries but apparently increase the *number* of these vessels that nourish the muscles.

Striding clears the mind and improves the disposition. Fifth-century Greeks believed that walking made their minds lucid and helped them crack problems of logic and philosophy. Former President Harry Truman always believed that his daily pre-breakfast walk was therapeutic. "They doubtless discovered," said Dr. White, "that their minds were clearer when they kept moving to bring more blood to the head and more oxygen to the blood."

Not only is logical thought helped by mental clarity, but so, it seems, is esthetic thought—appreciation of beauty. It may be that some of the visual splendors in William Wordsworth's poems, such as "The Daffodils," are linked to the fact that he was one of the great walkers of his time. His writer-friend Thomas DeQuincey believed that "to walking, Wordsworth was indebted for a life of unclouded happiness, and we for much of what is most excellent in his writings."

It's folklore knowledge that walking also helps dispel a temper, and when we go off down the block to "cool off" we don't saunter—we stride. I once accompanied a friend who plunged out into the night after a disagreement in which others had kept their tempers and he had lost his. After ten minutes of striding, he was feeling less explosive; and when we returned, the discussion was resumed with equanimity. Later, he told me he was surprised at how much the others' dispositions had improved by the time he returned.

Dr. White emphasizes striding's tranquilizing effects. "A brisk long walk in the evening," he says, "may be more helpful as a hypnotic than any medicine, highball or TV show."

Striding cuts fatigue. Once striding has been entrenched as a daily habit, you get bonuses from being in shape. Few constant brisk walkers need laxatives. Lower-back muscles, which benefit from striding, are likely to resist ache, even in old age, and to permit easier bending movement. Above all, the in-shape body is not so easily fatigued. Even when pushed hard, it is able to call on special reserves and keep from being overwhelmed by weariness. (Consider the aborigines who inhabit Australia's bleak, dry interior, striding mile upon mile in search of water and food—yet who seem untiring.) This prevention of early fatigue not only helps one feel better during exertion; it represents a safety quotient—more strength when needed.

Experts are cautious about making claims that daily striding will increase one's life-span. There is no hard proof that it will, and the most that experts will say is that with brisk daily walking you can remain youthful in condition, if not in chronological years.

A PRIME point in favor of brisk walking is that you don't have to schedule it; you can just incorporate it in your daily life-style. If you have a few blocks to go on an errand, walk them briskly. The short distance between transportation point and office—the same. Hit your stride down corridors; don't amble. Since a short brisk walk is worth two miles of ambling, you can easily get in a minimal amount of good exercise every day. And, as striding becomes a habit, you will soon get more exercise, willingly.

You will become aware that your mind is clearer, your eyes brighter. You'll feel as though you're looking out of newly cleaned windows, and you'll know you are adding to your body's resources. Not bad benefits—and they are all within walking distance.

INSULTS TO THE BODY

What Happens When You Smoke

by Walter S. Ross

ACCORDING to John A. Yacenda, who in the early 1970s was running a smoking withdrawal clinic for the Ventura County Health Department in California, the question teen-agers most often ask about smoking is: "How long does it take for cigarettes to harm you?" His answer: "About three seconds."

Or less. The fact is that the instant you inhale cigarette smoke, that rich country flavor goes to work—on your heart, your lungs, your whole body. It starts your heart pounding an extra 15 to 25 beats per minute, raises your blood pressure by 10 to 20 points. It corrodes the delicate membranes of your lips and palate. In your lungs, it chokes the airways and rots the air sacs, leaving a residue of cancer-causing chemicals. It deposits these and other dangerous poisons in your stomach, kidneys, bladder. All of this happens with *every* cigarette you smoke; no smoker is immune.

And when you exhale, up to 90 percent of that true tobacco taste stays with you—in the form of billions of microscopic particles comprising 1200 chemicals. In this balanced blend of fine aromas are acids, glycerol, glycol, alcohols, aldehydes, ketones, aliphatic and aromatic hydrocarbons, phenols. None is a health food; many will do you harm.

For years, some scientists scoffed that it wasn't possible for one substance—smoke—to attack so many parts of the body in so many ways. Research has proved, however, that tobacco smoke isn't a single substance. At least 60 percent of the country-fresh flavor you inhale is gas—20 different noxious vapors, including aerolein, hydrocyanic acid, nitric oxide, nitrogen dioxide, acetone and ammonia. And now science is zeroing in on one that's even deadlier: colorless, odorless, lethal carbon monoxide (CO).

Present in cigarette smoke in a concentration 640 times the safe level in industrial plants, this insidious poison has 200 times the affinity for your red blood cells that life-giving oxygen does—and those cells are designed to carry oxygen throughout your body. Therefore, in a smoker, blood is transporting five to ten times more life-denying CO than is normal. His body is forced to compensate by making more red cells.

Mainly, CO prevents red cells from picking up enough oxygen; but it also inhibits them from giving up oxygen as fast as your tissues demand. Because of this whipsaw CO effect, cigarette country is always about 8000 feet above sea level. A cigarette smoker who lives at zero altitude is getting as little oxygen as someone who's nearly two miles high.

There's no age limit on the effect, either. A teen-age tyro smoker may feel winded under mild stress, even if he smokes only five or six cigarettes per day. Every smoker who is a sportsman will find himself out of breath more quickly than his nonsmoking competitors. And this is only one of the less deadly results of CO. Consider what happens when its effects join up with those of nicotine, a poison found in nature exclusively in tobacco.

Studies indicate that a pregnant woman who smokes is smoking for two: nicotine constricts the blood vessels in her unborn child, cutting down on fetal blood flow, while CO cuts down the amount of oxygen in the reduced blood supply. The fetus just can't get enough blood or oxygen to grow as fast as it normally would. The babies of mothers who smoke during pregnancy weigh an average of six ounces less at birth than those of non-smoking mothers. Smoking mothers also have more miscarriages and stillbirths, and more of their babies die within one month of birth.

It's the nicotine in cigarettes that gives you a "lift"—it lifts your blood pressure, your heartbeat and the amount of blood pumped by your heart. It does this by releasing substances known as catecholamines (the main one is adrenalin) into your tissues. The catecholamines push your heart so hard it requires more blood in its coronary arteries to keep up with the demand. Healthy hearts rise to the occasion. But in people with coronary-artery disease, the hard-working heart does not get enough additional blood.

The adrenalin released by nicotine also hits fat cells all over your body, causing them to pour free fatty acids into your blood. Every time you smoke, the level of free fatty acids in your blood goes up. These elevated levels of fatty acids may have an accelerating effect on clotting. Some studies have shown that platelets, a clotting factor in the blood, also become more adhesive in smokers.

Moreover, animal studies show that carbon monoxide makes artery walls more permeable to fatty substances. This may be one of the mechanisms leading to the deposit of fatty plaques which narrow arterial passages—atherosclerosis.

Smoking doesn't cause all the heart attacks in the United States. But one scientist calculates that tobacco products are responsible for about 225,000 of the 748,000 U.S. deaths from heart and artery disease each year.

What produces most of the flavor in your cigarettes is those billions of chemical particles mentioned earlier. Condensed from smoke, they form viscous, smelly tar. A pack-a-day smoker each year inhales about a full cup—eight ounces—of tar in his smoke that satisfies.

Even as it pours tar into your lungs, smoke neutralizes the lungs' defenses: mucus, to trap dirt and microbes; cilia, tiny hairlike structures lining the airways, beating steadily to move the mucus toward the throat; and macrophages, hard-working vacuum-cleaner cells which gather and dispose of harmful substances. The cigarette smoke you gulp directly into your lungs produces excess mucus while slowing down and eventually stopping the cilia, and hampering the macrophages' ability to digest foreign matter.

In that tar—against which you now can't defend yourself— animal studies show there are about 30 chemicals which help cause cancer. Several are "complete carcinogens," which means they can start malignant tumors all by themselves. One such is beta-naphthylamine, a specific cause of bladder cancer in human beings, and so powerful that many countries have restricted its manufacture (it's used in dyes). A medical researcher has calculated that 35 percent of bladder cancers in the United States are smoke-related, resulting in 9800 deaths a year.

But tar itself is a more powerful cancer-causing agent than

the sum of its parts. Wherever it touches tissue, it produces abnormal cells. These aren't cancer, but it is among these deformed cells that cancers start. In pipe and cigar smokers who don't generally inhale, the common smoking-caused cancer areas are lip, tongue, mouth, larynx and esophagus. In cigarette smokers who inhale, the cancers also include lung, bladder and pancreas. Lung cancer is more than 90-percent fatal. Some 81,000 of the 90,500 annual U.S. deaths from lung cancer are smoking-related. (Most of the dead are men, but the percentage of women is on the rise.)

Cigarettes cause other lung diseases, which let you smoke yourself to death more slowly. Most smokers know well that first-thing-in-the-morning coughing spell. It starts the day because during the night your anesthetized cilia began to wake up and move the mucus. As smoking continues, the cough becomes chronic. Steady hacking and spitting are the symptoms of chronic bronchitis. Overproduction of mucus caused by this disease provides a breeding ground for bacteria while reducing the lungs' ability to fight off infection—one reason why smokers get more colds and other respiratory infections. Chronic bronchitis can kill, too.

Chronic bronchitis and its steady companion, emphysema—of which, the U.S. Surgeon General says, cigarettes are the most important cause—kill about 45,000 Americans a year. There is good reason to believe that 99 percent of heavy cigarette smokers (more than a pack a day) have some emphysema, a disease that destroys the lungs' air sacs. Recently, a pathologist studied the lungs of some 1800 deceased men and women and classified them by the amount of emphysema apparent. More than 99 percent of those who had smoked heavily had the disease, and in 19 percent it was far advanced; 90 percent of the nonsmokers had no emphysema, and there wasn't a single advanced case among them. Even among coal miners and others exposed to lung-damaging dust, smoking plays a significant part in death from emphysema.

"Lung cancer is a comparatively merciful death," says one doctor. "With emphysema you start gasping, and you may gasp for 15 years." It creeps up on smokers. We all start with about 100 square yards of interior lung surface. But we almost never need all of this; most of us live on a small part of our lung capacity (about 20 percent of it). The first hint a smoker gets of emphysema is when he finds himself out of breath after a small exertion. He may think this is an early warning; it isn't. It means that most of his lung reserve has been destroyed.

Even when warned, many smokers bravely refuse to give up cigarettes until it is too late. Visit the respiratory ward of your local hospital and you'll see them—never more than a few yards from their oxygen tanks and respirators, their entire lives devoted to one thing: breathing.

The list of smoking-related diseases goes on yet further. Smokers have more gastric ulcers than non-smokers, and take longer to heal; more periodontal disease, which attacks teeth and gums, and more trench mouth; more severe upper respiratory infections. And evidence is beginning to show that cigarette smoke attacks the central nervous system.

The damage is "dose-related." Each cigarette does some harm. Each additional smoke repeats the insult. Eventually these incessant attacks on the body may turn into disease. With about one million puffs, or 100,000 cigarettes—a pack a day for 15 years—smokers edge into the lung-cancer danger zone.

There's no such thing as a safe level of smoking. But since the harm *is* dose-related, research shows that cutting down on the number of cigarettes, and smoking those with efficient filters and less tar and nicotine, will reduce the risk of serious illness. However, the real payoff comes from quitting.

What happens if you do? First, your chronic bronchitis begins to clear up; no more hacking and coughing. Fewer colds. A cleaner mouth—and breath. Stay off cigarettes for a year, and your risk of heart attack goes down sharply. Keep it up for two years, and you begin to move out of the lung-cancer danger zone. The symptoms of emphysema may even improve—although the lung tissue destroyed by smoking will not regenerate.

The big thing to remember is that when you stop assaulting your lungs with air that tastes good like a cigarette should, whatever breathing capacity you have left, you'll *keep*.

Poisoning Ourselves With Noise

by James Stewart-Gordon

A FEARFUL thing happened to us on the way to the 1970s and 1980s: we became trapped in a dangerous web of noise. Whether it comes in loud, sudden blasts or as a steady high level of sound, noise is loaded with threats to the health of us all. And, ever-increasing, it must now be recognized as a plague that has reached epidemic proportions.

Since 1939, the sound intensity of "community noise" in the power-packed, unmuffled hives of American cities has increased a thousandfold. Some two million automobiles, trucks and buses pound the streets of New York, Chicago and Los Angeles every working day, creating a continuous roar. Add to this the sounds of industry and construction: jackhammers, compressors, air-conditioning units, power generation and materials handling. The loudest noise to which city dwellers are exposed continues to rise—at an estimated one decibel* each year.

Man's annoyance threshold for intermittent sounds, according to the Conservation Foundation, is from 50 to 90 decibels. His pain threshold is 120 decibels. Measure against these the sound of a noisy sports car or truck (90 db.); a pneumatic

---

*Sound is measured in decibels, or tenths of a *bel* (named for Dr. Alexander Graham Bell). A decibel is the lowest sound detectable by the human ear in quiet surroundings. Decibels increase logarithmically rather than arithmetically, so an increase of three decibels means double the intensity of sound.

jackhammer (94 db.); a loud power mower (107 db.); a riveter (130 db.); a jet plane on takeoff (150 db.).

Perception and response are affected not only by the loudness, pitch and duration of the sound, but also by the hearer's own physical and mental state. Noise, in fact, is defined by acousticians as "meaningless sound." Thus the sound of a sports car revving up, or the 114-decibel twanging of a group of electric guitars playing rock music, can be informative, gratifying or a giant earache, depending on how "tuned in" you are. Noise is most dangerous when it is loud, meaningless, irregular and unpredictable, and when it reaches a quick angry peak as in the sudden roar of a motorcycle, the stuttering blast of a jackhammer, or a chain saw's grating whine.

In a landmark series of experiments in the early 1960s, Dr. Gerd Jansen, then with the Max Planck Institute in Dortmund, Germany, established the limits above which noise ceases to be harmless. Over a two-year period he and his associates tested 1005 workmen in West German steel mills and ironworks: 665 who worked under the noisiest conditions, 340 in quiet jobs. In another experiment, under laboratory conditions, men were exposed to bursts of sudden, unpredictable noise at varying sound levels, for periods of from ½ second to 90 minutes.

Dr. Jansen discovered that the body's autonomic nervous system—that network of nerve fibers and ductless glands which regulates such involuntary responses as heartbeat, temperature, digestion and respiration—begins to react at 70 decibels, equivalent to the sound of traffic on a relatively quiet city street. At that level, vaso-constrictive effects were noted—narrowing of the arteries, which raises the diastolic blood pressure and also lessens the supply of blood to the heart. As the intensity of sound increased, the effects grew stronger: dilation of the pupils, drying of the mouth and tongue, loss of skin color, contraction of leg, abdomen and chest muscles, sudden excess production of adrenalin, stoppage of the flow of gastric juices, and excitation of the heart. These effects were automatic, unaffected by the subject's health, his annoyance, or whether he was accustomed to noise on his job.

Though amazingly resilient in its adaptability to most environmental changes, the body shows no sign of an ability to become conditioned to noise. In 1962 and 1963, Dr. Samuel Rosen, professor of ear surgery at New York's Mount Sinai

School of Medicine, together with Dr. Jansen and a team of scientists, tested the hearing of Mabaan tribesmen in the Sudan. Living in an atmosphere as nearly noise-free as any on earth, the Africans showed no evidence of hypertension or heart disease, and their hearing remained acute in old age. Yet when exposed to loud impulsive notes taped in a German steel mill, they exhibited the same autonomic responses, at the same noise levels, as the steelworkers.

The toxic force of noise makes itself felt in these areas:

Hearing Loss. "The length of time it takes for the body to return to its normal state after exposure to loud noise," said Dr. Rosen, "is roughly the same as the duration of the noise itself. But if the noise lasts for hours, recovery may take a good deal longer."

Dr. Rosen tested the sound output and hearing reactions of a rock-music group, and noted a very high decibel level of 114. He was not surprised to learn that the young leader had experienced a spell of transient deafness in his right ear. From the severity and duration of this "temporary threshold shift," as it is called, otologists can determine a person's susceptibility to noise, and predict the likelihood of permanent hearing loss with continued exposure to loud sounds over a length of time.

Millions of Americans suffer from some degree of hearing loss, more than suffer from all other disabilities combined. An estimated two out of three working males are victims of work-connected perceptive deafness, caused by the continuous impact of loud sounds (over 80 decibels) on the supersensitive hearing mechanism of the ear. There are some 34 million Americans who are exposed to such sounds during the working day. Fifty percent of those exposed to more than 95 decibels—in shipyards, foundries, boiler factories and other noisy industries—will have a compensable hearing loss after ten years. The loss is irreversible.

Industry and discotheques are not the only threats. We are surrounded by hundreds of noise-makers, including vacuum cleaners (81 decibels), kitchen blenders (93 decibels), outboard motors (102 decibels), and power mowers (103 decibels), capable of causing hearing loss.

Effects on the Sick. Dr. Irving Fish, director of pediatric neurology at New York University's Medical School, says: "Sufferers from diseases such as heart trouble, asthma, ulcers and gastrointestinal spasms, may all be adversely affected by prolonged or sudden noise."

Cardiac patients are particularly vulnerable. Loud noises, such as a bursting paper bag close to the ear, the backfire of a truck, the blast of an auto horn, may produce an autonomic response which can bring on an anginal seizure in a heart patient.

Continuous noise is also coming under investigation as a stress factor. In his examination of steel-mill workers exposed to the steady pound of high-volume noise, Dr. Jansen noted an unusually large number with cardiac disorders—apparently the cumulative result of the disturbance in the autonomic nervous system caused by the noise.

The experience of Dr. Vern O. Knudsen, physicist and former chancellor of U.C.L.A., provides a classic example of the effect of noise. While in a hospital undergoing treatment for stomach ulcers, he noted a recurrent pain. Scientific-minded, Knudsen traced the cause to a series of noisy trucks which passed by his hospital window, shocking his ulcer into activity. In self-defense, he invented an earplug to shut out the truck sounds. (It has been used by millions of GIs to protect their hearing.)

Emotional Damage. "Stress," says Dr. Hans Selye, a world authority on the subject, "becomes dangerous when it is unduly prolonged, comes too often, or concentrates on one particular organ of the body." The body, exhausted, loses its ability to resist and so is unable to deal with danger.

During the Korean war, a favorite means used by the North Koreans to weaken the resistance of captured GIs was to put upended buckets over their heads and bang the buckets with a stick. This clanging torture, a combination of noise superimposed on fright and anxiety, broke human spirits more rapidly than did starvation, cold or the nonstop third degree.

Ordinarily, noise by itself would not unhinge a well-adjusted person. But combined with other stress factors—domestic, financial or health—it can be the "triggering trauma" for emotional as well as organic reactions. Thus in New York City a sleepless and out-of-patience housewife, worried about a sick husband, dumped a bucket of water on the garbage man when he ignored her repeated requests to juggle the garbage cans more gently. And a man shot a 13-year-old boy playing in the street, whose shouting, combined with the traffic noise, was making it impossible for him to sleep.

Loss of Sleep. Noise does not relax its grip on you even when you are sleeping. Dr. Jansen and Dr. Gunther Lehmann, among others, have used electrocardiographs and electroencephalographs to demonstrate that bursts of sounds—even when mild enough at 55 decibels not to wake the sleeper—are recorded by the brain. And the autonomic nervous system responds just as it does during the waking hours. The effect is to turn a long restorative slumber into a less beneficial series of catnaps.

Chronically noise-interrupted sleep can have violent effects, particularly on aged or sick people. Dr. Julius Buchwald, a psychiatrist at Downstate Medical Center of the State University of New York, testifying before a state legislative committee on jet noise, cited paranoid delusions, hallucinations, suicidal and homicidal impulses as some of the possible consequences.

Inaudible Sound. Intense noise or vibration at infrasonic levels (below the hearing range) also presents a potential threat to health. These low-frequency waves pass easily through an eight-foot-thick wall. Directly affecting the brain, they can cause headaches, loss of equilibrium, and nausea, as well as damage to the middle ear.

Some machines produce infra-sounds that are too small to have any effect. In experiments, however, Vladimir Gavreau, head of the French government's Electro-Acoustic Laboratory in Marseille, found that old industrial ventilators, air-conditioning units and family oil burners all may produce infra-sound at "dangerous" levels. The infra-sound generated in the oil burner, for example, is multiplied by the chimney, which acts as an organ pipe, then multiplied again by nearby rooms whose proportions are responsive to the resonance. Such effects, Dr. Gavreau suggested, may help explain such afflictions as "housewife headache."

At the other end of the scale is ultra-sound, made up of very short wavelengths, *above* hearing range. Workers in an English factory began complaining of unaccountable headaches, fatigue and nausea. Measurements showed the noise volume to be a tolerable 76 to 80 decibels. When complaints persisted, scientists examined the drilling, welding, soldering and washing devices and discovered that high-intensity ultra-sounds were also being produced. Once these were got rid of by adjustment of the machines, there was an immediate drop-off in symptoms.

Antidotes. Noise is a very real and growing national health problem, and steps must be taken to stop it. This will mean setting realistic health standards, and enforcing them. It will also mean redesigning a lot of machinery and equipment.

Suppression of noise depends on isolating the source and by simple mechanical readjustments eliminating its vibrations, or changing the sound-wave energy into heat and dissipating it. Devices designed with noise-inhibition in mind usually cost about five percent more to manufacture than their noisy counterparts, but less than that when produced in mass quantities.

A public demand for quiet is beginning to be felt. In 1968 the Evinrude Company produced its first quiet-model outboard motor, which was mounted on rubber and fired its noisy exhaust into the water instead of the air. "But outboard owners *want* noise—it gives them a sense of speed," some said. Yet in its first year more quiet Evinrude outboards were sold than all its noisy competition combined.

In the past, whenever limitations for traffic, construction and industrial noise were discussed, the figures mentioned were usually between 85 and 90 decibels. But if a level is to be set, logically it should be set where it can eliminate the health hazard. In the light of present medical knowledge, that means a 70-decibel limit.

Many U.S. states, cities and towns do have anti-noise ordinances, but in most cases the language of the law is so out-of-date as to make enforcement impossible. Thus New York City, perhaps the noisiest city on earth, issued only 184 summonses in 1979 for violations of the general anti-noise regulations. California, employing a more practical approach, set up electronic measuring devices to check the volume of noise in its cities and highways, and has been designing freeways with noise abatement in mind.

In Britain, under the prodding of the Noise Abatement Society, cars must be well enough muffled to pass a road-noise test. In Paris, blowing your horn is specifically forbidden by law, except to avoid an imminent accident.

West Germany—the industrial city of Dortmund, in particular—has been the leader in effective noise-suppression. Several years ago, noting that Dortmund was being tortured by a noise plague, deputy city manager Helmut Hillman called in the experts. They fashioned a noise map of the city (a technique later borrowed by San Francisco) and set out to quiet the worst portions. Persuasion was used first. But when owners of one factory refused to muffle their machinery on grounds of cost, the case came to trial and a law was invoked that says, "Public health is above any economic consideration." Dortmund is quiet these days—and with no resulting wave of bankruptcy cases.

A similar tough policy has to be followed here. Only then will the relentless shock wave of sound which pollutes our daily environment and assaults our health be brought under control.

Alcohol and Your Brain

by Albert Q. Maisel

IT IS A fact of life in present-day America that more than 85 million adults—about 79 percent of all men and 63 percent of all women—drink alcoholic beverages. One drinker in 18 (more than 4,800,000 Americans) is an outright alcoholic. Four to five million more are "heavy" drinkers—meaning their alcohol consumption is great enough and frequent enough to cause serious personal problems. That leaves more than 75 million of us who are so-called moderate or social drinkers. We may take a cocktail or two before dinner, wine with a meal or a few beers at a cookout, but we seldom, if ever, come anywhere near getting drunk.

Until the late 1960s, almost all researchers believed that such occasional imbibers suffered no permanent ill effects from their drinking. Physiologists were convinced that even when such moderate drinkers did get "high," their slurred speech and slowed-up reactions evidenced only a transitory effect upon their brains and nervous systems. Now, however, strong evidence indicates that there is no guarantee of a "safe" level of drinking, no absolute threshold below which alcohol fails to damage or destroy groups of cells in the brain and other vital organs

Let's look at what happens when we drink. Whether we swallow beer or wine or whisky or vodka, the substance that affects us is ethyl alcohol, which is extremely soluble in the water that is the principal component of almost all the tissues of our bodies. It is so soluble, in fact, that a part of every sip of alcohol you take is absorbed right through your tongue and gums before you have time to swallow it!

Nor is the rest of it broken down or digested like ordinary foods. Instead, it is absorbed directly into your bloodstream through your stomach's walls or the lining of your small intestines—so rapidly that, on an empty stomach, fully 90 percent of the alcohol you consume may enter your bloodstream within an hour. Dissolved in your blood, the alcohol is quickly carried to every organ of your body—especially those which, like the brain, have a high water content and a rich blood supply.

Physiologists have long recognized that many of the familiar effects of drinking are really manifestations of alcohol's effect on our brains. In fact, they have established a direct relationship between the quantity of alcohol we put into our bloodstreams and the area of our brain the alcohol affects. If, for example, a 150-pound man consumes two bottles of beer on an empty stomach, the level of alcohol dissolved in his blood will reach about five hundredths of one percent. At this level, the normal activity of the cortex, or outer layer of the brain—particularly in the centers concerned with worry or anxiety—will be affected. The drinker will feel falsely "lifted up," because the inhibitions that usually hold him steady have, in effect, been paralyzed.

If he drinks enough to raise his blood alcohol to about ten hundredths of one percent, activity in the motor centers at the back of his brain will be depressed and he'll begin to lose the ability to control his muscles. If his blood alcohol level rises to 20 hundredths of one percent, the deeper portions of his midbrain will become affected and he'll become increasingly sleepy. Should the level pass one half of one percent, the respiratory centers in the lowest part of his brain may become paralyzed and the drinker will quietly pass from stupor to death.

Just how alcohol exerts these successive effects on the brain long mystified physiologists. Over the last four decades, however, increasing numbers of them have come to believe that alcohol acts indirectly upon the brain's various layers by depriving them of the oxygen essential for the functioning of their cells. This theory derives strong support from the fact that a direct deprivation of oxygen—such as that experienced by mountain climbers or aviators—produces exactly the same sequence of effects as does alcohol. (Numerous studies have shown that as a flier climbs over 9000 feet he begins to experience a sense of exhilaration that closely parallels that of a drinker after a cocktail or two. Should he rise above 18,000 feet—without an oxygen mask—his respiratory centers will stop functioning and he will die.)

The mystery of *how* alcohol deprives the brain of oxygen was solved by a brilliantly simple series of experiments conducted by the late Prof. Melvin H. Knisely and two associates, Drs. Herbert A. Moskow and Raymond C. Pennington, at the Medical University of South Carolina. Dr. Knisely's work had long centered upon studies of the blood, and he was recognized as one of the outstanding experts on the strange phenomenon known as "blood sludging."

In a normal, healthy individual the heart pumps the blood through a series of ever-smaller arteries until it reaches the minute capillaries that spread through every tissue of the body. It is in these tiny, narrow blood vessels that the red cells yield up their oxygen, thus maintaining the life of the cells that surround the capillary walls. For reasons not yet completely clear, a large number of disease conditions—from malaria to typhoid fever—bring about the production of a substance that coats the red cells and makes them stick together in clumps. As these bits of "sludge" reach the capillaries, they pile up into a wad that may entirely plug the capillary. When sludging is extensive and many capillaries become plugged, cells in entire areas of an organ will starve for oxygen.

To see this sludging directly, as far back as the early 1940s Dr. Knisely was illuminating the eyeball, where numerous capillaries lie just below the transparent surface. He thus observed through a microscope all the variations of sludging and capillary-blocking that occur in more than 50 human diseases. For his investigations he needed a sludge-causing substance that might be administered to a healthy person in precisely controlled amounts; one that would permit him to create, and observe, any desired degree of sludging. Alcohol proved to be the perfect substance for his purpose. He could give it in controlled quantities to laboratory animals or student volunteers, determine precisely the percentage of alcohol that appeared in the blood and observe exactly its effect on the eye's capillaries.

One key question remained: Were the capillaries in other organs affected in the same way by alcohol-induced sludging? Dr. Pennington gave alcohol to rabbits and then examined internal organ tissues. In each test animal he found sludged blood plugging capillaries in every organ and tissue that could be properly illuminated for microscopic study.

The experimenters quickly discovered they could detect sludging of the blood in the eye capillaries of students who had consumed as little as one large glass of beer. They went on to study every intoxicated person admitted to one private sanitarium over a 17-month period. They found that with every increase in alcohol in the blood, the number of wads of red cells also increased, and the rate of blood flow slowed. In patients with higher blood alcohol levels, they observed an increasing number of fully plugged capillaries. At the highest concentrations, a substantial number of the capillaries had been ruptured, producing microscopic hemorrhages.

The researchers felt justified in concluding they had discovered the mechanism by which alcohol injures and destroys cells throughout the body—by depriving them of the oxygen they need to survive.

The drinker who consumes enough alcohol to reach a stuporous state will thus incur a substantial number of small brain hemorrhages, and an even larger number of plugged brain capillaries. Around each of these minute points, some brain cells will die for lack of oxygen. Our bodies are incapable of creating new brain cells. But since the average adult brain contains more than 17 billion individual cells, the destruction of even a few thousand in a single drinking bout leaves the heavy drinker with his brain powers apparently intact.

If his drinking bouts continue year after year, however, millions of irreplaceable brain cells will be lost to him. Gradually, the accumulation of such losses will show up as the slowed wits and impaired judgment of the alcoholic. And when he dies—probably some years sooner than if he had been a non-drinker—an autopsy of his brain will reveal enormous numbers of small areas of atrophy in which brain cells have been destroyed. In some cases, Dr. Knisely observed, entire convolutions of the brain are so shrunken that the loss of tissue can be seen the moment the brain is exposed to view.

But what of the moderate or occasional drinker? He, too, the researchers suspect, might incur some loss of brain cells every time he drinks. And, once again, the cells he loses are irreplaceable. The only real difference between his loss of brain tissue and that of the heavy drinker is one of degree.

The significance of these discoveries extends far beyond the question of how alcohol injures the brain. Physicians have long known that cirrhosis of the liver develops about eight times as frequently in alcoholics as in non-alcoholics. But they have not known *how* alcohol creates or exacerbates this often deadly disease. Now, Dr. Knisely's group has shown that alcohol causes the same plugging of capillaries in the liver—and other organs—as in the brain. Here, too, whenever we drink, lack of oxygen may cause cells to die. Fortunately, however, the liver differs from the brain in its ability to produce new functioning cells, and its degeneration can be stopped if drinking is discontinued.

Dr. Knisely's work has also implied that liquor (once advised as a medication for victims of heart disease to help dilate the blood vessels that nourish heart muscle) may actually damage heart-muscle tissues by the very same capillary-clogging action it evokes in the brain. Most cardiologists no longer prescribe drinking as a means of improving circulation.

What should all this mean to the millions who are moderate or social drinkers? Obviously, each of us will come to his own conclusions.

Super Athletes—or Monsters?

by Ron Clarke, with Alan Trengove

As A BOY I was awed by Tarzan, played on the screen in those days by champion swimmer Johnny Weissmuller. That big hunk of man had won his second successive 100-meter Olympic freestyle title, in 1928, in 58.6 seconds. Yet a couple of summers ago an East German schoolgirl, Barbara Krause, was able to swim the same distance more than three seconds faster.

A decade before I was born, the running feats of Finland's Paavo Nurmi were considered almost superhuman. In 1924, "Peerless Paavo" set an Olympic 1500-meter record of 3:53.6. Yet today, Steve Ovett of Great Britain has run that distance an astonishing 22 seconds faster. And—shades of the "impossible" four-minute barrier—Ovett as well as Sebastian Coe have each run the mile in world-record times under 3:49. That's 11 seconds better than what was so recently considered the absolute limit.

Even these achievements don't illustrate the extension of human capacity as dramatically as Bob Beamon's amazing broad jump at the 1968 Olympics in Mexico City. All of us there watched as, exploding like a shot out of a cannon, the lithe American leaped 29 feet 2½ inches, exceeding the then world record *by 22 inches*.

There is, in fact, a universal advance in sporting standards. Better nutrition and the expansion of physical education have played a part. So has size. Today's average English high-school boy would be too big to wear a medieval knight's armor; U.S. children are ten-percent taller than in 1880. And, maturing earlier, these young people reach their physical peak during the period of their lives when they have most time to train for sport. So the typical crack athlete of the '70s was younger, taller, and possessed markedly more muscular strength and cardio-respiratory capacity than his predecessor.

Improvements in sports equipment and facilities are significant. So is the widening of opportunity. Yet, there are aspects of the rising standards which appall me. Today, the fun in big sport is fast vanishing, with athletic careers being blueprinted so thoroughly that champions seem in danger of becoming robots manipulated by biologists, chemists and computer specialists.

Valery Borzov, a rugged post-graduate physical-education student, was one of several sprinters selected by the U.S.S.R. in early 1970 as potential competitors in the 1972 Olympics. Comprehensive information was compiled about their physiology and strength, past performances, mental attitudes, even eating habits. These data were fed into a computer, which helped officials decide that Borzov had the best chance of winning gold medals. A computer was also used to analyze Borzov's sprinting action, and to devise a special training schedule to assist him in perfecting his technique. The computer monitored his workouts for 2½ years, until the Soviet athlete coolly won the 100- and 200-meter dashes at Munich, arms held triumphantly aloft.

"To turn Borzov into a ten-second sprinter was the work of a whole team of scientists, not unlike the mathematical designing of a car or airplane," said his coach, biologist Valentin Petrovski. "In the near future, success in sport will depend more on science laboratories than on the athletes."

If this attitude spreads, athletes will become machines, programmed by scientists and technicians on behalf of governments hungry for national prestige. Already in some eastern countries, small children are being physiologically assessed by sports technocrats. "We are working with two- and three-year-olds," a Soviet minister said in 1972. "The aim is to inculcate the sporting culture in them, so that the drive for sports becomes something organic that is beyond their control."

In East Germany, whose big investment in sports medicine has made it—with a population of only 17 million—one of the world's leading sports nations, 90 percent of the children are taught to swim by age four. The most talented children in all sports are sifted out at *spartakiades*—periodic, state-run competitions—and then encouraged to go to special schools where they can train under the supervision of physicians, biochemists and psychologists, as well as coaches.

In 1956, when I carried the Olympic flame at the opening of the Melbourne Games, it was rare to find more than one or two doctors attending a major sporting event in their professional capacity. Eleven years later, at a "Little Olympics" at Mexico City, the French team alone included 27 doctors, equipped with the most sophisticated machinery. And today, sports medicine is increasingly exploited.

Some of the worst abuses involve drugs. As noted by Drs. Robert Dugal and Michel Bertrand, of the National Institute for Scientific Research in Canada: "Coaches and trainers often have an impressive stack of powders and liquids which young athletes may indiscriminately take, hoping to improve their abilities faster."

In 1960, the world was horrified when a drugged road cyclist, Kurt Jensen of Denmark, collapsed and died at the Rome Olympics. Then in the 1967 Tour de France, an ashen-faced British rider named Tom Simpson fell off his bicycle in oven-like heat near the summit of Mount Ventoux. He died within seconds. The cause: a lethal mixture of amphetamines (which delay and subdue the *feeling* of fatigue), heat, altitude and physical exhaustion.

As a result of these and other malpractices, it has become standard Olympic procedure to make random blood and urine checks, after each competitive performance, to determine if athletes have taken drugs.

In recent years, most of the world's leading weight lifters and throwers have used anabolic steroids. These derivatives of the male sex hormone, intended for invalids, can add muscle power and body mass to any man or woman in training—and can also cause liver and kidney damage. British shot-putter Jeff Teale at first took only part of a tablet daily. After winning a silver medal at the 1970 Commonwealth Games, he confessed that he began taking up to ten tablets a day before competitions. He felt "stronger, faster and more aggressive," and added more than four feet to his shot-putting performance. (He was suspended from international and domestic amateur competition for life in 1974.)

Certain gadgets and practices also seem to me to breach the spirit of sport. In several countries, an electronic device attached to an athlete's chest measures his heartbeat and transmits details of his performance to his coach on the sideline. It paces the athlete, enabling him to adjust his training to maintain a prescribed heart rate. Weight lifters at the Moscow Institute of Physical Culture strap to their biceps electrodes carrying tiny charges that cause the muscles to flex rhythmically. The scheme is said to create bigger and stronger muscles.

Perhaps the most ingenious aid of all is computerized biomechanical analysis, as developed in the Department of Exercise Science at the University of Massachusetts. An athlete's action is filmed in slow motion. Then the movements of his joint centers are converted into mathematical relationships, and the figures are fed into a computer—where every segment of each joint's action is assessed, its dynamic forces calculated. In 1971, computerized analysis found that certain muscles in javelin thrower Bill Schmidt's left leg were working against his hurling action rather than helping it. He concentrated on using that leg correctly, increased his distance by 19 feet in the U.S. Olympic trials, and went on to win a bronze medal at Munich.

In Melbourne, Australia, researchers measure by electrocardiogram the time it takes for an impulse to move through the heart, thus learning the organ's size and its capacity to respond to hard training. First applied to racehorses, the test is now being used to discover young athletes' potential in stamina events. "Why subject a child to running round a track for five years before telling him he's not going to make it as a distance runner?" asks Dr. Gordon Steward, senior lecturer in veterinary pharmacology at Melbourne University.

But what if the boy runs for the sheer joy of running? Surely it's wrong to suggest that the only reason for anyone to be involved in sport is to achieve great success. The real fun is in trying to improve one's performance, and uncertainty is one of sport's most attractive features.

The successes of distance runners like Filbert Bayi, of Tanzania, who grew up in a village near Mount Kilimanjaro, have shown that at altitude, where the air is thin, athletes can train their bodies to transport oxygen more efficiently. As a result, hundreds of Olympians now spend months of preparation in mountain camps. How long—if it's not already occurring— before athletes attempt a shortcut by conditioning themselves in low-pressure chambers?

There are other ways in which today's science can give

athletes an extra edge, as I learned at the 20th World Congress in Sports Medicine at Melbourne in 1974. Among them:

• By removing two quarts of a person's blood over a period of a week, storing it and then re-infusing it, that person's endurance may be temporarily improved by up to five percent. So far confined to laboratory experiments, with athletes working out on treadmills, the process increases the supply of oxygen-bearing hemoglobin. "It appears that no method can be developed to check whether an athlete has received the treatment," Prof. Per-Olof Astrand, of the Swedish College of Physical Education, told me. "Because, after all, it's his own blood which has been re-infused."

• Dietary manipulations, combined with prolonged exercise, can double or treble the store of energy-giving glycogen in the liver and muscles. An athlete first clears his muscles of glycogen by training on a carbohydrate-free diet, then switches for three days to a diet rich in carbohydrates. "You can store up an extra 1.5 kilograms (53 ounces) this way," explains Dr. Eric Hultman of Beckomberga Hospital, Stockholm, Sweden.

If science and technology are to be prevented from dehumanizing sport completely, it will be the human spirit that does it. For the fact is that athletic barriers are in good part psychological. Athletes of the caliber of Paavo Nurmi, Emil Zatopek and Filbert Bayi have ingredients in their personalities which enable them to respond heroically to stimulus, overcoming discomfort and pain to turn in epic performances. For example, Zatopek, the sturdy Czech, ran his first marathon at the 1952 Olympics—after having won the 5000- and 10,000-meter events. For 16 miles he kept at the shoulder of the favorite, Britain's experienced Jim Peters. Then he turned and said in halting English, "Excuse me, Peters, but I have not run a marathon before. We go a little faster, yes?" Poor Peters struggled on for a while, then dropped out, while the iron-willed Zatopek went on to win.

Sports medicine, in its pursuit of ultimate performance, has begun to explore the minds of athletes. But it cannot yet—thank goodness—fabricate the kind of determination epitomized by Zatopek.

Marijuana: More Dangerous Than You Know

by D. Harvey Powelson, M.D.

LEGALIZE POT. That was the headline in the *Daily Californian*, our campus newspaper, on April 12, 1967. "Marijuana is harmless," the article quoted me as saying. "There is no evidence that it does anything except make people feel good. It has never made anyone into a criminal or a narcotics addict. It should be legalized."

At the time I made those remarks, I was chief of the department of psychiatry in the student health center at the University of California, Berkeley, and deeply involved in the debate over hallucinogens and "mind-expanding" drugs. LSD and mescaline, I thought, were very dangerous. But marijuana was different. I had tried it myself two times—once in the 1950s and again in the early 1960s—without noticing any ill effects. I had read the medical literature which, although sparse and out of date, indicated that it was non-addictive and produced no harmful effects.

Within five years I knew I was totally wrong. What caused me to change my mind? It was the consequence of observing some 200 students whom I counseled.

The catalyst was a 24-year-old student named Mike whom my wife Joan, a psychiatric social worker, and I treated privately. Mike was a bright and agile young man who was getting his law degree and Ph.D. simultaneously and working toward his pilot's license. He had just begun using grass that year. I'd known Mike previously, but now he wanted to see me professionally. He told us he had come to realize he had only acquaintances and no friends.

In therapy sessions, we noted that Mike's thinking often became cloudy and unreal. At such times he was certain, however, that his thinking was more insightful and clearer than ever.

"I feel like everyone is my friend," he observed one day.

"Do you mean criminals are your friends? Can you trust everybody?"

"Yeah, I can trust everybody," Mike said.

One afternoon, as we were walking back to our house, Joan was thinking out loud about our session with him. I said, "It sounds like organic brain damage." "He was at a pot party three days ago," Joan mused. It seemed unlikely there was a connection.

At that time, there was no medical evidence that marijuana affected, or remained in, the brain; but after more observation it became clear to us that the times Mike had the most trouble thinking clearly always followed the times he had smoked marijuana or hashish (a more concentrated form of marijuana). We told Mike we thought there was a connection, and asked him to stop smoking marijuana as an experiment. It was obvious that such an experiment would not hurt him, yet his reaction was hostile; he was not going to stop.

As he became more involved with marijuana, both his gullibility with others and his hostile suspiciousness of us were aggravated with each use of pot. Meanwhile, he was having trouble concentrating on his studies and couldn't finish his work. Six months later, Mike was piloting a small plane which crashed, killing him and two companions.

An inability to think logically, a tendency to speak in clichés and generalities, a temporary loss of memory and a growing paranoia—these were the symptoms Mike had displayed after using marijuana. Would we find them in other patients as well? It didn't take us long to conclude there was a definite correlation. The patients who used pot told us it heightened their "awareness" of particular experiences and made them feel mellow and peaceful, with real insights about the world. These self-observations were simply not true. They were part of what we have come to recognize as the marijuana illusion.

What they didn't tell us—because they didn't know—was that even small amounts of marijuana interfered with the sense of time and with memory storage. They didn't realize they were becoming less adequate in areas where judgment, clarity, memory and reasoning are necessary. They couldn't see that their own pathological forms of thinking were becoming more entrenched and that they were becoming paranoid. Heavy users lost their will to do anything sustained, and all users became vulnerable to the lures of easy solutions to personal and societal problems. For many, the search for highs meant other hard drugs.

John, a young graduate student, was typical of many patients who used marijuana every day. He couldn't sleep regular hours and had trouble concentrating. He spoke in all the current clichés and was unable to focus his attention. He followed me out of a lecture where I had talked about marijuana, then came to see us regularly to argue about pot. It was a year before he gave it up. But the effects of smoking so much marijuana over so long a period remained. Even as I write, a year and more after he stopped using it, John has to consciously focus his attention before he can do what other people do spontaneously.

A sensitive coed named Helen told us she smoked "only" two or three joints a month. But every time she lit up, she heard voices. On several occasions she had to be hospitalized. After months of treatment she regained self-control, but every time she shared a joint she began to have her old symptoms. Her reaction—disturbing because it was so extreme—was not typical. But it served as a needed reminder that, with marijuana, as with all mind-altering drugs, it is impossible to predict the effects on users.

Tom, a college graduate, was drafted into the Army but got out by pretending to be crazy. He came to us wondering if indeed it had been an act. He had used so much marijuana that he didn't know. Like all marijuana users, he was totally unable to evaluate a person's character. Normally shy and reserved, Tom had become promiscuous, and was constantly involved with emotionally disturbed women. In the process of therapy he learned for himself that he could not smoke dope. The withdrawal process lasted two years, but today he is totally involved in running his own flourishing business.

The chronic heavy use of marijuana, we found, leads to a deterioration of bodily functions that is difficult, sometimes impossible, to reverse. Heavy pot smokers lose their normal appetite. They have trouble sleeping regular hours. They can become sexually impotent.

Even more serious is the seemingly permanent loss of mental

ability. Consider the case of Steve, an athletic young junior faculty member who had earned a degree in mathematics and then gone on to take graduate work in philosophy. Soon after he started the daily use of hashish, he dropped out of school and did nothing for 18 months. When he discovered that the drug affected his athletic timing, he gave it up and returned to Berkeley to study for his Ph.D. But the effects remained. He told me he could no longer handle mathematics at his prior level. He simply couldn't follow the arguments anymore. As I write, three and a half years later, he still cannot. He is convinced that the change is permanent and was drug-induced.

By the spring of 1970, I had seen more than 1000 patients, both in consultation and in therapy sessions. I could no longer avoid the conclusion that my first opinion of pot was wrong, and publicly said so. Subsequently, medical-research groups, after a generation of neglect, began to attribute long-range ill effects to the use of pot. As a result of these findings and my own, I now believe that marijuana is the most dangerous drug we have to contend with today for these reasons:

• *Its early use is beguiling.* Pot smokers are so enraptured by the *illusion* of warm feelings that they are unable to sense the deterioration of their own mental and physiological processes.

• *Its continued use leads to delusional thinking.* And along with the delusions comes the strong need to seduce others into using drugs. I have rarely seen a regular marijuana user who didn't actively attempt to influence friends to use the drug.

Across the country, state legislatures have been considering proposals to legalize marijuana. This is a mistake. Legislators and parents should realize there is *no* argument *for* marijuana. Rationalizations such as "society is sick," "everybody else does it," "the laws are hypocritical," "it's no worse than alcohol, tobacco, etc.," are smoke screens. Responsible parents, teachers and clergy need all the help they can get. At present the backup of the law is all the help there is. The law should remain on the books and be enforced.

Once we legalize marijuana or remove penalties for its use or possession, hundreds of thousands of young people who have refrained from using it will be tempted to experiment. And many of them will suffer serious consequences.

PERSONAL EXPERIENCES

Return From Despair

by Mackey Brown

DEPRESSION. A small word. Nothing to terrify. As a mood, it may mean blue Mondays or disappointments. But the millions of people who tumble headlong into a melancholy so deep and pervasive that it changes their whole character know a different depression. Unreasonable guilt and anguish overwhelm them, and all joy and hope disappear. Well-meant advice—Get out more! Try helping those less fortunate!—aggravates rather than helps.

Some people slide slowly into the quicksand of depression. I was propelled down a long slick chute where I could grasp nothing to stop the swift descent. One January day I found myself in the kitchen with my hands in dishwater and tears cascading down my face, not even knowing why I cried. Next thing I knew, my once lively mind grew muzzy, incapable of the least decision. In the supermarket, a choice between peas and beans put me into a panic. If a friend spoke to me, I couldn't connect face with name, and would stammer or flee. I gave up driving, fearful my reflexes would fail me.

If the phone at home rang, I did not answer. At the sound of a car in the driveway, I would hide, shaking, huddled behind a chair or bed.

In the beginning, my husband, Walter, tried to get through to me. He searched my empty eyes, asking what he could do. My pathetic attempts at pretending to enjoy his lovemaking angered him. And I sensed his growing exasperation at my fumble-fingered confusion in everything I did. Finally he forced me to go to a physician.

After a thorough examination, the doctor put the tips of his fingers together in a tent and, avoiding my eyes and tears, pronounced me healthy as a horse. I was "... a little too concerned with my own *symptomatology,* perhaps." He advised involvement, getting out more. He shrugged when I told him I'd come *because* those activities were impossible for me. I went home with new despair: a hypochondriac, a self-pitying complainer.

I found myself unable to break free of a leaden lassitude, until simply sitting in a chair, looking not *through* but *at* a window, siphoned off the hours of the day. I had abandoned housekeeping. Toward evening, I would force myself to get a semblance of a meal on the table, but dishes crashed, misbegotten casseroles miscarried, food burned. "Holy cow," Walter would wail, "can't you do anything right?" Helplessly, I also saw my high-school son Mark's disdain grow.

How long could they put up with me? How long could I stand the pain of watching their love turn to rancid dislike? I was sleeping in the guest room to spare Walter my predawn awakenings: the worst moments of the day, sky still black and stars not yet faded when I opened my eyes, paralyzed with dread of the day to come.

After weeks, months, I became obsessed with the only way out: death. Erasing my horrid self was—to my depressed mind—all I had left to give my family.

The night I laid me down to die, everything finally seemed simplified. After dinner, I said good-night to Walter and Mark, who were off to the movies, and asked them not to wake me when they came home.

I poured a glass of whiskey from a bottle I'd hidden and choked down some barbiturates. I tried to feel sorrow, but my frozen emotions could not muster a response. I crawled in the unmade guest bed and turned off the light.

THREE DAYS LATER my eyes opened to the strangeness of an intensive-care unit. Was this the anteroom to hell? No. I had simply failed. Even death had rejected me. I struggled with the straps that bound me to the bed and kept the needles in my arms from ripping loose. My doctor appeared and stood looking down at me with condemnation. "Stop trying to tear those needles out," he censured.

"You had no right to interfere," I whispered hoarsely.

"Your husband called me. I had no other recourse," he said stiffly. "He and Mark found a long line waiting at the movie, so they came home. When your other son called from college, they went to wake you to see if you wanted to talk to him."

Now Walter and Mark would come and stare reproachfully. I would have to plot the whole dismal business over again.

"Mrs. Brown, I can't help you. I want you to see a psychiatrist."

"I don't *want* help."

He turned away angrily, and left.

Two men came, trundled me away to the lock-ward of the hospital. The rooms had barred windows, locked doors with judas-holes and seals over electric outlets. Dr. F, the psychiatrist, came to see me there.

Clipped seal mustache, brown tweed instead of doctor-white, he seemed to have empathy rather than repugnance in his face. (But of course I knew better.)

"On a scale of one to ten, how do you feel?" he asked.

"Minus," I whispered.

"I don't blame you," he said. (Sympathetically?)

"Everyone else does." (Damn those tears!)

"Yes, but I know what makes you feel the way you do. You've been very ill with a dreadful disease."

I didn't answer. My doctor had found nothing wrong.

"Did you ever hear of the manic-depressive syndrome?"

"Sure," I whispered. "Down one day, dancing naked in the streets the next. I haven't been doing much of that lately."

"A lot of people think that," he said. His smile was nice. "Actually, victims don't go up and down like a yo-yo. Mania can persist for weeks, depression for months, sometimes even a lifetime. But the underlying cause for both lies in brain chemistries that can alter mood."

"I'm sorry," I pleaded. "I know you want to help, but it's my life. Why can't I choose to end it?"

"If you felt as happy as you used to, would you still insist on dying?" he asked. "It's a pretty irrevocable decision, you know." I turned my face away. If even a psychiatrist couldn't understand . . .

"Don't trust me, right?" His tone was warm, not reproachful. "Well, just listen, give me a chance." I shrugged. Let him have his fun.

"We know that certain chemicals in the brain, or lack of

them, can cause moods that interrupt normal eating, sleeping, behavior and feeling patterns. What triggers depression? Sometimes events like divorce or getting fired. But often it seems to come out of nowhere, for *no* reason. And because it causes such pain and anguish, we've been working on drugs to get that old neuron network moving again.

"Are you willing to take a chemical trip with me, Mackey Brown? The drugs take time to work, and you will doubt me as many times as you believe me before you really get well. Are you game?"

What did I have to lose? Only time, while I found a new and surer way to kill myself. I nodded yes.

They kept me in the hospital, knowing many suicides try again when they fail. I took the drugs when they were brought to me every four hours. And, despite my doubts, over the weeks my despair began to lessen. Regressions? Yes, especially the first time I saw Mark and Walter. But progress, too.

Suddenly, one day, I was hungry. Not much to brag about? Ah, but after months of trying to force food into a mouth that did not have enough spit to swallow, it was a triumph to make bells ring! I noticed birds nattering about stuff for nests, saw the glow of sunset through the barred windows, began reading the books about depression Dr. F brought me.

His visits were never hurried, abrupt. He would talk about how I was feeling, discuss what I read. Nathan Kline's *From Sad to Glad,* and *Moodswing* by Ronald Fieve, a New York psychiatrist, helped me most.

One day I demanded angrily, "Why didn't my doctor recognize what was wrong with me?" Dr. F said thoughtfully that, if you were looking for them, the symptoms were easy to read. But many doctors had gone to school before the new brain discoveries had been made. "My great-great-aunt died of a ruptured appendix. Was it her doctor's fault that he was born a decade too early?" He touched my shoulder, transmitting the special tenderness of medicine men who care about people. "But I'm delighted to find you in a tantrum, even a tiny one."

In four weeks I was my old self again. I was almost giddy with feeling, with sight and sound, with pleasure in my family as I learned that many of the gestures I had taken for contempt had actually been grief that I'd interpreted wrongly.

The day I went home, the first buttercup had pushed its way out of the earth. I knelt to touch it gratefully; at long last my fingers could feel the petals, my eyes rejoice in the bright color.

As I opened the door, a long-forgotten emotion rose to the surface: pride. I itched to get at spring cleaning. My son deluged me with questions, listened to the answers as if I were a person rather than an idiot mother. The longed-for reaction to my husband's arms around me returned, overflowing, intoxicating.

And now, instead of hiding in misery, ducking the telephone, closing myself into a chrysalis, I need to speak out in gratitude for the miracle that gave me back my life.

I long to call to all my fellows who live in that horror called clinical depression: "Put away your guilt and self-hatred, resist what you take for harsh moral or professional judgment from doctors who do not yet know of the new discoveries. Ask them for a specialist in psychopharmacology. For you, too, should be able to treasure the gift of life again, as I do today."

Chemotherapy as a Treatment

For an estimated 15 million Americans, depression is more than a transitory case of the blues. It is a significant illness, requiring professional attention. Many doctors consider the best treatment for it to be a combination of psychotherapy and chemotherapy. To find out more, The Digest interviewed Dr. Nathan S. Kline, director of the Rockland Research Institute, New York State Office of Mental Health, Orangeburg, N.Y., and a leading exponent of chemotherapy as the treatment of choice for depression.

Dr. Kline, what are the signs of depression?

The most characteristic early symptom is the absence of joy or pleasure. The depressed person is unresponsive to events which normally would bring elation. Chronic fatigue, poor concentration, lack of interest and indecisiveness are also common. Remorse and guilt, very often accompanied by uncontrollable anxiety and irritability, can also occur. It is important to recognize these symptoms, because in its early stages depression is relatively simple to treat. If it is not treated, the person may become worse and, at the extreme point, suicidal.

We all feel blue at times. What distinguishes somebody who really has the illness from somebody who doesn't?

Clinical depression *persists*, uninterrupted, day after day. And over a period of time, it will interfere with one's capacity to function.

What kind of treatment do you recommend for depression?

For people like Mackey Brown, with clinical depression, I recommend chemotherapy. It will markedly help about 85 percent of these individuals.

How does chemotherapy work?

In between each nerve cell in the brain is a little space called a synapse, which is filled with fluid and activity. A nerve impulse has to cross this gap to get from the end of one nerve to the beginning of the next. And it does this by chemical transmission. The nerves excrete certain substances called biogenic amines (proteins formed in part by amino acids produced in the body) into the synapse and then reabsorb them. The amines transmit the impulse from one nerve to the next.

Normally this process goes on continuously. In the depressed person, this doesn't happen. Either the depressed individual doesn't produce enough amines, or the amines are destroyed too rapidly. In other words, there seems to be a deficiency. Two groups of drugs—tricyclic antidepressants and monoamine-oxidase inhibitors—appear to increase the amount of amines available in the synapse.

How do I find a doctor who uses chemotherapy to treat depression?

Ask your family doctor. He should know if you are more or less depressed than normal. And you may be taking another medication that as a side effect causes such symptoms. If you are clinically depressed, ask him to recommend a specialist.

How I Solve My Energy Crisis

by Bob Hope

EVERYONE seems to be worrying about the energy crisis. And no wonder—it has even caused a smog shortage on the Los Angeles freeways. I wish the energy crisis had come along when I was much younger, before I had an energy crisis of my own. Actually, it hasn't caught up with me yet. I'm speaking of the energy that makes *us* run—not our cars or our furnaces or our jet planes. We've all got a lifetime supply of that precious ingredient—if we just take care of it.

A lot of people have commented on my energy and I suppose I do have a reasonable amount of bounce to the ounce for a man age 49 and holding. (Actually I've been in show business so long I can remember when John Wayne was playing cowards.) How do I keep going? I guess the answer is that I have been blessed with an abundance of energy, and I try to take good care of it. I don't smoke, and I drink less than Dean Martin spills. Above all, I like to stay busy. I believe that keeping active, doing what you enjoy, whether it's work or relaxation, is the secret of abundant and lasting energy.

My favorite exercise is golf. I'm up early every morning I'm at home, sweating over a golf ball, until my staff presses my nose to the grindstone. My wife, Dolores, and I live just a chip shot away from the Lakeside Golf Club of Hollywood, and we have our own one-hole course right behind our house.

But you don't have to have your own one-hole course to enjoy the game. The real satisfaction I've had from golf is the sheer fun, friendly competition and exercise it affords. In fact,

I don't think there's any better way of keeping fit, or restoring your energy, than swinging a golf club, walking around a course, breathing the good air. If there isn't time for golf, I just go for a brisk walk. I like to walk around late at night after a performance. Or run—depending on the neighborhood and the performance.

Our energy often declines as we grow older; yet it need not, if we remain physically active. Larry Lewis, a San Francisco man, was still jogging almost six miles every morning, and walking five miles to work for an encore, when he was 106. Sen. Strom Thurmond of South Carolina, 77, jogs two or three miles every day—then does exercises and pushups. And he has fathered three children since he was 68! George Abbott, 93, plays golf periodically, dances, and directed his 119th Broadway show in 1978, when he was 91. Lowell Thomas, 88, is always flying off to the ends of the earth to try some new ski slope.

Asked the secret of his father's success, Will Rogers, Jr., answered in one word—"energy." "He'd rope calves, play polo and do a benefit, all in the same day," Will, Jr. said. "His energy was amazing."

I get impatient with people who say they would do more exercising if they just had the time. Certainly none of them is as busy as the President of the United States, and most Presidents have *made* time for some sort of physical exercise. President Eisenhower played golf every chance he got. President Kennedy played golf and touch football, sailed and was a crack swimmer. Probably the most energetic President we ever had was Teddy Roosevelt: T.R. hiked, boxed, rode, hunted, even climbed the Matterhorn.

Energy, like anything else in nature, declines with disuse. We should never allow our energy to stagnate. Like an old vaudeville juggler, I enjoy keeping a lot of balls in the air at once, the more the merrier. Apart from my show-business work, I've been involved in real estate, professional football and baseball teams, oil wells and raising cattle—and found all the activity very challenging and absorbing. The very variety seems to act as a stimulant that creates energy as it burns it, enabling me to do more than I thought possible.

It seems to me we all have more energy than we realize or use. Most people who have participated in the more strenuous sports have experienced the phenomenon known as "second wind." When we reach what seems to be the absolute end of our physical endurance, we somehow suddenly achieve an amazing fresh charge of energy—or second wind—which enables us not only to continue but to increase our pace. Even in everyday life, I've discovered that when you reach a point where you feel you cannot possibly go on, you often get, as if by magic, an infusion of energy that pulls you through.

I've experienced this mysterious second wind often on my overseas trips. I may have a cold, be running a temperature, or be exhausted to the point of collapse, but when that music plays, and I realize there is a show to do, my exhaustion vanishes. Suddenly, I have enough adrenalin flowing to run Grand Coulee Dam.

Still, it is possible to make excessive demands on your energy. I remember the rude awakening I got one year on a 16,000-mile trip to entertain the troops in the Azores, North Africa, Spain, Italy and Germany. We would do a two-hour show, and then I'd head for bed—only to find I was booked for a party or a hospital visit or a golf match or something else I couldn't refuse. Finally, my blood pressure went AWOL, my pulse started doing a rock 'n' roll beat, and I starred in a couple of blackouts that weren't in the script.

I snapped out of it, after some rest, and was able to finish the trip. But I still have a problem with one eye as a souvenir of the incident. It taught me not to push myself beyond a certain limit. Now I have an early-warning system—and I always heed it. If I pick up a golf club and it feels heavy, that means my barometer is dropping. Then it's time to log a little "rest and rehabilitation" until my batteries recharge.

Of course, proper eating is also an important way to keep up your energy. I'm no nutritional expert, but I try to eat plain foods and in moderation. Back when I was in vaudeville, playing around the country, I'd always try to find the local tea room, since those places served such dainty portions. The stagehands would look at me as if I was some kind of pantywaist, and they were half right—I was thinking of my waistline.

I must admit, though, that in my travels since then I've sometimes lost control of the cuisine. The worst place was in France, where I made a picture called *Paris Holiday*. The French really take their eating seriously. They served three courses and three kinds of wine for lunch on the set. By the time lunch was over, everybody had forgotten the plot. Soon we were three weeks behind on filming and six weeks ahead on wine. I was so stuffed I couldn't lift a fallen soufflé; and, to make things worse, as producer I was paying for it all. I emerged from the experience heavier, wiser and poorer. When the picture ended, I went on the Wallet Watcher's diet and eventually regained my normal weight and energy.

I think another thing that has kept my energy perking is being around young people—our own four kids, the G.I. audiences I played to for over 30 years, and the college crowd. Any audience gives me a lift, but when I play for a college audience, a little of their youth and enthusiasm rubs off on me. I'm sure that anyone can profit by involving himself with young people, listening to their music, listening to *them*. We can learn a lot from the young, especially about staying young and vital.

I've found there is also a lot of restorative power in human camaraderie, in communicating, in sharing. Since I'm a ham, my idea of ecstasy is performing for 50 million people on television. But I also enjoy just talking with friends on the phone, and the way I do it, Ma Bell enjoys it, too. I like to sit around at night and call old friends all over the country. It may not be as exciting as the White House hot line, but I get a lot of warmth out of those calls.

The ability to relax is important to anyone, especially in conserving energy. And if we all laughed a little more, especially at ourselves, we'd all be more relaxed. Humor helps to relieve strain and restore energy. "It is to a man in anxious and exhausting crisis the natural restorative, good as sleep," Emerson wrote. (My caddie told me that. I was so surprised I put down my right score.)

In some ways, at least, I think the energy crisis may turn out to be a blessing if it forces us to leave our cars in the garage more and use our own energy to get around. Energy is self-renewing and virtually inexhaustible. It's the only thing I know that is free, legal and non-fattening—and still makes you feel great.

Anatomy of an Illness

by Norman Cousins

EVER SINCE THE PUBLICATION of Adam Smith's much-talked-about *Powers of Mind* in 1975, people have written to ask whether his account in it of my recovery from a supposedly crippling, incurable disease was accurately reported. I had not written until now about my illness because I was fearful of creating false hopes in other persons similarly afflicted. However, since my case has surfaced in the public press, I feel justified in providing a fuller picture than was contained in Mr. Smith's account.

In August 1964, I flew home from a trip abroad with a slight fever and a general feeling of achiness, which rapidly deepened. Within a week, it became difficult to move my neck, arms, hands, fingers and legs. I was hospitalized when my blood sedimentation rate—the speed with which red blood cells settle in a test tube—hit 80 mm per hour, a sure sign of more than a casual health problem. It later reached 115.

I had a fast-growing conviction that a hospital was no place for a person who was seriously ill. The surprising lack of respect for basic sanitation, the extensive and sometimes promiscuous use of X-ray equipment, the seemingly indiscriminate administration of tranquilizers and painkillers, more for the convenience of the staff in managing patients than for therapeutic needs, and the regularity with which hospital routine takes precedence over the rest requirements of the patient—all these and other practices seemed to me to be critical shortcomings of the modern hospital.

My doctor did not quarrel with my reservations about hospital procedures. Dr. William Hitzig and I had been close friends for more than 20 years; he knew of my own deep interest in medical matters, and he felt comfortable about being candid with me. He reviewed the reports of the specialists he had called in as consultants—there was a consensus that I was suffering from a serious collagen illness, a weakening of the connective tissue. I had considerable difficulty in moving my limbs and even in turning over in bed. Nodules appeared on my body, gravel-like substances under the skin, indicating the systemic nature of the disease. At the low point of my illness, my jaws were almost locked.

I asked Dr. Hitzig about my chances for full recovery. He leveled with me, admitting that one of the specialists told him I had one chance in 500. Up to that time, I had been disposed to let the doctors worry about my condition. But it now seemed clear that if I was to be that "one case in 500" I had better be something more than a passive observer.

Residue of Stress. I asked Dr. Hitzig about the possible cause of my condition. He said that it could have come from any one of a number of causes—for example, from heavy-metal poisoning, or as a result of a streptococcal infection.

I thought hard about the sequence of events immediately preceding the illness. I had gone to the Soviet Union in July 1964, as co-chairman of an American delegation to consider the problems of cultural exchange. In Moscow, our hotel room was on the second floor. Each night a procession of diesel trucks plied back and forth. It was summer, and my windows were wide open. I slept uneasily each night and felt somewhat nauseated on arising. Could the exposure to the hydrocarbons from the diesel exhaust have anything to do with the illness? Moreover, as I thought back on the psychological and physical stresses of my experience abroad, I found myself increasingly convinced that I had had a case of adrenal exhaustion, which lowered my resistance.

From my reading, I knew that the full functioning of my endocrine system—in particular, the adrenal glands—was essential for combating any illness. In his classic book, *The Stress of Life*, Hans Selye shows that adrenal exhaustion can be caused by emotional tension; he details the negative effects of the negative emotions on body chemistry. The inevitable question arose in my mind: If negative emotions produce negative chemical changes in the body, wouldn't positive emotions produce positive chemical changes? Is it possible that love, hope, laughter and the will to live have therapeutic value?

Battle Plan. Obviously, putting the positive emotions to work is nothing so simple as turning on a garden hose. But even a reasonable degree of control over my emotions might have a salutary physiologic effect.

A plan began to form in my mind for systematic pursuit of the salutary emotions, and I knew that I would want to discuss it with my doctor. But first I wanted to find out more about my medication. The hospital had been giving me maximum dosages of anti-inflammatory drugs: 26 aspirin tablets a day, and 3 phenylbutazone tablets four times a day. If that medication was toxic to any degree, it was doubtful whether my plan would work. So, with Dr. Hitzig's support, we took tests—and discovered that I was hypersensitive to virtually all my medication. No wonder I had hives all over my body.

When I looked into research in the medical journals, I found that aspirin is quite powerful and warrants considerable care in its use. The medical press reported that the chemical composition of aspirin impairs platelet function. Did the relation between platelets and collagen mean that aspirin, so universally accepted for so many years, was actually harmful in the treatment of collagen illnesses? The history of medicine is replete with instances involving drugs and modes of treatment that were in use for many years before it was recognized that they did more harm than good. Living in the second half of the 20th century confers no automatic protection against unwise drugs and methods.

Suppose I stopped taking aspirin and phenylbutazone? What about the pain? The bones in my spine and practically every joint in my body already felt as though I had been run over by a truck. Yet I knew that pain could be affected by one's attitude. I could stand pain so long as progress was being made in restoring my body's capacity to halt the continuing breakdown of connective tissue.

But if we dispensed with the aspirin, how would we combat the severe inflammation? I recalled having read in medical journals about the usefulness of ascorbic acid—vitamin C—in combating a wide number of illnesses. Was it possible that it could also combat inflammation by "feeding" the adrenal glands? I had also read in the medical press that vitamin C helps to oxygenate the blood. If inadequate oxygenation was a factor in collagen breakdown, couldn't this circumstance be another argument for ascorbic acid? Also, according to some medical reports, people suffering from collagen diseases are deficient in vitamin C. Did this lack mean that the body uses up large amounts of vitamin C in the process of combating collagen breakdown?

Medicine of Mirth. Dr. Hitzig listened carefully to my speculations concerning the cause of the illness, as well as my layman's ideas for a course of action. He said that what was most important was that I continue to believe in everything I had said. He shared my sense of excitement about the possibilities of my recovery and liked the idea of a partnership.

A systematic program for the full exercise of the affirmative emotions as a factor in enhancing body chemistry was indicated. It was easy enough to hope and love and have faith, but what about laughter? Nothing is less funny than being flat on your back with all the bones in your spine and joints hurting. A good place to begin, I thought, was with amusing movies. Allen Funt, producer of the spoofing television program "Candid Camera," sent films of some of his "CC" classics, along with a projector. The nurse was instructed in its use.

It worked. I made the joyous discovery that ten minutes of genuine belly laughter had an anesthetic effect and would give me at least two hours of pain-free sleep.

If laughter did in fact have a salutary effect on the body's chemistry, it seemed at least theoretically likely that it would enhance the system's ability to fight the inflammation. So we took sedimentation-rate readings just before, as well as several hours after, the laughter episodes. Each time, there was a drop of at least five points. I was greatly elated by the discovery that there is a physiologic basis for the ancient theory that laughter is good medicine.

Next, arrangements were made for me to move my act to a hotel room—which, happily, would cost about one third as much as the hospital. The other benefits were incalculable. I would not be awakened for a bed bath or meals or medication or a change in the bed sheets. The sense of serenity was delicious and would, I felt certain, contribute to a general improvement.

What about ascorbic acid and its place in the general program for recovery? I wondered whether a better procedure than the injection series we had planned would be to administer the ascorbic acid through slow intravenous drip over a period of three or four hours. In this way we could go far beyond the usual 3-g injection. My hope was to start at 10 g and then increase the dose daily until we reached 25 g.

Dr. Hitzig's eyes widened when I mentioned 25 g. He cautioned me about the possible effect on the kidneys, and on the veins in the arms with such a massive infusion. However, it seemed to me we were playing for bigger stakes: losing some veins was not important alongside the need to combat whatever was eating at my connective tissue.

To know whether we were on the right track, we took a sedimentation test before the first intravenous administration of 10 g of ascorbic acid. Four hours later, we took another sedimentation test. There was a drop of nine full points.

Seldom had I known such elation. The ascorbic acid was working. So was laughter. The combination was cutting heavily into whatever poison was attacking the connective tissue. The fever was receding, and my pulse was no longer racing.

The Life-Force. We stepped up the dosage gradually, until at the end of the week we had reached 25 g. Meanwhile, I was completely off drugs and sleeping pills. Sleep—natural sleep without pain—was becoming increasingly prolonged.

At the end of the eighth day I was able to move my thumbs without pain. By this time, the sedimentation rate was somewhere in the 80s and dropping fast. It seemed to me that the gravel-like nodules on my neck and the backs of my hands were beginning to shrink. There was no doubt in my mind that I was going to make it back *all* the way.

Two weeks later, my wife took me to Puerto Rico for some sustained sunshine. Friends helped support me in the breaking surf. Within a week I was able to jog—at least for a minute or two. The connective tissue in my spine and joints was regenerating. I could function, and the feeling was indescribably beautiful.

I must not make it seem that all my infirmities disappeared overnight. For many months I couldn't get my arms up far enough to reach for a book on a high shelf. My fingers weren't agile enough to do what I wanted them to do on the organ keyboard. My neck had a limited turning radius. My knees were somewhat wobbly and, off and on, I have had to wear a metal brace. But I was back at my job as editor of *Saturday*

Review full time again, and this was miracle enough for me.

Is the recovery a total one? Year by year the mobility has improved. In 1976–77 I became fully pain free, except for my knees, for the first time since I left the hospital. I can ride a horse flat out and hold a camera with a steady hand.

What conclusions do I draw from the entire experience?

The first is that the will to live is not a theoretical abstraction, but a physiologic reality with therapeutic characteristics. The second is that I was fortunate to have as my doctor a man who knew that his biggest job was to encourage to the fullest the patient's will to live. Dr. Hitzig was willing to set aside the large and often hazardous armamentarium of powerful drugs available to the modern physician when he became convinced that his patient might have something better to offer. He was wise enough to know that the art of healing is still a frontier profession.

Something else I have learned: Never underestimate the capacity of the human mind and body to regenerate—even when the prospects seem most wretched. The life-force may be the least understood force on earth. William James said that human beings tend to live too far within self-imposed limits. It is possible that those limits will recede when we respect more fully the natural drive of the human mind and body toward perfectibility and regeneration. Protecting and cherishing that natural drive may well represent the finest exercise of human freedom.